'Marketing' Reproduction?
Ideology and Population Policy in India

'MARKETING' REPRODUCTION?

Ideology and Population Policy in India

Rachel Simon-Kumar

zubaan

An Imprint of Kali for Women

'Marketing' Reproduction?: *Ideology and Population Policy in India*
Rachel Simon-Kumar

Published in 2006 by
Zubaan, an imprint of Kali for Women
K-92, First Floor,
Hauz Khas Enclave,
New Delhi – 10016, INDIA
Email: zubaanwbooks@vsnl.net and contact@zubaanbooks.com
Website: www.zubaanbooks.com

Zubaan is an independent feminist publishing house based in New Delhi, India, with a strong academic and general list. It was set up as an imprint of the well known feminist house Kali for Women, and carries forward Kali's tradition of publishing world quality books to high editorial and production standards. "Zubaan" means tongue, voice, language, speech in Hindustani. Zubaan is a non-profit publisher, working in the areas of the humanities, social sciences, as well as in fiction, general non-fiction, and books for young adults that celebrate difference, diversity and equality, especially for and about the children of India and South Asia under its imprint - Young Zubaan.

ISBN-81-89013-02-5

Typeset at Print Services, B-17, Lajpat Nagar, Part II, New Delhi – 110024
Printed at Raj Press, R-3, Inderpuri, New Delhi – 110012

ACKNOWLEDGEMENTS

This book marks a milestone in a long—and often, arduous—journey of change and self-discovery. I am indebted to my friends and colleagues who supported me with advice, insights and critique through both the writing of this book and the research that preceded it—a good ten years, two continents and several 'life changes' in the making. Thanks to—

Priya, who was there from the beginning, when the ideas in this work were only inarticulate thoughts. From the minutiae of proof reading, through the tedium of methodological finesse and the exhilaration of scholarly discovery, your professional support and personal friendship has been a vital anchor in A sea of dislocation.

Mohan Rao, who kept seeing potential in this work even when I was dispirited, refusing to let me give up.

Yvonne, Bill, Hee, and Phyllis for reading drafts at very busy times in their lives, and at such short notice. Their excitement at this work was an important leap in confidence.

Urvashi, Jaya, Manisha and Preeti—invisible hands at Zubaan shaping surprises out of raw form.

Sindhu—who insisted that it was my 'karma' to complete this and so made it easier to take that next step.

Lee and Anna-Marie, all those years ago, urging me to send in that first prospectus.

Jenny, and the other Jenny, Leena, Dianne and Allan, Simon and Aruna.

Bill, again, for the sustenance in that last push to the finish.

Te Puni Kokiri, past employer, for time to write.

All those mentioned in the previous research especially the participants, my supervisory panel, and colleagues who helped with the data collection.

And to my friends in New Zealand and India, for their unfailing welcome—each time.

Parts of the book have drawn on articles already published:

'The Public Sphere and Emancipation: Negotiating women's rights in the time of neo-liberal development', *International Feminist Journal of Politics.*, Vol. 6, No. 3 (2004) pp. 490–506.

'Claiming the State: Women's Reproductive Identity and Indian Development', chapter in Kum-Kum Bhavnani, John Foran and Priya Kurian (eds), *Feminist Futures: Re-imagining Women, Culture and Development*, Zed Books, London (2003).

'Gender-Sensitive Policy? The ideology of "gender" in the Reproductive and Child Health Policy in India', *Economic and Political Weekly*, Vol. XXXVII, No 32 (2002) pp. 3369–3377.

Contents

For Naomi

1

Introduction

The International Conference on Population and Development (ICPD) held at Cairo in 1994 is considered a landmark event in the history of population and development thought. The Conference coalesced ideas about reproduction and women's empowerment that had been fermenting within women's movements in the North and the South for nearly two decades. The ICPD brought together women's groups, heads of governments, academics, and representatives of religious bodies who vigorously debated and gave shape to an ever-evolving concept: Reproductive and Sexual Health and Rights. At the end, there was a new understanding and—as many have later pointed out—an international 'consensus'. The Secretary-General of the Cairo ICPD, Nafis Sadik, captured the significance of the Conference thus:

> The ICPD is often referred to as a benchmark conference. Indeed, it was. It galvanised political will, forged new partnerships, crafted a new approach to population and development and focused the spotlight on women's rights and their pivotal role in achieving sustainable development.[1]

---

[1] Statement by Dr. Nafis Sadik, Executive Director, United Nations Population Fund (UNFPA), Second Anniversary of the International Conference on Population and Development, ICPD News, No. 5, September 1996.

http://www.un.org/popin/unfpa/taskforce/icpdnews/icpdnews9609.html

The ICPD will be remembered for its unprecedented departure from the discourses that conventionally mark debates on population policy. To the discerning observer, there was a perceptible shift in the ethos of the Conference discussions—away from a Malthusian focus on population control to a broader concern with reproductive health and rights. The ICPD represented the start of a new global rhetoric on population policy which drew on feminist visions and had the sanction of the mainstream population community. Fred T. Sai, the President of the International Planned Parenthood Federation noted:

> Cairo signalled an understanding that population is at last seen as part of the necessary investment in people, without which none of our development or environmental problems will be solved. Educating girls and making women truly equal partners in development, reducing infant and child mortality, promoting safe motherhood, giving access to quality family planning, tackling the problems of STDs, and providing clean water and adequate food and nutrition are all connected with improving reproductive and family health and reducing family size (Sai 1997).

By the end of the nine-day conference, approximately 179 states had ratified the resolutions negotiated at the conference. A Programme of Action (POA) was charted that outlined definitional issues, key concerns in specific areas of reproductive health and proposed forms of actions to improve or redress reproductive health violations. A fifteen-point chapter on the Principles of the POA firmly embedded the debates of the ICPD within the language of 'dignity and rights' (Principle 1), 'gender equality and empowerment' (Principle 4), 'universal access to health care' (Principle 8) and 'sustainable development' (Principle 2, 6, 7, 15).

It is now over a decade since the Cairo ICPD. There is a voluminous record of the spectacle that has unfolded since the conference. Academics, policy-makers, health practitioners, demographers and activists have all contributed to the outpouring of introspective analyses of the ICPD and its aftermath. Reviews have examined the effect of the ICPD on health status, programmes and services, women's empowerment, and so on. Yet, what makes the Conference a lively and relevant subject of study even today is that it represents a watershed commentary on fundamental ideas of our contemporary society—human rights, women's rights, economic growth, globalisation, population, and the State. In 1994, these ideas were still nascent as governments, civil society and academia wrestled with what the concepts meant for each of them, independently and in tandem. Retrospectively, it is easier to see that although these groups were speaking similar words, they were communicating in very different languages. Beneath the veneer of consensus, the Programme of Action reflects multiple, and sometimes conflicting, expectations.

Yet, a new language, a new rhetoric did emerge from the Cairo Conference—Reproductive Health, Quality of Care, Gender Empowerment, Women's Rights. These are ideas that have had immense consequences in the global landscape of population thought and practice and must not be underestimated. Research has shown that national level policies in both developing and developed countries are directly influenced by debates in the international arena, and that what are likely to be codified as national programmes and policies would have been discussed in earlier international conferences and forums. Conventionally, the International Population Conferences have tended to provide the basis for a shared, if fraught, action on population and development. The UN-sponsored decennial Conferences (in 1974, 1984 and 1994) have been the international platform where diverse and often contending politics—and academic opinions—are played out. From the first Conference (held at Bucharest), the ICPDs have been an important benchmark of ideas and visions that influence population policy-making of individual countries. As Barret and Frank (1999: 217) point out, international discourses, in effect, 'precede and predict' national population policy. The ideas legitimised at the Cairo ICPD, therefore, became all the more important for the influences they bring to bear on national population policy-making. A 1999 study that examined the progress of the ICPD on the reproductive health programmes of eight developing countries concluded that '... excellent progress has been made in placing Cairo on national health agendas ... [M]ost respondents (in the study) said that the (Cairo) conference recommendations provided the impetus to design new programs or redesign existing ones using a client-centred approach to integrated care' (Hardee et al. 1999: S8).

However, as a researcher with a background in feminist politics, to me the Cairo Conference raised questions about consequences that were not contained in statistics or programme redesign but rather manifest, if at all, in social change: what became of the countries that took the language of reproductive health back to their respective homes, once the hype of Cairo had died down? How did the ideas that were proliferated at the Conference, many of them foreign to their native cultures, translate into the everyday machinery of government? What is lost or altered in translation from the global to the local? Beyond the health programmes, beyond the delivery of contraceptives, beyond the statistical records of health and contraceptive achievement—what processes underlie the diffusion of ideas from one context to another? The discourse of women's empowerment, which made the Cairo Conference noteworthy, is of particular interest. Has the ideology of women's empowerment and agency been embedded or transformed as the state institutionalised reproductive health discourse? Or, was the global discourse of reproductive health merely new wine poured into old bottles, subsumed by long-standing ideologies of patriarchal states?

It is these questions that drive the research presented in this book. In seeking answers, the issue of reproductive health is moved from the domain of demography and health to that of the political and the social. Rather than focus on abortion rates or quality of health services, this research examines the settings in which reproductive health has been embedded as a state intervention. Institutional arrangements and tacit rules, historical processes, value systems and individual interpretation—all create an environment where ideas are translated into specific forms of practice.

India and the ICPD

The influence of the ICPD in India forms the backbone of this book. Historically, India has been a forceful voice in the International Conferences on Population and Development. At the first inter-governmental conference, India raised the successful maxim: 'development is the best contraceptive' (see Finkle and Crane 1975; Gulhati and Bates 1994; Harkavy 1995). The slogan challenged the persuasive stance of the North that was trying to enforce strict population regulation in 'population-ridden' Third World countries. While the developed countries tried to impress a collective perspective that excessive population increases stymied economic growth, the Indian position countered this with a reverse argument: namely, countries that achieved certain levels of economic and social development automatically seemed to register falling fertility rates. The solution to the population problem in the Indian view—and which became a rallying point for developing nations—was for the West to support development in these countries in order to make a lasting change in fertility levels. At the 1984 ICPD held in Mexico, however, India had a reversal of fortune and philosophy; the Indians now directly favoured strengthening population control. Weighed down by increasing population growth during the past decade, the official stance was to garner international support for more population regulation programmes (Finkle and Crane 1985). Given the change of position, India kept a low profile in Mexico than a decade earlier and played less of an influential or adversarial role at the 1984 ICPD.

The ideological position of the U.S. at Mexico was also contentious and further compromised the position of strength held by India at the previous Bucharest conference. The U.S. withdrew from its earlier position that population was a serious obstacle to economic growth and at Mexico promoted population as a 'neutral' factor in development. The real route to economic growth, the U.S. advocated, was the free market and privatisation. The main reason for the volte-face of the U.S. stand was the growing pro-life lobbies within America. The impasse in the discussions was evident; in all, the draft version of the Mexico Declaration was "vague, non-committal, poorly documented and badly structured paper ... a working group was created and instructed to re-write the draft version and formulate a plausible text" (Cliquet and Thienpont 1995: 62).

India went to the Cairo Conference in 1994 with this continued concern about its population growth but also with the optimism that market development would salvage its endemic problems of poverty, unemployment and low economic growth. In his speech to the ICPD on 6 September 1994, B. Shankaranand, the Indian Minister for Health and Family Welfare at the time, spoke of the stranglehold of population growth:

> Poverty as the biggest challenge remains the central issue in developing countries as over 90 per cent of the current growth in population is taking place in the developing countries. High rates of population growth, poverty and under-development are all inter-linked. Therefore it is all the more necessary to break the nexus between high fertility, poverty, ill-health and illiteracy in the context of population stabilisation and sustainable development ... [R]apid population growth has also brought unprecedented increase in the working age groups. Employment opportunities for new entrants to the labour force are dominating the economic agenda of the developing countries. The economic reforms have raised new hopes of more employment opportunities in the developing world.[2]

India was a signatory to the Programme of Action at the ICPD and among the first countries to act upon its commitments (Finkle 2002). The Ministry of Health and Family Welfare in New Delhi took decisive steps to reformulate its family welfare programme. The introduction of the Reproductive and Child Health Programme (RCH) in 1995 was a direct response to the shift in discourses in the international arena. The government removed the decades-old system of incentives and replaced it with a Target-Free Approach (TFA). The conventionally top-down Family Welfare programme was reinstituted as a participatory and decentralised form of population planning. The shift in policy was, in large part, prompted by the government's concern that there was a 'neglect of the quality of services' in the existing family welfare programme (Government of India 1997: 1). Particular emphasis was on making 'the RCH programme gender-sensitive or responsive to the needs of women' (GoI undated). The government's approach to family planning was more than the initiation of new family planning services; increasingly, the

---

[2] Statement of Indian Health Minister at the International Conference on Population and Development, United Nations Population Information Network (POPIN) UN Population Division, Department Of Economic And Social Affairs, 1994. http://www.un.org/popin/icpd/conference/gov/940906154452.html (accessed 26.10.2003)

government and the donor agencies referred to a shift in 'ethos', 'paradigms' and 'ideology'. Saroj Pachauri (1996: 245), of the Population Council of India, noted that, 'implementing reproductive health services within the national programme in India would, therefore, require an *ideological shift* ...' (emphasis mine). The emphasis on ideological transformation was noteworthy. The RCH was the first in a line of approaches—almost the *first generation* of reforms—that the Government of India (GoI) adopted in response to the international vision of reproductive health. This translation was quite significant; overshadowed by a historical legacy of population control and thrust into a radical 'paradigmatic shift', the RCH represented a critical juncture in the thinking underpinning India's population policy.

This book is a political study of the ideology of reproductive health in the first generation of programmes in India, the RCH, that followed soon after the ICPD. There is an implicit argument here that the book builds on—the RCH represents the onset of a particular narrative that is juxtaposed against other ideologies in the policy environment. The outcome for the ideas of reproductive health is uncertain: it merges, and simultaneously is in conflict with, reflects, and produces new hybrids of ideology. The research presented in this book attempts to capture the confrontation of the many ideologies that dot India's political and policy landscape. *First, this book explores the confrontation of pre-existing family planning values in contact with new discourses.* The Family Welfare programme in India is rooted in a history of fertility control. The reproductive health discourse brings with it ideological norms that are radical in content and that, at the very least, challenge the paradigms on which conventional population policy in India has tended to be framed. The shift from population control to reproductive agency is a stark shift in institutional norms. This book explores the unevenness created when existing institutional ideologies encounter new rhetoric. From targets to target-free, numerical quotas to informed choices, this book examines the use and effect of the new ideology of reproductive health in an institutional setting already entrenched with a particular language, expectations, ways of working and thinking.

Second, this book captures the confrontation between competing discourses. The reproductive health discourse entered (segments of) the Indian political landscape at the time that the collective conscious was being bombarded with yet another discourse—that of market liberalisation, which has touched most aspects of economic and political life. Ideas around government interventions, public policy and governance structures have changed radically in the past fourteen years since the Congress government initiated its New Economic Policies in 1991. The rolling back of the state in social development programmes, the privatisation of the public sector and the devolution of central government responsibilities to the state and local levels have formed the main parameters of market liberalisation in India. But market development is more than a mere cobbling together of economic strategies. It represents an ideology around political and institutional relationships in its ideas about the respective roles, rights and responsibilities of the state and its citizens in determining an individual's well-being. This book analyses how the market ideology in India has adapted itself (or not) around the ICPD discourses of reproductive health.

Third, this book presents an analysis of the ideology of the state. From yet another perspective, in examining the structures of discourse and ideology, this book moves beyond the specific context of reproductive health to an analysis of the Indian state. As the key interpreter of international discourses, the Indian state reveals its existing ideological stances in its policy and programme vision and content. Undeniably, a reproductive health discourse is also a gender discourse. The state's interpretation of policy will invariably reflect ideologies surrounding gender (drawn from economic, nationalistic, cultural and other discourses) that the state subscribes to. This study implicitly builds on the proposition that the discourses around reproductive health subscribed to by the practitioners of policy are intimately associated with discourses around women, and gender per se, that the state in India embraces. Women's identity in the state, therefore, forms the main theoretical foundation for exploring the expression of ideologies around reproductive health.

The discourse of the market or neo-liberalism is, again, significant here. Feminist critiques of neo-liberalism have argued for decades that neo-liberalist tendencies of the state will compromise women's social rights and jeopardise efforts to represent women as equal citizens within the public sphere. The state's perception of women's political identity under dominant neo-liberalism is central to the way that a reproductive health discourse is likely to be interpreted. This book will explore the production of discourses around women as subjects of the state, and the political positioning of women within the reproductive health and neo-liberal discourses. This book, in sum, is both an evaluation of policy, and an attempt to develop a feminist analysis of how women are positioned as citizens within a developmental state in transition to market-directed growth. The feminist dimensions of this study will be outlined in the following chapter.

Sources and Methodology

This book is based on research that I began in 1996—two years after the Cairo Conference, when expectations of a new awareness were high and the world seemed poised on the brink of new beginnings. At the time, my interest in the impact of the conference was sparked by the optimism of change. Like a breath of fresh air, the discourse of reproductive health offered promise of new life. The RCH programme was in its very early stages when the main bulk of the research was conducted. The programme was in the process of being instituted at various levels of the Family Welfare Ministry, and key staff were only just being trained in the precepts of the programme. This propitious timing proved both an advantage and a limitation. The advantage was that the research captured ideologies in transition, in the process of interpretation by the state. The research cannot, however, predict the material outcomes of a well-honed ideological stance.

Studying the discourses of the state offers a wide range of choices, and drawing institutional and material boundaries is important. I wanted to trace the elements of ideology at the national, state (regional) and local levels, while simultaneously looking at influences from, and implications for, other institutions in the discursive arena. At the time of the research, the main agency of the state that produced discourses of population policy in India was the Ministry of Health and Family Welfare (MoHFW) situated in Delhi. The extension of the Government of India's MoHFW at the state level is the Department of Family Welfare (DFW). The DFW provided the administrative control for the functioning of the Directorate of Health Services (DHS) in which family welfare services form a significant component. The DHS supervised the office of the District Medical Office (DMO) located in every district in a state.

Kerala was chosen as the state where the production of local discourses would be explored. Following the announcement of the Reproductive and Child Health Programme (RCH), the Government of India instituted the Target-Free Approach (TFA) in two states on a trial basis, Kerala and Tamil Nadu. Kerala, particularly, with its history of being a 'model of development' offered a strong site for exploring how ideologies of empowerment are embedded in an institutional context.[3] The reproductive health indicators in Kerala at the time were (and are) impressive. Kerala ranked the highest among states in India on the Reproductive Health Index (RHI) figures released in 1996 by the Population Foundation of India.[4] The Kerala value was at 87 while the all-India value was 46.[5] According to the 1997 figures, the average woman had less than two children (or a total fertility rate, TFR, of 1.8).[6] Further, 92.3 percent (24.5 percent in India) of births in Kerala were conducted in an institutionalised setting. The Maternal Mortality Rate (MMR) in 1998 was approximately

---

[3] There is a wide range of writings that capture Kerala's "unique" model of development. See for example, AKG Centre Conference Proceedings (1994), Centre for Development Studies (1975), Franke and Chasin (1996), Jeffrey (1992), Parayil (2000).

[4] The RHI is computed by including the following variables: infant mortality rate, life expectancy, type of medical attention received at birth, birth order and birth interval (Population Foundation of India 1996). The RHI index is being used with some caution as it is ideologically closer to the ideas of population control than reproductive health. See Ramanathan (1998).

[5] RHI indices range in value from 0 to 100. The higher the value, the better the placing of that state in relation to others.

[6] Figure from National Commission of Population Policy, http://populationcommission.nic.in/npp_app3.htm (accessed 12 August 2005).

198 (deaths per 100,000 live births) whereas in India as a whole it was 407.[7] Literacy among women in 2001 was estimated at 88 per cent as opposed to the Indian average of 54 per cent.[8] Kerala has the record for having one of the most efficient health systems in the country; in fact, the government claims to have achieved all the major health indicators targeted under "Health for All by 2000 A.D" (Government of Kerala undated). Furthermore, it has impressive historical and contemporary achievements in the area of women's empowerment. Its matrilineal system, distinctly higher levels of women's literacy, relative absence of gender bias in several social development indicators, and women's participation in political and social life have been the subject of much research and popular writing. Kerala, therefore, presents a fertile ground for the 'best case scenario' possible in the interpretation of a reproductive health discourse in India. Without the pressing need to provide for basic health levels or raising levels of gender awareness as in the rest of the country, the health department in Kerala can, in principle, address fundamental issues ingrained within the global discourse of reproductive health.

To understand the ideologies of the state, this book goes to the discourses of the state that are reproduced in text, graphic and oral forms by institutional structures and representatives of the state. The primary textual source for this study is government policy; the main data source used in this research included key documentation that emerged around the mid-1990s when the RCH was being designed and implemented. This documentation comprised strategy documents, budget statements, implementation plans, annual reports, publicity material, proposals for funding, research and consultation reports, among others, put out by the Central Government and the state of Kerala. In addition, I perused reports and research from other population agencies and non-governmental groups such as the Family Planning Association of India, HealthWatch, the World Bank, and the Population Council. The readings of these documents

---

[7] Figure from http://www.undp.org.in/programme/undpini/factsheet/kerala.pdf (accessed 12 August 2005).

[8] Figure from http://www.undp.org.in/programme/undpini/factsheet/kerala.pdf (accessed 12 August 2005).

were supplemented with interviews conducted with a range of officials from the MoHFW (New Delhi) through to DHS (Kerala) to medical providers, including doctors and auxiliary nurse midwives in two Primary Health Care centres, in Vellanad in Trivandrum district and Palathara in Quilon district. I also spoke to members of HealthWatch, Family Planning Association, World Bank, and consultants who had provided advice to the Government on instituting the RCH.[9]

Defining Ideology and Discourse

Given that the terms 'ideology' and 'discourse' are central to this book, it seems appropriate to provide an operational understanding of these terms as used here. As a concept, ideology has long had a negative association with the Marxist notion of 'false consciousness'—it is the political propaganda of a select elite that is imposed on the masses. A newer tradition of ideology appearing in social science research, and drawn upon in recent critical perspectives in development studies, aims to understand the norms, values, and beliefs that underpin social and political ideas. Teun van Dijk, in his book *Ideology* (1998: 8), stresses that ideology is a multidisciplinary concept that may be defined as the 'basis of the social representations shared by members of a group'. Ideology, according to van Dijk, is not 'simply a "world view" of a group, but rather the principles that form the basis of such beliefs'. Ideologies play an important role in social life. At one level, ideology is a frame of reference that helps individuals organise their ideas and interpret the world around them. At another, it integrates the individual's ideas, opinions, views, attitudes, and so on with a wider set of beliefs of particular groups. These groups may or may not be a recognisable or physically cohesive entity with an apex forum that communicates these ideologies. Yet, many belief structures, ranging from fundamental to liberal, are held cohesively together with remarkable internal consistency. This is, in large part, because individual and group ideologies are intricately linked to everyday social expressions, be it spoken or written language, texts, visual

[9] A list of people I interviewed is given in the Appendix.

imagery, institutional relationships, or social practices. To understand ideologies, one must scrutinise these social expressions or manifestations in discourses.

The term *discourse* is another term that does not easily lend itself to definition. Teun van Dijk considers discourse as simply a 'communicative event' (van Dijk 1998), one of the many ways in which social actors convey their ideas. Discourse, especially in talk and text, is a principal way in which ideology is expressed, although ideology can manifest in other ways as well (action and inaction, for instance). The idea of discourse is popular in current social theories because it emphasises the constructedness of social life. Scholars draw on the post-structuralist understanding that language constitutes the social world. The term discourse has been defined as a 'series of rules' to construct the object to which they refer (Fischer 1995: 208). Discourses set parameters to the way people are able to describe and act within their 'knowable' world. Discourse, through language, not only expresses the social reality of an individual, it equally constructs it. To study discourse is to understand how a social order in a particular context is defined—it reveals the 'common sense' reality that underlies social practices.

The idea of 'discourse' was popularised by the social analyses of Michel Foucault (1926-1984). For Foucault, the fundamental codes of culture, namely those governing its language and its practices, lay the parameters within which individuals understand and act in their worlds. Individuals evolve within the discourses of institutions and social structures; they form the 'discursive field' wherein individuals develop their subjectivity or identity. Using examples of madness, sexuality, criminality and penalty, Foucault showed that the very foundations of society and the world-view of individuals are produced as part of discourses (see among others, Foucault 1979, 1981). Foucault argued that because all human beings are constituted in discourses, their knowledge of the world is set by the system of language statements that particular discourses offer them.

Discourse and Ideology are important because they imply 'social situatedness', which in turn implies power. Foucault used the concept of a 'discursive field' to understand the relationship between language, social institutions, subjectivity and power. He contended that discourses and power are established on the principle of *exclusion*—that 'in every society the production of discourse is at once controlled, selected, organised and redistributed according to a certain number of procedures, whose role is to avert its powers and dangers to cope with chance events, to evade its ponderous, awesome materiality' (Foucault 1972: 215). Certain discourses become historically fixed over time as 'truth' and 'fact', constituting the formation of a dominant discourse or "truth regime" (Foucault 1980). To be situated within a dominant discourse means that only certain types of realities are highlighted while others are not. In what is popularly known as his 'genealogical' works, Foucault sought to understand the 'analytics of power'; i.e., how power was tied to the production of discourses. In particular, he studied the ways in which the organisation of knowledge in human sciences, such as statistics had been co-opted by the institutions of the state for making certain kinds of knowledge and discourses more valid than others. The more entrenched in the language of knowledge, such as medicine or law, the more likely that a particular discourse would be credited as being truthful. This partial vision of the social world is reflective of power relationships in society, and is manifest in individual and institutional bodies of knowledge and practice. The key to unravelling the power embedded in society is to analyse society's discourses (represented in talk, text, visual or other forms). By analyzing discourses, it is possible to 'view the strategies implicit in the creation of different discourses' and show 'the links between how it is constructed and how it can function to establish a group's political power' (Fischer 1995). Examining the structures of discourse can determine the political practices that are engendered and/or excluded.

Although the terms 'discourse' and 'ideology' are often used synonymously, there are important distinctions between the two. The similarities between the two are that they refer to the same aspect of social life—that is, it is the way that people understand and comprehend their social worlds. Both ideology and discourse set directions for the ways in which people think and act. Purvis and Hunt (1991) offer an interesting study of the differences between the two terms. They suggest a use of the notion of 'discourse' and 'ideology' not as oppositions or in exclusion of the other, but as complementing each other, so that discourse is a *process* of constructing social meanings and ideology the *effect* of such constructions, especially if they maintain relations of domination-subordination. Not all discourses are ideological (Fairclough 1992); however, it is ideology that develops a particular system of linked signs. As Purvis and Hunt (1991: 497) point out 'what makes some discourses ideological is their connection with systems of domination. *Ideological discourses* contain forms of signification that are incorporated into lived experience where the basic mechanism of incorporation is one whereby sectional or specific interests are represented as universal interests'. Ideological discourses are communicated through specific discourse mechanisms such as language structure, use of specific lexicons, metaphors, style, emphasis/suppression of specific content and highlighting distinctions between the Us and Them (van Dijk 1998). The production of discourses (and reproduction of ideology) occurs in social contexts, in the presence of other social actors where certain beliefs are legitimated and others excluded.

Within the field of development studies, the analysis of ideology as a form of academic critique has gained currency since the 1980s. The work of scholars such as Arthuro Escobar, Ignatius Sachs, Majid Rahnima, and others interrogate assumptions and theories about people in 'developing societies' that form the basis of most development strategies. The argument advanced is that operational development, even (or especially) of international organisations such as the World Bank, more often than not, is based on certain constructions of the Third World and its peoples—their 'needs', their 'poverty' and so on. These constructions, argue proponents of development critique, reflect less the reality of people in these societies and more the projections of policy-makers in the First World. In other words, western *ideology* tends to form the basis for the knowledges and praxis of development at local levels in developing societies.

In a similar way, the landscape of population/demographic fact and practice is heavily influenced by strands of dominant ideologies (mostly derived from western societies). Demeny (1988) provides insights into the history of the field of demography itself and how political interests deemed what was legitimated as science, and what was set as the intellectual foundation for policy, especially Third World policy. Western ethnocentrism and a western paranoia of unrestrained population growth in the Third World directed population policy design (Grimes 1994, 1998; Sen 1995). Betsy Hartmann (1987) critically demonstrates that the magnitude of material and institutional support provided by international actors had persuasive effects on developing countries to accommodate certain population strategies. Gould (1995) highlighted the role of ideology in population policy-making in Kenya where the government founded its population policy on the basis of a perceived inverse, if weak, link between fertility decline and contraceptive prevalence. The Kenyan population policy, therefore, primarily encouraged programmes to increase contraceptive use among people. According to Gould, "these policies have been formulated more from ideological presumptions and preferences than from explicit dependence on systematic policy analysis" (1995: 213), and reflects the neo-Malthusian ideologies of the state and international development agencies that aid these programmes. First World mindsets also imposed qualities of 'rationality', valorised in the western liberal subject, onto reproductive decision-making capacities of people in the South (Amalric and Banuri 1994). Dubois (1991) takes this argument a step further; he argues that the institutionalisation of contemporary population discourse is a means to ensure neo-colonial ideological dominance of the Third World (Dubois 1991).

Organisation of the Book

A word of counsel to the prospective reader of this book. For those seeking a linear plot development with a climax as its finale may feel a sense of frustration at the unfolding of the book. Because, in truth, in exploring the discourses of reproductive health, I unfurled not one but *several* debates relevant to understanding the larger picture of market ideologies, states and gender. The book sets out these various arguments, sometimes in snapshot perspective, in order to preserve the key theses that

I am putting forward. To that extent, the book's argument does not strictly move forward—instead, it reveals systematically and laterally the various threads of a core question, each of which are linked to expose a web of connections that shape the way the policy is eventually practiced.

This book is organised into eight chapters. This introductory chapter sets the context for the various theoretical, empirical and analytical threads in the book. It introduces the ICPD 1994, as the starting point of the global discourses on reproductive health that have influenced state governments to review the foundations on which they base their population policies. The significance of analysing reproductive health as a political discourse (rather than as a demographic discourse) is emphasised, and it is against this theoretical canvas that the research objectives have been laid out. Chapter 2 develops the idea of reproductive health as a political discourse torn between feminist and neo-liberal influences by developing two main themes. First, the chapter reviews the recent history surrounding the emergence of reproductive health as a global discourse, focusing on the role of the trans-national women's health movement of the South in the 1980s/1990s. Secondly, I evaluate this history using the theoretical model of social discourse articulated by Fraser (1989). Drawing on Fraser, I argue that reproductive health discourse endorsed by the women's health movement in the 1990s was akin to an oppositional discourse within the context of neo-Malthusian and neo-liberal population politics. These two contrasting influences on reproductive health have significantly different ideological imports; the interpretation of reproductive health will vary vastly depending on which vantage point one chooses to position oneself in. However, policy is not implemented in a vacuum. It is institutionalised through the structures of the state. The State, as feminist political theorists contend, interprets policy based on its own perceptions and constructions of women. Policy cannot be studied apart from an analysis of the state and its dominant ideologies around gender and women. Chapter 3, in a sense, presents a second dimension to this analysis. In this chapter, I review feminist theorisations around the nature of the state and women's political identity, first, in the context of western states, and second, in the context of India. My argument is that the way women are constructed as citizens in the state is relevant to the way the state interprets development policy, in this case, reproductive health policy.

The later chapters focus specifically on the RCH in India. Building on the theoretical arguments of the early chapters, I go on to empirically identify ideological constructions within reproductive health policy, i.e., the RCH. I emphasise that the RCH is an outcome of two dominant strands of ideology, the state's neo-liberal agenda and the international discourses on reproductive rights. The policy's integration of these divergent discourses reflects the state's perception of women's political identity in contemporary Indian society. Chapter 4 provides an overview of the RCH policy. As a prelude to the discourse analysis of policy, this chapter describes the RCH and its various elements. The antecedents to the policy are discussed, particularly the earlier policy regimes that the Indian Family Planning Programme operated under. The key features of the policy are described: the goals that the government has set for itself, the programme's design, the services the state hopes to institute, the main sources of funding, and the institutional structures that will be implicated in the RCH. Towards the end of the chapter, I focus on the implementation of the RCH specifically in Kerala.

Chapters 5, 6 and 7 present and interpret the results obtained from deconstructing the discourses of the RCH. Chapter 5 demonstrates the neo-liberal/market ideologies of the RCH policy and shows that traces of the market are reflected primarily along two discursive locations in the policy, namely, (a) in discussions of what is perceived as the functional role of the state as provider of family welfare services, and (b) in the construction of users of the programme. In this chapter, I argue that the ideologies of the market reinforce certain relationships between citizen and the state, which can have implications for the state's constructions of women's needs. Chapter 6 focuses on the dominant gender ideologies that are reflected in the RCH. The chapter throws light on, and critiques, the state's understanding of gender-sensitivity in reproductive health policy. I also examine the state's understanding of equality and equity for women in development. In Chapter 7, I continue the qualitative evaluation of the RCH. In particular, I examine how the gender and market ideologies form a framework that influences health providers' interpretation of three key elements of the feminist discourse on reproductive health—namely, 'empowerment', 'rights' and 'choices'. I show that, in practice, these are hybrids of a feminist and neo-liberal/ market discourse. The analysis offers significant insights into the manner in which ideology colours the directions and norms of policy.

The evaluation of RCH policy ideologies, however, is not the sole end product of this research. This research also attempts to theorise the implications of policy ideology on women's claims to the state and, ultimately, on their political conditions. Finally, Chapter 8 examines the implications of the neo-liberal and gender discourse and explores whether the ideologies of the state can actually, through the RCH, effect positive improvements in the fundamental political conditions of women. The chapter concludes that the state's discourses actually offer limited chances for women's empowerment, and further that these ideologies contribute to reifying discriminatory notions of public reproduction and private empowerment. The concluding chapter sums up implications for the study of ideology for wider feminist praxis and policy improvement.

References

AKG Centre for Research and Studies (1994) International Congress on Kerala Studies: Abstracts, 5 volumes, AKG Centre for Research and Studies : Trivandrum, Kerala, India.

Amalric, F. and Banuri, T. (1994) "Population: malady or symptom?" *Third World Quarterly*, Volume 15, No. 4, 691–706.

Barret, D. and Frank, D.J. (1999) "Population Control for National Development: From World Discourse to National Policies" in J. Boli and G. M. Thomas (eds) *Constructing World Culture: International Non-Governmental Organizations since 1875*, Stanford University Press: Stanford, California, pp. 198–221.

Cliquet, R.L. and, Thienpont, K. (1995) *Population and Development: A Message from the Cairo Conference*, Kluwer Academic Publishers: Dordrecht, Boston.

Demeny, P. (1988) "Social Science and Population Policy", *Population and Development Review*, Vol. 14, No. 3, pp. 451–480.

Dubois, M. (1991) "The Governance of the Third World: A Foucauldian Perspective on Power Relations in Development", *Alternatives*, Vol. 16, pp. 1–30.

Fairclough, N. (1992) *Discourse and Social Change*, Polity Press: Cambridge

Finkle, J. L. and Crane, B. B. (1975) "The Politics of Bucharest: Population, Development, and the New International Economic Order", *Population and Development Review*, Vol. 1, No. 1, September, pp. 87–114.

Finkle, J. L. and Crane, B. B. (1985) "Ideology and Politics at Mexico City: The United States at the 1984 International Conference on Population", *Population and Development Review*, Vol. 11, no. 1, March, pp. 1–28.

Finkle, J. L. (2002) "Impact of the 1994 International Conference on Population and Development". Publication of the United Nations Social and Economic Development Agency.url: http://www.un.org/esa/population/publications/completingfertility/RevisedFINKLEpaper.PDF

Fischer, F. (1995) *Evaluating Public Policy*, Nelson-Hall Publishers: Chicago.

Franke, R. and Chasin B. (1996) 'Is the Kerala Model Sustainable? Lessons From the Past — Prospects for the Future'. Presented at the International Conference on Kerala's Development Experience: National and Global Dimensions. Sponsored by the Institute of Social Sciences, 9–11 December.

Foucault, F. (1972) *The Archaeology of Knowledge and the Discourse on Language*, Pantheon Books: New York.

Foucault, F. (1979) *Discipline and Punish: The Birth of the Prison*, Penguin Books: Harmondworth.

Foucault, F. (1980) "Truth and Power" in C. Gordon (ed.) *Power/Knowledge: Selected Interviews and Other Writings 1972–1977, Michel Foucault*, Pantheon Books: New York, pp. 109–133.

Foucault, F. (1981) *History of Sexuality*, Penguin Books: Harmondsworth.

Gould, W.T.S. (1995) "Ideology and data analysis in African population policies: the case of Kenya", *Applied Geography*, Vol. 15, No.3, July, pp. 203 –218.

Government of India (1997) *Manual on Target Free Approach*, Ministry of Health and Family Welfare: New Delhi.

Government of India (undated), *Reproductive and Child Health Programme*, Ministry of Health and Family Welfare: New Delhi.

Government of Kerala (undated—web page) Health Status of Kerala, Department of Health and Family Welfare. Url found at http://www.kerala.gov.in/dept_health/healthstatus.htm

Grimes, S. (1994) "The ideology of population control in the UN draft plan for Cairo" *Population Research and Policy Review* , Vol. 13, No. 3, September, pp. 209–224.

Grimes, S. (1998) "From 'population control' to 'reproductive rights' : ideological influences in population policy", *Third World Quarterly*, Vol. 19, No. 3, pp. 375–393.

Gulhati, K. and Bates, L.M. (1994) "Developing Countries and the International Population Debates: Politics and Pragmatism in R. Cassen and Contributors, *Population and Development: Old Debates, New Conclusions*, ODC: Washington, pp. 47–75.

Hardee, K., Agarwal, K., Luke, N., Wilson, E., Pendzich, M., Farrell, M., and Cross, H. (1999) "Reproductive Health Policies and Programs in Eight Countries: Progress since Cairo", *International Family Planning Perspectives*, Volume 25, Supplement, January, S2–S9.

Harkavy, O. (1995) *Curbing Population Growth: An Insider's Perspective on the Population Movement*, Plenum Press: New York and London.

Hartmann, B. (1987) *Reproductive Rights and Wrongs: The Global Politics of Population Control*, Harper and Row: New York.

Jeffrey, R. (1992) *Politics, Women and Well-Being: How Kerala Became 'a Model'*, Macmillan: London.

Pachauri, S. (1996) "A Shift from Family Planning to Reproductive Health: New Challenges" in K. Srinivasan (ed.) *Population Policy and Reproductive Health*, Population Foundation of India: New Delhi, pp. 243–266.

Parayil, G. (2000). (ed). *Kerala: The Development Experience. Reflections on Sustainability and Replicability*. Zed Books: London.

Population Foundation of India (1996) *India: Population, Reproductive Health and Human Development* (statistics brochure), Hindustan Publishing Corporation: New Delhi.

Purvis, T. and Hunt, A. (1991) "Discourse, ideology, discourse, ideology, discourse, ideology..." *British Journal of Sociology*, Volume 44, No. 3, pp. 473–499.

Ramanathan, M. (1998) "Reproductive Health Index: Measuring Reproduction or Reproductive Health?" *Economic and Political Weekly*. 33(49). Dec, 5–11, pp. 3104–3107.

Sai, F. T. (1997) "ICPD Programme of Action: pious hope or a workable guide?", *Health Transition Review*, Supplement 4 to Volume 7, pp. 1–5.

Sen, A. (1995) "Population: Delusion and Reality" in M. Cromartie (ed.) *The Nine Lives of Population Control*, The Ethics and Public Policy Centre and Wm. B. Eerdmans Publishing Company: Michigan, pp. 101–128.

van Dijk, T. A. (1998) *Ideology: A Multidisciplinary Approach*, Thousand Oaks: London, Sage: California.

2

Feminist Frameworks

Policy and Ideology

> If there was a 'paradigm shift' at Cairo, women were at the very heart of it.
>
> Johnson, 1995

> … [t]his concept of population, which transforms living people into mere numbers makes it possible … even for a UN document to compare the growth of the 'car population' with that of the 'human population'.
>
> Mies and Shiva, 2001

Conventionally, mainstream discussions of population policy are projected as being around programme design or service provision, the availability, supply and use of contraceptives, and so on—seemingly arid technical and demographic debates devoid of any vested interests, and driven solely by the logic of population determinants. Successive ICPDs, however, have revealed the deeply political nature of these administrative debates. If anything, Cairo revealed much the same. However, there was an exception. The debates at Cairo, unlike other ICPDs, pertained primarily to women; the discourse of reproductive health cannot be viewed apart from its emphasis on rights and emancipation for women. This added dimension created some volatility at the Conference. It aroused an array of opinions, each of which underscored a deeper value system that had definitive views on the roles and needs of women in society. Not surprisingly, what was learnt at Cairo was that gender ideologies underlining the discourse on reproductive health are intimately linked to wider social, historical, cultural, juridical values and beliefs—that definitions of women's reproductive needs are influenced by their perceived role in population issues, their societies, and in the globalising world. These are areas where intense gender research of the last three decades has already highlighted that particular constructions of women are both widespread and insidious, often with discriminatory impacts on women.

Constructions about women and their social position are not scattered attitudes in individuals' minds but part of a highly organised belief system: an ideology. The linkages and ramifications of gender ideology are complex. They run from the everyday behaviour of a single person to the institutionalised rituals of the most modern organisations. Ideology and discourse effects also manifest in policy and are expressed in the production of policy, in the interactions between provider and recipient of services. Effects of ideology are captured in the languages privileged in the machinery of government, in its visions, in the priorities set across sectors, and the services it delivers/does not deliver. Gender ideologies also overshadow the wider structures of the state that are involved in the policy process; the state draws on ideologies from fields afar, such as, history, myth, culture and religion, all of which frame the processes and outcomes of gender policy. In this chapter and the chapter that follows, I aim to explore the ways that gender 'ideology' and 'discourse' are embedded in the workings of the policy machinery. I trace theoretical perspectives that lay out the fundamental concepts underlying the links between social/ political ideologies and constructions of women, women's roles and needs in policy. I explore influences of discourse studies in two fields of feminist thought. These include studies on the production of policy discourse, and studies of the state and women's identity. The present chapter will focus on the former—how discourses translate into the policy field. In elaborating this, I first review feminist theoretical perspectives on discourse and policy. The theoretical literature that I draw on has its source in research around women and policy in the 'First' World and with caution is applied to the context of women in developing countries. The chapter then moves from the theoretical to a survey of the recent history of the reproductive health discourse—its emergence in the international arena and integration into the main/malestream of population policy leading up to the Cairo Conference. The next chapter focuses on ideology and discourses within the domain of the state.

Gender, Discourse and Ideology

A scholarly interest in gender and discourse emerged in the mid-to-late 1980s with an increasing number of feminist adherents to the post-structuralist school of theorising power. Until then, feminist explanations of women's subordinate roles were drawn from Liberal, Radical, Marxist and Dualist accounts of social relations, or what are sometimes called the 'traditional' schools of feminist thought.[10] The Liberal theorists upheld that women's inequality stemmed from their lack of access to various spheres of public life, be it education, politics, the paid work force and so on. Their rebuttal of male dominance in society was primarily through demonstrating that women were equally capable and had a 'right' to participate in the affairs of 'men's' world. Women's rights were justified through their 'sameness' with men, and through juridical changes, liberal feminists expected that women would participate equally with men. Unlike Radical feminists, Liberal theorists never questioned the system they strived to enter—their main effort was to remove perceptions of female inadequacies and to be equal participants in all spheres of life. Radical feminists, on the other hand, attributed women's subordination to biological differences between the sexes and women's role in reproduction. Women's capacity to reproduce, they argued, was used against women as a tool for subjugation. Radical feminists also highlighted that institutions, political, educational, and religious as well as the media in contemporary society, were underpinned by widespread values of patriarchy

[10] For a review on the various schools of feminist thought, see Jaggar, A. and Rothenberg, P. (1993).

that discriminated against women. Radical feminists believed that the only long-term hope of an egalitarian society for men and women was a revolutionary new order that would replace patriarchy. Marxist feminist theories of women's disempowerment were closely tied to understandings of capitalism and class power—women's unpaid domestic labour and underpaid market work provided the lever for capitalist growth. Marxist feminist analyses underscored capitalism as the source of women's exploitation. The economic system, in their view, had to be overhauled if women's subordination was to be addressed. Dual theorists built on both a socialist and radical feminist perspective arguing that a capitalist structure in conjunction with patriarchy was responsible for women's subjugation.

These theories, incisive as they were, failed to address some key issues that underpin any account of gender oppression in society. One was that in any social order, not all women were equally disempowered. Oppression was also a matter of location—some women in some positions of society were more likely to be subordinated than others. Class, race, ethnicity, religion and sexual orientation all accounted for a different experience of oppression (this issue tends to be referred to as the contradiction of 'differences' among women in feminist theory). Furthermore, often women themselves were the perpetrators of women's oppression. Similarly, contrary to the proponents of the biology-based theories, not all men were oppressors either. Men, depending on their location, experienced subordination as well. The relativity of location, gender and power led to the need for theoretical perspectives that tackled gender-relations as an outcome of their social roles and the social meanings attached to these roles, rather than biology or economic structure. Who produced these meanings? How were these meanings or constructions used to maintain power? How were women's experiences in societies shadowed by these meanings? Over the course of the last two decades, feminist theorisations have moved to a focus on the study of the interactions between production of meaning (usually through language and discourse) and power. This is broadly what is covered by post-structuralist thought.

Without digressing into a detailed discussion of post-structuralism, I will briefly outline the fundamental concepts that make up this theoretical position. According to post-structuralists, power is exercised through myriad ways in social settings. I draw on notions of power used by Foucault which refute an idea of power that is centralised and necessarily only manifested in physically oppressive ways. Rather, power is ubiquitous, its use and abuse is complex, and its effect culminates in the production of pliant subjects, people who so identify with the social meanings/representations attributed to them that in an extreme view there is no room for stepping outside of the constructions and acting with agency. As Elizabeth Grosz points out:

> ... he (Foucault) refuses to equate power with a social structure (such as patriarchy), or with social institutions and practices (such as the family or the practices of socialisation exercised by it), or with interpersonal force or strength (as in heterosexual sexual and aggressive relations). Rather, power is both (a) historical system aligned across structures, institutions, rituals, practices, and individual lives, bringing them together in some contexts, and dividing them in others—a 'substratum of force relations; and (b) the particular use of the products of these alignments (e.g., knowledges, practices) to interrogate, regulate, supervise, observe, train, harness, and confine the behaviours and subjectivities of individuals and groups (Grosz 1990: 87–88).

Post-structuralists point out that social meanings, representations and subjectivities are produced through economic, political and social discursive practices. Subjectivities refer to the conscious or unconscious thoughts and emotions of an individual, her/his sense of self and her/his way of relating to the world around her/him (Weedon 1987: 32). Since power is exercised in subjectivities, it is important to query the discourses that produce certain constructions and meanings. Post-structuralists consider text (which reveals discourses and ideologies) as the major site of struggle for women's emancipation. Herein lies the power of one group over others in society.

Individuals do not occupy only one subject position at a time. It is more likely that people slip from one subject position to another. So the "demure wife" at one moment can become the "overbearing mother-in-law" or the "selfless mother" in another. However, discourses limit the number of subject positions that can be taken up and the freedom within a subject position. And when discourses are institutionally embedded, subjectivities can constrain women's ability to experience autonomy and agency. Chris Weedon summarises feminist post-structuralism as follows:

> Feminist post-structuralism, then, is a mode of knowledge production which uses poststructuralist theories of language, subjectivity, social processes and institutions to understand existing power relations and to identify areas and strategies for change. Through a concept of *discourse*, which is seen as a structuring principle of society, in social institutions, modes of thought and individual subjectivity, feminist post-structuralism is able, in detailed, historically specific analysis, to explain the working of power on behalf of specific interests and to analyse the opportunities for resistance to it ...discourses represent political interests and in consequence are constantly vying for status and power. The site of this battle for power is the subjectivity of the individual and it is a battle in which the individual is an active but not sovereign protagonist (Weedon 1987: 41, emphasis in original).

There is one important point to note here. Although feminist post-structuralism has drawn on Foucault's description of power, feminist theorists do not totally concur with his views on power. Feminist critics of Foucault argue that in conceptualising power as being neither an institution nor structure, Foucault does not acknowledge role-constitution as resulting from domination of one group by another. An analysis of power without an understanding of gender domination is futile to the praxis of feminism. Rather, feminist scholars, while drawing on Foucault's analysis of power and discourse, seek to understand the constitution of gender relations from a more critical perspective. Feminists explicitly argue that the inability to have control over production of discourses relates to the social location of individuals and groups, and that, in challenging dominant discourses, social relations can also be altered. Such a perspective of power and gender discourse supports the feminist project of social transformation and activism (Hartsock 1990).

Gender, Discourses and Policy

These basic postulates on power from post-structuralist theorists are significant—they provide an important lens to analyse representations of gender in diverse fields, from literature and media to economic and scientific theory. So, how do these theorisations of discourse reflect in mainstream policy-making and the context of politics?

Although unacknowledged in traditional texts on policy studies, public policy, like any other political discourse, is suffused with ideological presuppositions. Conventional policy analysis tends to idealise the policy-making process as being a rational one, where policy analysts are engaged in systematic problem solving. Policy analysis—as epitomised in the model of the Policy Cycle—is represented as being a process progressing systematically from a phase of problem definition, analysis of alternative solutions, the adoption of a solution, and its implementation and evaluation. The aim of policy analysis is to weigh up empirical evidence to select the most relevant option to solve public needs. This image of policy analysis has come under considerable criticism because it misrepresents policy making as an 'orderly sequence of stages as if on an assembly line' (Stone 1988: 7). A growing number of policy theorists argue that it would be more pragmatic to view policy-making as a site where various political, social, ideological and value judgments influence the shape and design of policy.[11] Rather than adhere to set stages, policy, in practice, arises from political *conflict*; it is a 'struggle over ideas' where concepts, definitions and criteria are susceptible to continuous scrutiny and compromise (Stone 1988:7).

Public policy, when enacted in the everyday world therefore, is messy and chaotic; it mirrors the volatile world of public sphere politics. The public spaces where politics is deliberated are sites where contending social discourses prevail and where social meanings are constantly contested. These spheres of struggle

---

[11] The name given to this genre of policy studies scholarship is post-postivism. Authors include Ascher (1987), de Leon (1998), Fischer (2003), Fischer and Forrester (1993) and Torgerson (1996).

are seldom fair or equal; for the most part, it is the voices and interests of the powerful or dominant discourses that are visibly represented. Discourses of marginal or oppositional groups are, at best, the "challengers" to dominant discourses.[12] Dominant discourses are institutionalised in the key discursive sites of society such as parliament, academia, courts and the mass media and become reference norms that exclude some discourses and include others. As a result, it is important to recognise that policy is not about identifying and satisfying needs of various groups of people, but equally about issues such as *who* has deemed certain concerns as needs and how these are interpreted (Fraser 1989a). Discourse also gives validity to specific knowledge systems that political and policy scientists work within. Both politicians and policy analysts have enduring visions of what constitutes public interests and appropriate policy interventions. The tendency for policy analysts to work within a technocratic framework or for politicians to emphasise certain kinds of policy outcomes is a consequence of the entire institution of politics being steeped in a particular discursive paradigm.

Furthermore, discourse also directs the language that constitutes politics. Fraser (1989a) argues that the language of the dominant discursive paradigm penetrates political reality in a variety of ways: from the officially recognised idioms in which one can press claims to the ways in which various discursive positions of people are defined, and the paradigms that are considered authoritative. In a democratic society where premium is placed on the use of language and debate at every stage of the political process, the transformative power of language cannot be undermined. An important distinction must be made. Political discourse is not political power itself; rather, 'discourse has a complex relationship to power.... [w]hile it is not power per se,

---

[12] It must be noted that dominant discourses may correspond but not necessarily be aligned to party politics. Ideology at the level I refer to in this book go far deeper than partisan politics. The case of the Women's Bill in India is an example that illustrates this. It is interesting that when introduced, the Bill was challenged across political parties, demonstrating that the dominant discourse is less about party ideology than, perhaps, a masculinist ideology.

political discourse produces and transmits power' (Fischer 1995: 225). It is also important to note that discourse is not immutable or irreversible; neither is power. Because discursive frames are mutable, challengers to a dominant paradigm can expect to make inroads into existing value systems, but these are likely to be gradual and incremental. Thus, political discourse can serve as a 'tool of either domination or liberation' (Fischer 1995: 225).

While there is little challenge to the proposition that ideology does play a role in the construction of gender policy, there is less certainty about its consequences. Nancy Fraser's writings in the late 1980s and throughout the 1990s provided an influential analysis of the process of producing gender policy in an environment charged with contradictory discursive forces. She postulated the theory of 'Needs Interpretation', which she explores in her 1989 book, *Unruly Practices*. The 'needs interpretation' thesis brings a critical perspective to the way discourses around (social) needs are articulated in late twentieth century welfare states, and aims to show how these needs find their way into policy frameworks. There are three aspects of this model that are particularly useful for examining the processes by which certain gender discourses attain currency in political life, namely: (1) the concept of runaway needs, (2) the three moments of needs interpretation, and (3) the major forms of needs-talk (i.e., the way needs are debated and constructed) discourses and their functions. To gain an understanding of these three components, I will first elaborate Fraser's (1989a) conceptualisation of the discursive structures in society.

According to Fraser, the welfare state in the late twentieth century was constituted by various social groups. Each of these groups made claims on the state to produce policy that satisfied what they regarded as crucial needs for their well-being. For Fraser, the actual content of the needs and how these may be satisfied is secondary to the discourses surrounding needs; that is, the focus should be on how needs are interpreted rather than only focusing on implementation of programmes to satisfy what have already been interpreted as needs. Among the reasons Fraser (1989a) gives for this shift of focus is that needs are not determined or satisfied in isolation from social and political processes in society. Fraser draws on Foucault's notion that discourses construct individuals as subjects, and emphasises the importance of giving due attention to the role of institutions and authorities that determine which groups' claims are articulated in the public arena. She points out that mainstream political theorists by focusing on satisfaction of established needs '... assume that it is unproblematic who interprets the needs in question and from what perspective and in the light of what interests; they thus occlude the fact that *who* gets to establish authoritative thick definitions of people's needs is itself a political stake' (Fraser 1989b:162, emphasis in original). Fraser also sees the establishment of needs discourses as closely tied to key zones in society: the political, economic and domestic dimensions. Fraser positions the domain of the political as "public-official" in opposition to the "private" spheres of the economic and domestic.

In Fraser's model, an issue that has not become a matter for political debate or action is entrenched within the personal sphere—either within domestic or economic institutions. Women's issues usually tend to be contained within the domestic sphere. However, the boundaries between the political and the personal are porous; under a variety of circumstances, an issue that is conventionally regarded as private escapes into the public sphere—a "runaway, leaky issue" that then becomes politicised. Furthermore, Fraser sees society being constituted mainly by three kinds of discourses that influence needs-talk: *oppositional discourses*, representing the voice of subordinate groups or discourses from "below", such as feminist movements; and *reprivatisation discourses* and *expert-needs discourses*—from "above"—that represent the discourses of the institutionalised problem solving structures in society. The discourses from above seek to deny the claims of oppositional movements of the legitimacy of a "runaway need". Reprivatisation discourses, representing the reactionary forces in society or the forces of economic gain, are in continuous conflict with oppositional claims to political legitimacy. Expert-needs discourses depoliticise oppositional needs by trying to institutionalise and 'normalise' them through the state's bureaucratic apparatus. Expert-needs discourses are the vehicle for translating "sufficiently politicised runaway needs into objects of potential state intervention" (1989b: 174). Both the reprivatisation and expert-needs discourses serve to depoliticise runaway needs that are articulated by oppositional groups. However, the struggle to establish a needs-discourse, or endow an issue with a political status, according to Fraser, is only the first of three interrelated *moments in needs interpretation*. A second stage in the needs struggle is defining the means to satisfy the need or the interpretation of the need. The third moment is the struggle to satisfy the need, or the process of allocating the resources and making provision for the satisfaction of the need.

The outcomes of discourse struggles for gender policy are not predictable. Policy changes are never completely new; fresh approaches, particularly gender perspectives, to policy are always introduced and implemented in the context of the legacies of the past, as well as current conditions. It is important to know how oppositional discourses translate into policy in contexts where values and ideologies are overwhelmingly male/mainstream. Fraser (1989a), for instance, argues that institutionalisation of oppositional feminist discourse tends to *two* possibilities: a pressure to reprivatise politicised issues, or conversely, appropriate them into the existing structures of bureaucracy, nullifying their political impact. In either case, the consequences for women are not in their interests. In the latter, in particular, the institutionalisation of policy in specific contexts has an ominous outcome—women's issues can become 'depoliticised' in the course of assimilation within public discourse. Alternatively, gender-sensitive recommendations are likely to become add-ons to an ongoing policy legacy (Beall 1997; Harding 1995). There could also be several orientations to policy, which may operate within the various levels of state, from global to local levels. In this form of policy accrual, there is a real danger that consistency in addressing women's issues could be compromised, and women's needs could well be marginalised.

Reproductive Health as a Political Discourse

A brief history

According to Mosse (1994), there are three broad phases in international approaches to population policy since the 1950s:

(a) the 1950s and 1960s emphasised a *family planning approach*, (b) the 1970s saw the emergence of the *maternal and child health approach* and (c) the late 1980s were the beginnings of a *reproductive health approach*. The family planning approach placed inordinate focus on fertility control through the promotion of contraceptive use. The maternal and child health focus emphasised conditions for safe maternal and child health, both as a health objective and because of its indirect implications for people's fertility decisions.

The genesis of reproductive health as a population discourse can be traced to several sources. A key influential force was the trans-national women's health movement of the 1970s and the 1980s. The international women's health movement was a loose coalition comprising several groups from various countries coalescing or networking through a few key organisations. One such key organisation was the Women's Global Network for Reproductive Rights or WGNRR (with headquarters in Amsterdam); another was the International Women's Health Coalition or IWHC.[13] With the spread of second-wave feminism in the West in the 1970s, one of the issues that emerged as a focal lobbying issue was women's health. The issue of reproductive rights was central to the activities of the women's movement, reflecting the political and legal debates at the time in Europe and North America, especially those surrounding women's right to abortion.[14] In the mid-seventies, spurred in part by the start of the UN focus on women's issues world-wide, there was an effort to link the North American and European feminist movements with women activists from other parts of the world. There was an increasing visibility in the presence of activists from the South at international conferences and as part

---

[13] For a history of the international women's health movement of the 1990s, see Correa and Petchesky 1994; Dixon-Mueller and Germain 1994; Garcia-Moreno and Claro 1994; Johnson 1995.

[14] Abortion was an important fuelling issue in the West in the 1970s following the landmark decision on the 1973 Roe vs. Wade case by the Supreme Court of the United States. The decision was the first in the country that allowed a woman, under certain conditions, to make the decision to terminate a pregnancy.

of informal trans-national networks. The diversity of women in the international arena brought to the fore various forms of reproduction-related oppressions faced by women. Women from the South highlighted, in particular, that oppressive family planning policies infringed their right to reproductive freedom. Development Alternatives with Women for a New Era (DAWN), the women's group spearheaded by women in the South, pointed to Third World women's concerns in the way reproductive freedom was being denied to them.

> Control over reproduction is a basic need and a basic right for a woman. Linked as it is to women's health and social status, as well as the powerful social structures of religion, state control and administrative inertia, and private profit, it is from the perspective of the poor women that this right can best be understood and affirmed. Women know that child bearing is a social, not a purely personal, phenomenon; nor do we deny that world population trends are likely to exert considerable pressure on resources and institutions by the end of this century. But our bodies have become a pawn in the struggles among states, religions, male heads of households and private corporations. Programs that do not take the interests of women into account are unlikely to succeed (Sen and Grown 1987: 49).

The women's health movement defined their key philosophy in their definition of reproductive rights, that women should have the right to decide 'whether, when and how to have children, regardless of nationality, class, ethnicity, race, age, religion, disability, sexuality or marital status in the social, economic and political conditions that make such decisions possible' (WGNRR newsletter 1993). For feminists, reproductive health is expected to encompass four dimensions: (1) the ability to enjoy sexual relations without fear of infections, unwanted pregnancy, or coercion, (2) the ability to regulate fertility without the risk of unpleasant or dangerous side effects, (3) the ability to go safely through childbirth, and (4) the ability to be able to bear and raise healthy children (Germain and Antrobus cited in Graham 1993). Ensuring high standards of reproductive health is thus central to the idea of reproductive rights. The women's health movement adopted the WHO definition of reproductive health which was defined not in the negative as the "absence of disease or infirmity", but as a condition to aspire to, that is, "a state of complete physical, mental and social well-being" (WGNRR newsletter 1993). Some of the issues that the women's health movement addressed as reproductive health concerns were around information (about sexuality as well as reproduction and contraception, about reproductive health and health problems, and about benefits and risks of drugs, devices, medical treatments and interventions, without which informed choice is impossible), good quality comprehensive and accessible reproductive health services, safe and legal abortions, safe and effective treatment for infertility, and freedom from population policies and social codes that pressure some women to have children and others not to (WGNRR newsletter 1993).

The heightened consciousness about the detrimental effects of mainstream population policy was increasingly a rallying point for women from various regions at international women's forums. The women's health movement was critical of narrowly constructed definitions of family planning programmes. A central tenet of the women's health movement is that women's health and rights, not macro-demographic objectives, are of paramount concern. The international women's movement emphasised the notions of rights of a woman to have control over her own body, her sexuality, and her reproductive life. The International Women's Year Conference, 1975, noted that, "...it should be one of the principal aims of social education to teach respect for physical integrity and its rightful place in human life. The human body, whether that of woman or man, is inviolable and respect of it is a fundamental element of human dignity" (United Nations 1976, cited in Freedman and Isaacs 1993: 23). Right through the 1980s, there was an increased awareness of women's issues in many areas of political and economic life. Research, teaching and practice of gender and development mushroomed. The United Nations processes were acknowledging gender and women's issues in many of their charters and conferences. Hilkka Pietila in her book *Engendering the Global Agenda* (2002) devotes a whole chapter to the idea that the 'United Nations Decade for Women changed the world'. Non-governmental international agencies were mainstreaming gender into their everyday organisational functions. Individual women (such as former US Congresswoman, Bella Abzug) were gaining immense credibility in their ability to lobby for women's issues at an international level. Alongside, it was becoming increasingly acceptable to run parallel NGO forums at UN Conferences. In the 1990s, Secretaries-General who organised the UN Conferences (Nafis Sadik was Secretary-General for the ICPD, Cairo) were open to working with women's groups (Pietila 2002).

All in all, by the early 1990s, there was considerable interest among the international women's health groups to be a compelling voice in the debates at Cairo. As the Conference drew closer, they made preparations to participate in the Prep-Comms or preparatory committees leading to the ICPD (Harkavy 1995). The women's health movement drafted the 'Women's Declaration on Population Policies' (The Declaration) in 1992 in time for the Cairo Population Conference. The Declaration was intended to convey the women's health movement's stand on a variety of issues around development and reproduction in the Third World. Between 1992 and October 1993, the Declaration was modified and finalised by over 100 women's organisations in 23 countries (Johnson 1995: 138). These organisations affirmed that[15]:

> [w]omen's fertility has been the primary objective of both pro-natalist and anti-natalist population policies. Women's behaviour rather than men's has been the focus of attention. Women have been expected to carry most of the responsibility and risks of birth control, but have been largely excluded from decision-making in personal relationships as well as in public policy.... [P]opulation policies must be based on the principle of respect for the sexual and bodily integrity of girls and women ... (cited in Germain, Nowrojee and Pyne 1994: 32).

The Declaration was finally adopted in January 1994. As a document, the singular achievement of the Declaration was that

---

[15] Not all women's organisations supported the Declaration. Some like the WGNRR were opposed to it and similar population frameworks on grounds that by compromising to accommodate official rhetoric, the WGNRR would lose its critical edge, dull its tools of analysis and divorce itself from the women it represents (Nair, Kirbat and Sexton 2004)

women from all over the world deliberated over it and supported the values and agendas it embodied.

The research and activism emerging from the women's health movement was reflected in a change in the focus of mainstream demographic scholarship. The medical understanding of fertility behaviour that had primarily focused on maternal health, was beginning to acknowledge a host of other influences on a woman's reproductive life. An influential early work within the medical/demographic field was by Sai and Nassim (1989). They pointed out that the foundations of health were laid down during childhood and adolescence and that a reproductive health approach, in principle, recognised aspects of nutrition, development, education and the socio-economic environment as key determinants of the health of women at the time of pregnancy and childbirth. According to Sai and Nassim (1989), a reproductive health approach recognises that maternal mortality, the main indicator of women's health, is just the "tip of the iceberg of problems" caused by sexuality and pregnancy. The focus on reproductive health, in many ways, compelled the medical community to review critically the fragmented approach to health that was conventionally provided in developing countries and the advantages of integrated health programmes which focus on the social determinants of people's lives.

International donor agencies also began to recognise that a reproductive health approach was a key development in population policy. In the mid-1980s, the Ford Foundation redefined its framework for thinking about population policy. In 1985, the Ford Foundation's work on population acknowledged the narrow conception under which most policies work and recognised that fertility decisions were in fact influenced by factors such as "a woman's education and her sense of her own opportunities" (Harkavy 1995: 188). By the 1990s, reproductive health became the fundamental theme for all grants made under population-related activities of the Ford Foundation. The MacArthur Foundation since 1988 has put primary emphasis on funding reproductive health programmes. The United States Agency for International Aid (USAID), under the Clinton administration, also chose to work in areas around women's status, although not directly labelled reproductive health.[16] The United Nations Foundation for Population Activities (UNFPA), alongside, collaborated closely with women's groups and was responsive to the change in direction that was impelled under the ethos of reproductive health (Harkavy 1995).

The rhetoric of reproductive health, which began in the women's health movement, thus began to challenge and redefine existing values that defined population policy. The final affirmation of efforts of the women's health movement was the adoption of ideas espoused in the reproductive health approach by the international population community. The movement's participation in international conferences and, especially, the processes that led to the International Conference for Population and Development at Cairo, 1994, were particularly significant in influencing the text of the document that emerged from the conference. The Programme of Action at Cairo (POA) centred women's well-being and rights as the pivotal concern that would impel the design and implementation of population policy. The phrase 'quality of care' was a new addition to the text of the POA, while concepts that had emerged from the women's movements' discourses around reproductive health like "bodily integrity" were implicitly acknowledged within the broad agenda of women's empowerment. The preamble of the POA notes that "... advancing gender equality and equity and the empowerment of women, and the elimination of all kinds of violence against women, and ensuring women's ability to control their own fertility, are cornerstones of population and development related programmes" (United Nations 1995: 8). It was the first time that reproductive and sexual health, and reproductive rights of women were central to an international agreement on population (Germain and Kyte 1995). As Correa and Petchesky (1994: 119) point out, "[y]ears of organising and advocacy by women's health groups throughout the world have clearly had an important effect

[16] There has, of course, been a radical change in the US government's policies since George W. Bush became President. Most funding from USAID is restrained by conservative views on relationships between men and women, and women's rights to reproductive choices.

at the level of official rhetoric on inter-governmental forums concerned with population issues" (emphasis in original).

Not surprisingly, the text of the POA of the ICPD is an interesting mix of ideas that have been drawn from feminist visions of reproductive freedoms and earlier international charters that enunciate criteria for reproductive rights. The POA adopted the World Health Organisation's (WHO) definition of reproductive rights as the "right of all couples and individuals to decide freely and responsibly the number, spacing and timing of their children ..., the right to attain the highest standard of sexual and reproductive health ..., the right to make decisions concerning reproduction free of discrimination, coercion and violence" (POA, Chapter 7.3, United Nations 1995). The POA also makes specific references to women's reproductive rights within reproductive health programmes. Chapter 4.4 (c) of the POA notes that "... countries should act to empower women ... assisting women to establish and realise their rights, including those that relate to reproductive and sexual health". Chapter 11.9 also emphasises the promotion of the notion of rights in programme strategies, stating that "... [i]nformation, education and communication efforts should raise awareness ... on such issues as: safe motherhood, reproductive health and rights ...". The POA further asserts that "... reproductive health programmes should be designed to serve the needs of women ... and must involve women in the leadership, planning, decision-making, management, implementation, organisation and evaluation of services" (POA, Chapter 7.7, United Nations 1995). The ICPD set five quantifiable goals for the twenty-year period between 1995 and 2015:

- universal access to family planning and reproductive health services;
- reduced infant and child mortality;
- reduced maternal mortality;
- increased life expectancy at birth; and
- universal access to and completion of primary education, with particular emphasis on girls.

Thus, the ICPD 1994 locates reproductive health and rights within a broader context of women's self determination and control over their reproductive and sexual lives. This is evident in the generous attention that the POA gives to women's empowerment and equality issues within reproductive and sexual health. The POA rejects the view of women's equality as simply a means to the goal of fertility control as is evident from the following quote: "... the empowerment and autonomy of women and the improvement of their political, social, economic and health status is a highly important end in itself" (Chapter 4). The POA links empowerment to decision-making capacities for women, thus implying reorganisation of existing gender relations in society (Chapter 4.4). The POA also emphasises the importance of male responsibility within the traditional sphere of women's activities (such as child-care, housework and sexual responsibility) (Chapter 4.11). Further sections such as 4.17 point out that "the value of girl children to both their family and society must be expanded beyond their definition as potential child-bearers and caretakers ...". Thus, the POA replaces both anti-natalist and pro-natalist ends with those of personal well-being, pleasure and freedom (Petchesky 1995).

Armed with a lexicon of feminist associations, the reproductive health discourse entered public conscience advocating a set of principles that were revolutionary. Firstly, the reproductive health discourse stood for *rights*. As a rights-based discourse, reproductive health took on several meanings. The most clearly articulated was that reproductive health was a 'human right'; in other words, reproduction was firmly embedded within a framework of human rights (Bunch 1990; Cook 1993, 1995a, 1995b; Correa 1994; Dixon-Mueller 1993).[17] In the early 1990s when feminists campaigned to recognise that 'reproductive rights as women's rights' and 'women's rights as human rights', the

---

[17] Cook (1993) draws on the following rights endowed by the Political Covenant (the International Covenant on Political and Civil Rights) and the Economic Covenant (International Covenant on Economic, Social and Cultural Rights) and applies them to reproductive health issues: the Rights to Life, Liberty, and Security, the Right to Liberty and Security, the Right to Marry and Found a Family, the Right to Private and Family Life, Rights regarding information and education, the Right to Reproductive Health and Health Care, and the Right to the Benefits of Scientific Progress.

onus was on these women's health groups to justify why and how women's issues equated with the first and second generation of human rights, i.e. civil and political rights and economic, social and cultural rights. The evidence of blatant reproductive discrimination, sometimes resulting in death, but more often in heightened morbidity was convincingly laid out.[18] As a human right, the denial of reproductive health, through prevailing laws that deny or limit availability of and access to reproductive health services, are seen as a violation of the 1979 Convention on the Elimination of All Forms of Discrimination against Women (the Women's Convention). By ratifying the Women's Convention, States are obliged to 'pursue by all appropriate means and without delay a policy of discrimination against women in the field of health care in order to ensure ... access to health care services including those related to family planning'(Article 12, Women's Convention). Two kinds of actions were expected of states in this regard: one was a positive action, where states would provide enabling conditions for individuals to exercise reproductive agency, and a negative action, where states would refrain from coercive policies that restrain women's reproductive freedom. A decade later, feminist writings were emphasising the indivisibility of the various generations of rights in making reproductive health effectively protected by human rights (Petchesky 2000). In Petchesky's words:

> a woman cannot avail herself of her right 'to decide freely and responsibly the number, spacing and timing of her children' (ICPD Programme of Action, 7.3) if she lacks the financial resources to pay for reproductive health services or the transport to reach them; if she cannot read package inserts or clinic wall posters; if her workplace is contaminated with pesticides or pollutants that have an adverse effect on pregnancy; or if she is harassed by a husband or in-laws who will scorn her or beat her up if she uses birth control (Petchesky, 2000: 13).

However, the positioning of reproductive health as a rights discourse has not been without contest, even among feminists. Staking a claim for reproductive rights as an individual's right

[18] For some of the literature that emerged at this time on reproductive health and human rights, see the publications in The Centre for Reproductive Law and Policy at www.crlp.org

within a liberal framework has been challenged; such a claim raises problems about the underlying *individualistic* bias which may be unacceptable in many cultural contexts. The alternative is to reframe reproductive rights from a 'social rights' perspective; Correa and Petchesky (1994: 110) note a social rights perspective of reproductive rights would 'shift the major burden of correlative duties from individuals to public agencies ... acknowledge the *communal* (relational) *contexts* in which individuals act to exercise or pursue their rights ... [and] ... foreground the substantive basis of rights in human needs and a redistribution of resources'. For women of developing societies, where an individualist concept of reproductive rights is contrary to their ideas of body and self, and to their allegiance to their community and family, the social rights perspective resonates closer to their understanding of their reproductive needs (Petchesky and Judd 1998).

A second idea associated with reproductive rights is that of *empowerment*. A term that is widely considered difficult to define or measure, empowerment has come to represent several aspects of women's ability to exercise agency in their lives.[19] A feminist discourse on reproductive health is grounded in *empowerment* of women, that is, a reproductive health policy is more than about providing services for women or ensuring that certain reproductive outcomes—no matter how necessary for women's health—have been achieved.[20] Instead, the feminist discourse of reproductive health is underpinned by a sense of 'power'. Reproductive empowerment is personal; it rests on one's ability to exercise decision-making and have autonomy over one's own body (Correa and Petchesky 1994). Equally, an empowering

---

[19] Kabeer (1999) notes that empowerment is about the ability to make choices and the ability to define one's goals and act upon them. Batliwala (1994) describes empowerment as the process by which the powerless gain greater control over resources (physical, human, intellectual and financial) and over ideologies (beliefs, values, etc.) that influence their life's circumstances.

[20] This is not to suggest that all feminists have a unified understanding about the various social and personal aspects of reproduction and reproductive health. Smyth (1998) provides a brief description of the ways in which the various major schools of feminist thought perceive reproduction.

reproductive health discourse is also about altering power relations both in a woman's external circumstances and in her internal state of being and capability (Sen and Batliwala 2000).

Thus, reflecting its origins in the feminist movement, the reproductive health discourse is embellished with notions of rights, freedom and power. As reproductive health became the ideological basis for population and development, there were potential implications for population policy and programmes. The reproductive health discourse challenged existing ideas of how population policy ought to be addressed, particularly, its espousal of the notion that women's well-being superseded the objectives of the nation-state and local communities. The institutionalisation of the discourse of reproductive health, as a result, involves a marked shift to a novel set of discursive themes. The state's negotiation of this discourse, and its consequent assimilation into the state's pre-existing ideologies, is a critical moment in the institutionalisation of reproductive health within health systems.

The Discourses from Above: Neo-Malthusianism and Neo-Liberalism

If the reproductive health discourse, emerging as it has from the struggles of the women's health movement resembles Fraser's (1989a,b) oppositional need, then the discourses of neo-liberalism and neo-Malthusianism reflect Fraser's (1989a,b) discourses from 'above'. The interpretation of the reproductive health discourse is particularly sensitive to the ideologies of other socially dominant discourses that mark the same international and national terrain. Both materially and ideologically, the discourses of neo-Malthusianism and neo-liberalism, which are fundamentally at odds with the reproductive health discourse, are likely to affect the way that reproductive health will be interpreted.[21] What these ostensibly divergent discourses are and

[21] Although neo-liberalism and neo-Malthusianism are distinct ideologies, there are overlaps in the way that they are used in practice especially in anti-natalist policies. In India, for instance, the ideology of economic growth is inseparable from an anti-natalist agenda.

how they conflate at the level of reproductive health policy will form the basis of the discussion that follows.

Neo-Malthusianism[22]

A description of mainstream population thinking would be incomplete without alluding to the work of the eighteenth century clergyman, Thomas Malthus (1766–1834). His renowned work, *Essay on the Principle of Population*, published in 1798, was a treatise on the contradictory forces of population and growth of food. His simply stated principle was that:

> Population, when unchecked, increases in a geometrical ratio. Subsistence increases only in an arithmetical ratio. A slight acquaintance with numbers will shew the immensity of the first power in comparison of the second. By that law of our nature which makes food necessary to the life of man, the effects of these two unequal powers must be kept equal. This implies a strong and constantly operating check on population from the difficulty of subsistence. This difficulty must fall somewhere and must necessarily be severely felt by a large portion of mankind (Malthus 1798).

In other words, according to Malthus, unless constrained, population would grow significantly faster than food production. This prediction for humankind was bleak; starvation would eventually ensue from this condition, leading, not surprisingly, to the end of (wo)mankind. Malthus's key contribution to economic theory was arriving at what is known as the Malthusian Equilibrium. Malthus argued that societies would arrive at a balance between fertility and mortality, both central components of demographic change. To understand how this balance or equilibrium would be reached, Malthus had a population model with two curves, representing two functional relationships. The first one represented real wages, or standard of living and the

---

[22] Rao (2004) distinguishes the conceptual difference between Malthusianism and neo-Malthusianism. Whilst both schools of thought are concerned with reducing fertility especially among the poor, neo-Malthusians were focused with population control in the 'Third' World. Moreover, while Malthusians advocated moral restraint, neo-Malthusians brought in technology to control fertility.

second described demographic behaviour. The starting point of his model is this: he referred to two checks on population—a positive check and a preventive check. A positive check occurs when mortality (particularly of the "lowest orders of society") reduces population. This happens because mortality rises as standard of living falls (an inverse relationship). A preventive check on population comes about with declining fertility—a control of population urged by falling standards of living, the "difficulties attending the rearing of a family" and because people are "disabled from giving the proper food and attention to their children".

There is a net increase in population if births exceed deaths and a decline if the opposite is the case. A rising population bears on the existing standard of living and lowers it, which brings population growth to a standstill. A lowering population improves the standard of living in the short term but this could be offset by an increase in population in one of the several scenarios Malthus predicts. An equilibrium between mortality, fertility and income would be reached at zero-population growth, and unless deliberately acted upon, society would continue to remain at that level. Malthus's conclusion was that any improvement in standards of living was possible only if population growth was minimal, either through fertility reduction or as an outcome of high mortality. As recommending that mortality be high was immoral, fertility restraint, according to Malthus, was the only viable way to increase standards of living in the long run. However, Malthus expressed some scepticism in containing population; as he said, "passion between the sexes was necessary and will remain nearly in its present state" (Malthus 1798). A vicar by profession, Malthus was opposed to the use of contraception and his solution was to check fertility by restricting early marriage. There are historical events, which illustrate the validity of Malthus's model. The Black Plague (1340s) and the Irish Potato Famine (1840s) are seen as examples of periods where high population growth put a strain on resources and led to falling standards of living. It was with the huge number of deaths that followed that standards of living began to rise again.

The Malthusian logic is widely paraded as the foundation for twentieth century anti-natalist population programmes. Neo-Malthusianism was certainly played out strongly in the ICPDs (particularly the 1974 ICPD) where a western paranoia of increasing Third World population was evident in the manner in which the debates around population growth were carried out. However, the ideology and practice of neo-Malthusianism has not been without challenge. Scholars like Julian Simon and Ester Boserup, for instance, pointed to the *beneficial* impact of increased population; that without a certain critical and growing mass of population, there is evidence of low economic development. Boserup showed how the 'strain of population' actually fosters use of better technological approaches in agriculture to boost food production.

With widespread public condemnation of the coercive history of population programmes in many developing countries (for example, sterilisation programmes in India in the 1970s and the Indonesian contraception safaris), and with the increasing use of human rights language in population policy, the neo-Malthusian tone of international population policies has been modulated. Still, as recently as 2001, the United Nations Commission on Population and Development in its Thirty-Fourth Session stated that:

> Population growth is generally regarded as the single most important force driving increases in agricultural demand. Most recent expert assessments are cautiously optimistic about the ability of global food production to keep up with demand for the foreseeable future (that is to say, until approximately 2030 or 2050) ... However it is important to note that these assessments are predicated upon the expectation that population growth rates will continue to decline... *The need to feed a growing population is placing mounting stress on water supplies in many parts of the world.*[23] (emphasis mine)

The legacy of Malthus's principle on population still continues.

---

[23] United Nations Economic and Social Council, Commission on Population and Development, Thirty-Fourth session (Follow-up actions to the recommendations of the International Conference on Population and Development), Concise Report on world population monitoring, 2001: Population, environment and development, Report of the Secretary-General, Para 53 and 54.

Neo-liberalism

The second ideology that overshadows the discourse of reproductive health is that of neo-liberalism. Given the extensive available literature (and equally extensive body of critique) that has proliferated in the last two decades, neo-liberalism as a concept and lived reality is familiar to many people across the globe today. Neo-liberalism originated within the discipline of economics as a set of rules to guide optimal profit creation in economies. The foundation of these principles is the rule of the market or what Adam Smith in 1776 called *laissez-faire*. In its twentieth century incarnation, neo-liberalism has seeped from within the boundaries of capitalist economies and currently underpins the political, social, and cultural contexts of many countries, apart from being a formidable influence on the processes of international relations (or what we know as 'globalisation').

The main objective of the neo-liberal or market principle is to enhance the profits/growth (that would, purportedly, trickle down to public good eventually) of society through the efficiency of the economic system guaranteed only by the market. Some of the mechanisms to augment the market are: removal of any restriction or regulations on the working of a free market, reduced intervention of the state in social programmes (a 'roll-back' of the state), privatisation of state-owned enterprises, a cutting down of expenditure in state institutions, and an emphasis on developing the cash-economy in order to kick-start economies into growth. The manifestation of the market world is best symbolised in the gargantuan increase of multi- and trans-national corporations in the past fifty years that concentrate a large proportion of world wealth and power. The diminished state presents a political dimension to the neo-liberal prescription, and throws into disarray the relationship between state, citizen, public good and private commercial interests. Equally, neo-liberalism has spread into a social and cultural ideology as well; the free market principle glorifies the 'rational' behaviour of the economic agent who interacts in the free market. For the lay (wo)man this translates into messages of individualism, consumerism, dynamism, competition, challenge of traditional norms and incessant youth as edicts for contemporary living.

Third World nations' tryst with neo-liberalism can be traced to two key events in recent economic history. The introduction of Structural Adjustment Packages from the mid-1980s onwards was the first stark jolt that abstract economic principles could become a reality of rule. Structural Adjustment Programmes (SAPs), in principle, aim to promote economic growth by cutting down 'wasteful' expenditure and reducing government spending in social programmes and creating conditions for market-led economies. Within the adjustment package, control of population growth is a key goal, as population growth is seen to impinge strongly on the other economic strategies undertaken in the package (Palmer 1991; Grown 1994; Mason 1993). In fact, the introduction of family planning policies has often been part of the conditionality of SAPs (Pearson 1997). At the same time, studies from developing countries indicate that auxiliary social services for women are on the decline (Sparr 1994; Dixon-Mueller 1993; Waylen 1992). Governments are keen to divert investment to sectors that directly produce outcomes that can be traded in the global economy.

The Washington Consensus was the second key event which solidified the neo-liberal discourse. The term 'Washington Consensus' was coined by John Williamson (1990, 2000) to refer to the "lowest common denominator of policy advice being addressed by the Washington-based institutions to Latin American countries as of 1989" and specifically advocated the following ten principles of economic management:

- Fiscal discipline
- A redirection of public expenditure priorities toward fields offering both high economic returns and the potential to improve income distribution, such as primary health care, primary education, and infrastructure
- Tax reform (to lower marginal rates and broaden the tax base)
- Interest rate liberalisation
- A competitive exchange rate
- Trade liberalisation

- Liberalisation of inflows of foreign direct investment
- Privatisation
- Deregulation (to abolish barriers to entry and exit)
- Secure property rights (Williamson 2000: 252)[24]

The Washington Consensus, in time, assumed the status of the operating doctrine that pushed ahead market fundamentalism, unthinking of the implications for poverty. The score card, upon surveying the impacts of neo-liberalism, is less than impressive—for a majority of those living in developing countries, poverty in the name of economic reform through the 1980s and 1990s was inescapable. The global protests against the conduct of the International Monetary Fund (IMF), the World Bank, the World Trade Organisation (WTO) and individual governments are remonstrations against an economic principle indifferent to the hardships of people's everyday lives.

The neo-liberal agenda, whilst retaining much of its original prescription of freeing the market, has since been through some revision in thinking. In the early 1990s, the state particularly was deemed a hindrance to the growth of healthy market competition and was to be diminished as much as possible. By the mid-1990s, there was a gradual shift to encompass the state again within the ambit of development. The state was recalled in the emerging discourses of 'governance' to take a rightful place in forming a sound political framework for the development of economic foundations (Leftwich 1994, World Bank 1997, World Bank 2000/01). Often referred to as the 'Third Way' (Giddens 1998), this revision of neo-liberalism has opened the way for a new role for the state. Through investment in social policy, practices of social inclusion ('roll-out' of programmes), and the language of localised democracy such as 'participation', 'devolution', and 'decentralisation', the state makes an attempt to rectify the serious social repercussions of an inveterate economic restructuring programme. Despite critique against some of the Third Way projects (see Craig and Porter's (2003) comments on Poverty Reduction Strategy Papers of the World Bank), there

---

[24] As an aside, Williamson argues that his term has become misused to symbolize a neo-liberal policy agenda of the US government and Washington-based institutions, which was not his original intent.

is wider recognition that the marrying of liberal democracy and the efficiency of the market can be a 'productive engagement' (Walby 2000).

Although neo-Malthusian and neo-liberal discourses are distinct ideological influences (the former emphasising fertility control and the latter economic rationalism), it may be argued that in the context of developing countries the two are intricately intertwined. In India, for instance, the ideology of economic growth is inseparable from an anti-natalist agenda. Neo-Malthusianism has long been a component of the economic ideology of the state, and under neo-liberalism this particular emphasis remains unchanged. In the aftermath of the Cairo conference, feminists were concerned that reproductive freedom had been compromised by these dominant discourses in existing population and development thought and practice. Grimes (1998: 389), for instance, notes that, "[w]ithin the feminist movement there are clear divisions between those who regarded the 1994 Cairo Conference as a step forward in the promotion of a more liberal approach towards the provision of 'reproductive rights' and those who regard the politically correct language of reproductive choice, women's empowerment and environmental concern as a clever repackaging of the population establishment's old agenda of fertility control." Correa and Petchesky (1994: 119) point out that, "perceiving the history of population control policies and programs as all too frequently oblivious to women's needs ... they [feminists] fear the language of reproductive rights and health may simply be co-opted by the Cairo process to support business as usual." It was not that neo-Malthusianism was abrogated at Cairo; rather, as scholars have pointed out, the consensus between the population discourse that focuses on rights and that which stressed control of population was possible only because the fundamental conflict between the two discourses—that is, to stabilise world population and respect people's rights—was never addressed (Amalric and Banuri 1994). The evidence from Cairo, Amalric and Banuri (1994) point out, seems to indicate that the global discourse on population still continues to be dominated by neo-Malthusian ideology. As they note, "...[s]uccess of the [Cairo] action plan rests on the belief that more contraceptives, more health services and more schools will be sufficient to bring down fertility rates" (Amalric and Banuri 1994: 703). As a policy discourse, therefore, reproductive health is likely to be interpreted from within the ideological standpoints of feminism and/or neo-liberalism/neo-Malthusianism, in what Smyth (1998:217) refers to as the "feminist vs. population control" debate.

Neo-liberalism and neo-Malthusianism are not the only forms of fundamentalisms that have challenged reproductive health discourses. Since the coming to power in 2000, the Bush Administration has revoked (and continues to do so) many of the advances that have been made by women's groups worldwide. In the past five years, the Bush administration's Global Gag Rule and the challenging of the ICPD document itself has threatened to erase all the work of the past two decades. Neo-conservatism is the latest in an array of "reprivatisation" discourses that act to disregard the rights discourses of reproductive health. For the rest of this book, I use the term 'neo-liberalism' to encompass the range of conservative ideas that are part of the discursive arena where reproductive health is under contestation.

Conclusion

To describe reproductive health as a political discourse is to open the proverbial Pandora's Box—out pours an unexpected array of value-inflected frames of references. At the heart of this chapter is the emphasis on meanings and the power of ideology in determining a particular interpretation of reproductive health. The feminist discourse of reproductive health resembles Fraser's oppositional discourse while neo-Malthusianism/neo-liberalism represents reprivatisation discourses of the policy arena. The contrasting perspectives of a feminist approach and neo-liberal/ neo-Malthusian ideology are played out in the site of reproductive health. The analysis in Chapters 5 to 7 illustrates the play of neo-liberal/neo-Malthusian discourses in the RCH in some detail; here, I will briefly signal a key area of difference. Whilst the feminist discourse of reproductive health emphasises rights and empowerment, the concerns of the latter revolve around the effective and efficient delivery of public services. Consequently, policy paradigms dominated by oppositional discourse or the discourses from 'above' are likely to have differing implications for population policy and its women beneficiaries. A central argument of this book is that the feminist discourse on reproductive health centres women as a constitutive category within the state and realigns their bargaining position in society whereas the neo-liberal debate sees women and their reproductive health as instrumental to the priorities of economic growth. A population policy interpreted from the feminist perspective of reproductive health puts women's needs on the centre stage of social rights and legal reconstitution to uphold these rights. Conversely, a reproductive health policy interpreted from the neo-liberal/neo-Malthusian perspective hovers on the verge of being added-on to a wider economic agenda, which in the long run can marginalise women's position vis-à-vis the state.

References

Amalric, F. and Banuri, T. (1994) "Population: malady or symptom?" *Third World Quarterly*, Volume 15, No. 4, 691–706.

Ascher, W. (1987) "Policy Sciences and the economic approach in a 'post–positivist' era", *Policy Sciences*, Vol. 20, No. 1, pp. 3–10.

Batliwala, S. (1994) "The Meaning of Women's Empowerment: New Concepts from Action" in in G. Sen, A. Germaine and L. C. Chen (eds) *Population Policies Reconsidered: Health, Empowerment, and Rights*, Harvard Centre for Population and Development, Cambridge, MA, pp. 127–138.

Beall, J. (1997) "In sickness and in health: Gender issues in Health Policy and their implications for development in the 1990s" in I. Baud and I. Smyth (eds) *Searching for Security: Women's Responses to Economic Transformation*, Routledge: London and New York, pp. 67– 95.

Bunch, C. (1990) "Women's Rights as Human Rights: Towards a Re-vision of Human Rights", *Human Rights Quarterly*, Vol. 12, pp. 486–498.

Cook, R. (1993) "International Human Rights and Women's Reproductive Health", *Studies in Family Planning*, Vol. 24, No. 2, March/April, pp. 73–86.

Cook, R. (1995a) "Gender, Health and Human Rights", *Health and Human Rights: An International Quarterly Journal*, Vol. 1. No. 4, pp. 309–312.

Cook, R. (1995b) "Human Rights and Reproductive Self-Determination", *The American University Law Review*, Vol. 44, No. 975, pp. 976–1016.

Correa, S. (1994) *Population and Reproductive Rights: Feminist Perspectives from the South*, Zed Books Ltd: London.

Correa, S. and Petchesky, R. (1994) "Reproductive and Sexual Rights: A feminist perspective", in G. Sen, A. Germaine and L. C. Chen (eds) *Population Policies Reconsidered: Health, Empowerment, and Rights*, Harvard Centre for Population and Development, Cambridge, MA, pp. 107–123

Craig, D. and Porter, D. (2003) "Poverty Reduction Strategy Papers: A new convergence", *World Development*, Vol 31, No. 1, pp. 53–69.

Dixon-Mueller, R. (1993) *Population Policy and Women's Rights: Transforming Reproductive Choice*, Praeger: Westport, Connecticut and London.

Dixon-Mueller, R. and Germain, A. (1994) "Population Policy and Feminist Political Action in Three Developing Countries" in J. Finkle and C. A. McIntosh (eds) *The New Politics of Population: Conflict and Consensus in Family Planning*, The Population Council: New York, pp. 197–219.

DeLeon, P. (1998) "Models of Policy Discourse: Insight vs. Prediction", *Policy Studies Journal*, Vol. 26, Iss. 1, pp. 147–162.

Fischer, F. (1995) *Evaluating Public Policy*, Nelson-Hall Publishers: Chicago.

Fischer, F. (2003) *Reframing Public Policy: Discursive Politics and Deliberative Practices*, Oxford University Press: Oxford.

Fischer, F. and Forrester, J. (1993) (ed.) *The Argumentative Turn in Policy Analysis and Planning*, Duke University Press: Durham, North Carolina, US.

Fraser, N. (1989a) *Unruly Practices: Power, Discourse and Gender in Contemporary Social Theory*, Polity Press: Oxford.

Fraser, N. (1989b) "Talking about Needs: Interpretive Contests as Political Conflicts in Welfare State Societies" in C. R. Sunstein (ed.) *Feminism and Political Theory*, The University of Chicago Press : Chicago and London, pp. 159–181.

Freedman, L. and Isaacs, S. (1993) "Human Rights and Reproductive Choice" *Studies in Family Planning*, Vol. 24, No. 1, Jan/Feb., pp. 18–30.

Garcia-Moreno, C. and Claro, A. (1994) "Challenges from the Women's Health Movement: Women's Rights versus Population Control" in G. Sen, A. Germaine and L.C. Chen (eds) *Population Policies*

Reconsidered: Health, Empowerment, and Rights, Harvard Centre for Population and Development: Cambridge, MA, pp. 47–61.

Germain, A., Nowrojee, S. and Pyne, H.H. (1994) "Setting a New Agenda: Sexual and Reproductive Health and Rights", in G. Sen, A. Germaine and L. C. Chen (eds) *Population Policies Reconsidered: Health, Empowerment, and Rights,* Harvard Centre for Population and Development : Cambridge, MA, pp. 27–47.

Giddens, A. (1998) *The Third Way: The Renewal of Social Democracy,* Polity Press: Cambridge.

Graham, W. (1993) "Reproductive health in developing countries: measurement, determinants and consequences", International Population Conference, Montreal, 24 August–1 September, pp. 571–577.

Grimes, S. (1998) "From 'population control' to 'reproductive rights' : ideological influences in population policy", *Third World Quarterly,* Vol. 19, No. 3, pp. 375–393.

Grosz, E. (1990) "Contemporary theories of power and subjectivity" in S. Gunew (ed.) *Feminist Knowledge: Critique and Construct,* Routledge: London, pp. 59–120.

Grown, C. (1994) "Structural Adjustment, Demographic Change and Population Policies" in I. Bakker (ed.) *The Strategic Silence: Gender and Economic Policy,* Zed Books: New York and London, pp. 61–70.

Harding, S. (1995) "Just add women and stir?", in Gender Working Group, United Nations Commission on Science and Technology for Development, *Missing Links: Gender Equity in Science and Technology for Development,* International Development Research Centre in association with Intermediate Technology Publications: Ottawa, and UNIFEM: New York.

Harkavy, O. (1995) *Curbing Population Growth: An Insider's Perspective on the Population Movement,* Plenum Press: New York and London.

Hartsock, N. (1990) "Foucault on Power: A Theory for Women?" in L. Nicholson (ed.) *Feminism/Postmodernism,* Routledge : New York, pp. 157–175.

Jaggar, A and Rothenberg, P. (1993) (ed.) *Feminist Frameworks: Alternative Theoretical Accounts of the Relations between Women and Men,* McGraw Hill: New York.

Johnson, S. (1995) *The Politics of Population: Cairo 1994*, Earthscan Publications: London.

Kabeer, N. (1999) Resources, Agency, Achievements: Reflections on the Measurement of Women's Empowerment, *Development and Change,* Vol. 30, 435–464.

Leftwich, A. (1994) "Governance, the State and the Politics of Development", *Development and Change,* Vol. 25, pp. 363–386.

Malthus, T. (1798, first edition) *An Essay on the Principle of Population*, online version available at http://www.econlib.org/library/Malthus/malPop.html (accessed 5 September 2005)

Mason, A. (1993) "The Response of fertility and mortality to economic crisis and Structural Adjustment Programmes during the 1980s: A Review", International Conference, IUSSP: Belgium, Montreal.

Mies, M. and Shiva, V. (2001, reprinted) "People or Population: Towards a New Ecology of Reproduction" in Kum-Kum Bhavnani (ed.) *Feminism and "Race"*, Oxford University Press: Oxford, pp. 331–347.

Mosse, J.C. (1994) "From Family Planning and Maternal and Child Health to Reproductive Health", in C. Sweetman and K. de Selincourt (eds) *Population and Reproductive Rights,* Oxfam Focus on Gender (No. 5), Oxfam: Oxford, pp. 6–12.

Nair, S., Kirbat, P. and Sexton, S. (2004) A Decade after Cairo: Women's Health in a Free Market Economy, The Corner House, Dorset, UK at http://www.thecornerhouse.org.uk.

Palmer, I. (1991) *Gender and Population in the Adjustment of African Economies: Planning for Change*, Women, Work and Development Series, ILO: Geneva.

Pearson, R. (1997) "Global Change and Insecurity: Are Women the Problem or the Solution ?", in I. Baud and I. Smyth (eds) *Searching for Security: Women's Responses to Economic Transformation*, Routledge: London and New York.

Petchesky, R. (1995) "From Population Control to Reproductive Rights: Feminist Fault Lines", *Reproductive Health Matters,* No. 6, November, pp. 152–161.

Petchesky, R. (2000) "Human Rights, Reproductive Health and Economic Justice: Why they are Indivisible", *Reproductive Health Matters,* Vol. 8, No. 15, May, pp. 12–17.

Petchesky, R. and Judd, K. (1998) (eds) *Negotiating Reproductive Rights: Women's Perspectives across Countries*, Zed Books: London.

Pietila, H. (2002) *Engendering the Global Agenda: The Story of Women and the United Nations*, UN Non-Governmental Liaison Service, United Nation, Geneva.

Rao, M. (2004) *Malthusian Arithmetic: From Population Control to Reproductive Health*, Sage Publications: New Delhi.

Sai, F. and Nassim, J. (1989) "The need for a reproductive health approach" *International Journal of Gynaecology and Obstetrics*, Supplement 3, pp. 102–114.

Sen, G. and Grown, C. (1987) *Development, Crisis and Alternative Visions—Third World Perspectives*, Monthly Press Review: New York.

Sen, G. and Batliwala, S. (2000) "Empowering Women for Reproductive Rights" in H. B. Presser and G. Sen (eds) *Women's Empowerment and Demographic Processes: Moving Beyong Cairo*, Oxford University Press: Oxford, UK.

Smyth, I. (1998) "Gender Analysis of Family Planning : Beyond the 'feminist vs. population control' debate" in C. Jackson and R. Pearson (eds) *Feminist Visions of Development : Gender Analysis and Policy*, Routledge: London and New York, pp. 217–238.

Sparr, P. (1994) (ed.) *Mortgaging Women's Lives: Feminist Critiques of Structural Adjustment*, Zed Books: London and New Jersey.

Stone, D. (1988) *Policy Paradox and Political Reason*, HarperCollins: USA.

Torgerson, D. (1996) "Power and Insight in Policy Discourse: Post-Positivism and Problem Definition" in L. Dubozinski et al. (eds) *Policy Studies in Canada*, University of Toronto Press: Toronto, Canada, pp. 266–298.

United Nations (1995) *Report of the International Conference on Population and Development: Cairo, 5–13 September 1994*, New York: United Nations.

Walby, S. (2000) "Gender, globalisation, and democracy" *Gender and Development*, Vol. 8. No. 1, March, pp. 20–28.

Waylen, G. (1992) "Women, Authoritarianism and Market Liberalisation in Chile, 1973–89" in H. Afshar and C. Dennis (eds) *Women and Adjustment Policies in the Third World*, St. Martin's Press: New York, pp. 5–21.

Weedon, C. (1987) *Feminist Practice and Post–Structuralist Theory*, New York: Blackwell.

Williamson, J. (1990) "What Washington means by Policy Reform" in John Williamson (ed.) *Latin American Adjustment: How much has happened?* Institute for International Economics, Washington, D.C.

Williamson, J. (2000) "What Should the World Bank Think About the Washington Consensus?" *World Bank Research Observer*, Washington, DC: The International Bank for Reconstruction and Development, Vol. 15, No. 2, pp. 251–264.

Women's Global Network for Reproductive Rights (1993) *WGNRR Newsletter*, No. 42, January–March.

World Bank (1997) *World Development Report 1997: The State in a Changing World*, Oxford University Press: Oxford.

World Bank (2000/01) *World Development Report 2000/01: Attacking Poverty*, Oxford University Press: Oxford.

3

The State and the Ideologies of Gender

Women in Indian Development

> Just as sexing chickens requires a close inspection of the genitalia of the bird, sexing the state involves a study of that entity's reproductive mechanisms.
>
> Charlesworth 1997

> In the South Asian context, the nation is represented as a motherland and the state as the father. In some cases, the patriarchal state exercises control with benevolent paternalism, and in others, in an authoritarian fashion. The paternalistic state offers protection to "its" women and children on the assumption that they cannot protect themselves. In return for this protection, it demands control over women's sexuality.
>
> Basu 1998

The state holds a unique place in the contestation of discourses; it is not only one of the 'stakeholder' groups that participate in the construction of meaning, it is also authorised to transform into policy the outcomes of the 'struggles for meaning' (Fraser 1989). As a stakeholder/participant, the state produces and subscribes to discourses around women and gender. These gender discourses are drawn from within the state (its existing policies, political agendas, the history of the state's development, the structure of the state's bureaucracy, for example) and from its continuing relationships with other formal and informal institutions (such as, religious bodies, cultural values, markets, and so on). The state, therefore, is an ideological structure in itself. An oppositional discourse such as the reproductive health discourse encounters the state and its ideologies en route to policy implementation. The analysis of the state and its gender discourses, in effect, become another focal point for understanding aspects of gender policy.

The Concise Oxford Dictionary of Sociology (1994) defines the state as:

> A distinct set of institutions that has the power to make the rules that govern society.... The state is not a unified entity.... It is rather a set of institutions which describes the terrain and parameters for political conflicts between various interests over use of resources and the direction of public policy (G. Marshall 1994: 635).

The "state" in question in this context is the development state. The role of the development state is distinct because, in principle, as a political structure it prioritises the socio-economic growth and development of the nation. From the inception of the field of development studies, the 'proper' role of the state in development has been contested and has fluctuated from decade to decade. Frank Petiteville, in his essay, *Three Mythical Representations of the State in Development Theory* (1998), points out that in development theory, three archetypes of the state can be identified: in the 1950s-60s, the image of the 'developer state' prevailed, in that the state was seen as playing an interventionist role that would advance economic development. In the 1970s, dependency theorists dubbed the state as a 'puppet' state of Western capitalists. By the 1980s and 1990s, with the emergence of neo-liberalism, the notion of the 'small-scale liberal' state was mooted. Under the last, the ideal state was minimal but intervened enough to provide stable governance structures for the unfettered and smooth development of the market. The model development state was typically liberal-democratic, protecting human rights and civic rights combined with a responsible administration untainted by corruption.

For feminist critics, these mainstream descriptions of the development state are informed primarily in relation to economic growth—i.e., how adeptly the state draws on capital, technology and resources—but shed little light on the gender dimensions of the development state. Rai (1996a, 1996b) argues that the conventional theories of the development state are "gender-blind" as they do not offer an understanding as to why women fare differently from men in the development state. Is the gender-blindness an anomaly of the structures of development policy or do the wider gender history and socio-politics of developing nations explain women's differential roles and benefits from development policy/programme? Gender and the functioning of the contemporary developmental state are intricately connected; what is missing is a coherent articulation of the 'how.'

This chapter attempts to profile the 'sex of the state'—it's ideologically-driven gender mechanisms—and has two specific aims. One, it attempts to describe the state from a gender standpoint, and second, it seeks to explore how women's identities /subjectivities are constructed by the state. The basic argument developed in this chapter is that ideologies impact on the constructions of women's political and economic identities. These identities, in turn, impact on the claims that women can make on the state as citizens, the leverage of power they wield, and the policy outcomes of contested discourses. Ultimately, gender policies for women will mirror these ideologies. What is significant to see is whether the state's gender policies will enhance women's political power as a final outcome. A caveat is needed here as in the previous chapter; western feminist political theories of the state have long offered the most sophisticated gender analyses of the (usually, welfare) state. These descriptions are clearly limited in their ability to explain notions of gender in the development state. As Rai (1996b: 5) notes, "western feminist state theory has largely ignored the experience of Third World women under the post-colonial state." Western-based theories do, nonetheless, proffer a foundation for generating a gender-lens to appraise the state. Consequently, this chapter summarises some of the relevant arguments that western feminists have put forward on which the research presented in this book later builds on.

Theorising the Western State

Feminist analyses of the state typically fall into one of two categories: a 'traditional' school and a recently emergent post-structuralist school (Rai 1996a, 1996b). Traditional schools—the Liberal, Radical, Dual theorists and Marxist-feminists—draw on existing left or liberal political theorisations of the state, underscoring MacKinnon's (1982, 1983, 1989) comment that feminism has no theory of the state. Feminist accounts of the state in essence extend the fundamental tenets of their respective world views; liberal feminists, for instance, see the state as sexist because it is dominated by men. Through increasing women's participation in formal political processes and using legislative structures to win rights for women, the state could be redeemed for women's interests—in other words, liberal feminists work *with* the state. Radical feminists contend that the state is inherently patriarchal, in that all its laws, policies and institutions are organised in ways that seek to control women's productive and reproductive roles. Radical feminists rarely see a role for women's interests within the existing structures of the state, and consequently, do not work with the state but *against* it.[25] For Marxist-feminists, the primary motive of the state is the promotion of capitalism. All gender discrimination and subordination is subsumed within the capitalist character of the state. Marxist-feminists, too, see a fundamental structural change as the sole way to restore women's interests within the state's priorities. Dual theorists argue that the state is both patriarchal and capitalist, and gender discriminations can be explained by one or other paradigm.[26]

Critiques of these traditional theories point to the simplistic and reductive portrayal of state actions, particularly, that the state is unilaterally oppressive to women (Pringle and Watson 1992, 1996; Watson 1990, 1992). In contrast, a contemporary genre

---

[25] 'With' or 'Against' the state was the catchword in the 1970s and 1980s that described the two polarities of feminist thought with regard to the state.

[26] For a detailed review of these schools, see Connell 1990; Franzway et al. 1989; Witz and Savage 1992.

of feminist theorists favours a post-structuralist view of the state (Allen 1990; Connell 1990; Franzway et al. 1989; Pringle and Watson 1992; Rhode 1994). At the heart of the post-structuralist perspective is the acknowledgement that the state is not a monolithic entity with unitary influences, but rather a plurality of forces. The post-structuralists see the state as a "process rather than ... as [a] thing" (Connell 1990: 509) and as a "network of power relations existing in co-operation and also in tension" (Rai 1996b: 5). Brown (1992: 12) notes that the state is a "significantly unbounded terrain of powers and techniques, an ensemble of discourses, rules and practices, cohabiting in limited, tension-ridden, often contradictory relation with one another." This 'process' is that the state operates within a culturally defined 'public' realm, but this is not historically or culturally fixed (Franzway et al. 1989). The post-structuralists build their theory of power around subjectivities created through discourse and language. Language creates identities, language constitutes needs, and language evokes politics. No identity, needs or politics are fixed but rather are temporally and historically constituted. In a post-structuralist analysis of the state, "discourse" and "subjectivity" rather than structures and interests become the key terms (Pringle and Watson 1992: 65). The post-structuralist's focus is on discourses that emanate from the state's laws and organisation of its institutions, and power is analysed in relation to the ability to control the meanings of those discourses.

This dispersed view of the state implicitly acknowledges a series of arenas that constitute the state both discursively and through practices. As Connell (1990) points out, because the state is not unitary, neither are the practices that connect the various capillaries of the state body. At different points in time, different kinds of connections mark the structures of the state. Depending on how intense these networks are, more or less power would accrue to the state (Watson 1990:7). Yet, the state, as post-structuralists note, is the "... node within that network of power relations that is one of the principal sub-structures of the gender order... [T]he state is the main organiser of the power relations of gender" (Connell 1990: 520). The state's impact on sexual and gender politics is, in the post-structuralists' view, dynamic, in that there is no one linear direction of oppressive activity or ideology. Unlike the 'traditional' accounts of the state, post-structuralists do not point to any singular intent that the state pursues to oppress women. Brown (1992: 13) notes:

> In so far as "the state" is not an entity or a unity, it does not harbor and deploy only one kind of political power.... [P]olitical power does not come in only one variety.... [E]ach works differently as power, produces different effects, engenders different kinds of possible resistance and requires a different analytical frame.

Another feature of the state that post-structuralists point out is that it plays a key role in *constituting* women's needs (Pringle and Watson 1992). As Connell (1990: 527) notes, the state "do[es] gender." It is not a neutral institution that merely reflects the sexual politics prevalent in society; the state equally shapes desires and plays a role in "legitimating, suppressing, or redirecting" women's preferences (Rhode 1994: 1189). Being the central locus of power, the state has "a considerable, though not unlimited, capacity to regulate gender relations in society as a whole" (Connell 1990: 527). Brown (1992: 29), in her essay, demonstrates convincingly that the state "mediates the *discursive*, *semiotic*, and *spatial* terms of women's political practices" (emphasis in original). Although the state is not likely to deliberately oppress or discriminate against women, building policies based on certain constructions of women can develop social structures and relationships where women are disadvantaged. As Moore (1988: 129) noted "according to prevailing assumptions and ideologies about the role of women, the nature of the family and the proper relations between man and woman ... the state [does have] a role not just in regulating people's lives but in defining gender ideologies, conceptions of 'femininity' and 'masculinity', determining ideas about what sorts of persons women and men should be."

Finally, the post-structuralist position veers away from an authentic notion of the category 'woman', but focuses instead on the multiple positions and identities that women (and men) assume in a social context. In this view, there is no longer a need to emphasise 'women's interests' in an essentialist way. Instead, it would be more fruitful to deconstruct the context in which needs are articulated. As Pringle and Watson (1992: 69) point out, "[i]nterests are produced by conscious and unwitting practices by the actors themselves in the processes of engagement. Feminists who engage with the state do so within a set of parameters that are discursively constituted and will formulate their interests accordingly."

Using the idea of the post-structuralist state, Brown (1992) argues that masculinity is the pervading ideology within the various structures of the state. The state does not have an essence of patriarchy at its core; however, the state functions as an institutionalisation of the power of men (partly because historically it has been masculinist and the modern state carries this legacy), and to that extent may be said to be patriarchal (Connell 1990; Franzway et al. 1989). This masculinity is multifaceted, takes many forms and is complex in its manifestation. In fact, Brown (1992: 14) points out that "the state can be masculinist without intentionally or overtly pursuing the 'interests' of men precisely because the multiple dimensions of socially constructed masculinity have historically shaped the multiple modes of power circulating the domain called the state." Brown points to four modalities of the state: the Liberal aspect, the Capitalist aspect, the Prerogative aspect and the Bureaucratic aspect. She contends that in all these areas, masculinity is a persistent theme—and women are identified against these criteria. But the masculinity that she refers to is complex; in the liberal modality, for instance, it is expressed in the form of the public and private divide and in the capitalist modality, it is expressed in the sexual division of labour. The prerogative state reflects its arbitrary powers which, Brown (1992: 26) notes, "whether expressed as the intervention of the police or as incessantly changing criteria for welfare benefits, is often all that stands between women and rape, women and starvation, women and dependence upon brutal mates." Finally, the ideology of its bureaucratic dimension, which is constructed upon socially masculine values of abstract rationality, formal proceduralism, rights-orientation and hierarchy, "creates *feminised* subjects and it excludes or colonises *female* subjects"[italics in original]. Masculinity is therefore institutionalised in diverse ways and, in the end, generates paradoxical outcomes rather than only oppressive ones as, for instance, conceptualised by Radical feminists.

Women's Identity in the Western State

Women's identity in western states is conventionally theorised in relation to the social spaces they occupy, viz., the public and/or the private. The idea of the public sphere has origins in the Greek concepts of *polis* or city and the *oikos*, the home or the domestic sphere. Classical liberal theory constructed women as beings of the private sphere. Based on notions of women's purported natural flair for reproductive work, women's relationships with the public sphere tended to be seen as an elaboration of their private domestic task. By the 'natural' make-up of the domestic world, women faced exclusion from the sphere of men. Pateman (1988, 1989) and Fraser and Gordon (1994a, 1994b) scour the writings of the eighteenth century to show that arguments for the separation between these spheres were associated with differential citizenship rights for men and women. Although the early utilitarians advocated the idea of the liberal individual/subject, the notion was never intended to include at least three specific categories of persons: offspring, slaves and women. Of these, male offspring could be expected in due course of maturity to evolve into independent subjects. As women lacked the attributes and capacities of individuals who can enter civil society and sell their labour power, they were denied the right to equal citizenship (the same was true also in the case of slaves). The idea of *coverture* was prevalent; it was taken as 'natural' that women's political inclinations could be played out through their husbands. Therefore, upon marriage, women were considered to have undergone a 'civic demise' (Thornton 1995), and their identity subsumed under the legal identity of their husbands.

Fraser and Gordon (1994a, 1994b) discuss other implications of the gendered public sphere on women's political identity. They argue that in the wake of the evolution of the gendered discourses of the private and the public from the eighteenth century, there emerged two kinds of exchange within these spheres. As the public sphere was dominated by 'liberal' subjects and imbued with the attributes of rationality, the main form of individual interchange was accepted as contractual—that is, "resources were exchanged for exact equivalents in discrete, monetarised transactions between self-interested independent individuals" (Fraser and Gordon 1994a: 100). Within the domestic sphere, resource flow was influenced by intimate social and kinship relations, which were outside of the circle of equal exchange. The contractual exchange was privileged over the domestic exchanges as it was predicated on the motives of rational self-advantage (Fraser and Gordon 1994a). As society developed, all significant relationships had been assimilated within the contractual exchange, except perhaps for labour and resource exchange within the domestic sphere. Any extra-familial relationship that could not be made contractual was defined by its opposite: charity. In charity, the exchange was not between equals, instead it was between a donor and a recipient—the latter had no claims on the donor's 'gift' and the donor was under no obligation other than voluntarism to provide one.

The representation of gender identity in western states has conventionally been framed within the 'contract/charity' dichotomy. Men's relationship with the state has a direct political basis as they are seen as individuals and as representatives of a family (B. Marshall 1994), while women do not enjoy a similar status. B. Marshall (1994: 136) points out "men are individuals, women are related to individuals." The main reason for the differential positioning of men and women in relation to the state has been traced to the places they hold in the public and private spheres. Men were seen to have capabilities that are exchangeable under the contractual doctrine, and it was usually these capabilities that formed the criteria for citizenship. Under nationalistic discourses, for instance, male constructions of citizenship were tied to their capacity for military service—a notion that was resonant of 'independence' and exchange in a contractual relationship (Fraser and Gordon 1994a; Pateman 1988, 1989). The masculinised form of the 'citizen-soldier-protector' (Fraser 1991: 263) model is one that is reflected through constructions of 'ideal' citizens. Women's relationship to the state, on the other hand, has been much less direct. Women have the capacity to produce future soldiers for the country (Sarvasy 1992), be caregivers for future and past generations (Pateman 1988) or be represented as symbols of nationalism (Yuval-Davis and Antias 1989). For women, their predominance in the domestic sphere entails that most of their exchanges with the public sphere are indirect and in their capacity as reproductive beings. These roles of women do not qualify for direct interchange with the state; as a result, women are seen as secondary citizens of the state.

With the emergence and development of capitalist ideologies within the state's discourses, the criteria of validity as citizens were increasingly linked to productive worth in the market. Jennings (1993) argues that the first separation of social spheres in Anglo-American society was between the family and the state, which developed in the seventeenth century. By the nineteenth century, however, the state was steadily losing ground to the primacy of the market. The market was increasingly the reference point for defining the public/private split, in which the public (the market) was privileged. As Jennings points out, "...the prominence of the 'economic man' is an artifact originating in nineteenth century cultural interpretations, which conflated man with dynamic market activity and woman with unchanging familial roles" (Jennings 1993: 122). A new definition of women as non-economic beings emerged, and this was more critical to the interpretation of their identity in society, whereas their former definition as non-political beings was no longer essential to that interpretation. Jennings (1993) argues that the shift of political identity in terms of economic value could explain why women were able to win political rights (like the right to vote) since the nineteenth century rather than economic rights. Fraser and Gordon (1994c), in their analysis of the idea of dependency in welfare states, also point out that it was with the rise of industrial capitalism that women as 'housewives' or non-wage earners were transformed from "partners to parasites" (p.11). Therefore, the development of the market went hand in hand with a definition of women's political identity that was tied to their perceived economic value.

The notion of economic worth continues to be the dominant value that frames citizenship and distinguishes the status of men and women in the state. Women's relationship with the western welfare state in the twentieth century is a case in point. Feminist scholars noted that women's relationship to the welfare state tended to be dominated by the ideology of charity (Fraser and Gordon 1994a, 1994b; Nelson 1990). In most social policies dealing with welfare, women are positioned as 'dependants' of the state and, therefore, as recipients of the state's charity. The term 'dependency' is loaded with connotations of moral/ psychological deficiencies; as citizens, dependents acquire an undesirable quality (Fraser and Gordon 1994c). Quite often, even this charity is not 'free'; it is tied to conditionalities to reciprocate the state's welfare, such as, undertaking training programmes or looking for employment. Catherine Kingfisher in her book *Women in the American Welfare Trap* (1996) addresses the welfare programme Aid for Families with Dependent Children (AFDC). She notes:

> ... [t]he model for the Family Support Act and the MOST program (training programmes) is the social contract, in which there is supposedly an exchange between recipients and the welfare system. Specifically, recipients participate in training programmes in exchange for a variety of services related to job placement and child and medical care. Recipients, in other words, are not 'entitled' to benefits, but rather are subject to the 'obligations' of citizenship (Kingfisher 1996: 21).

In contrast, men are designated as deserving of the state's welfare—their pensions, unemployment supplements or sickness benefits are the state's support for otherwise contributing members of society. Critics of this 'dual-welfare standard' point out that this biased perception of the state arises because women's contributions to housework and childcare are not perceived as economic work, whereas men's engagement in paid work—no matter how sporadic or unskilled—still qualifies them as better citizens.

Women's citizenship, therefore, is founded on layers of social meaning and ideology. In his classic work *Citizenship and Social Class* (1950), T.H. Marshall describes three stages of citizenship in capitalist societies: the first, a civil citizenship (where individual rights are recognised as separate from the state); the second, a political citizenship (where individuals participate in political rights) and a third and final stage of social citizenship, where the mark of being a citizen is expressed in terms of availability and use of social entitlements, i.e., the right to share to the full, in the social heritage and to live the life of a civilised being according to the standards prevailing in the society. For women, to solely attain political citizenship (through universal franchise) would be a limited achievement if the ultimate aim is to encourage their active and inclusive participation as citizens of a state. Recent writings on women and identity are moving towards a meaningful conceptualisation of citizenship that encompasses questions about women's social and economic entitlements (see Rai 2002:189-193). What is important for us, in the present context, is to raise questions about the ideologies that the *development* state propagates about women's identities: how are women constructed? Do these constructions enable women to lay claims to rights or are they able to influence needs discourses in ways that are empowering for them?

The Development State

Given that notions of the public-private spheres, women's identity and citizenship have developed within a specific western context, there is, understandably, criticism about making this gendered framework universally applicable to non-industrialised, non-western societies whose political and social evolution has followed their own trajectory. The essence of these arguments can be summarised. First, the idea of the domestic (private), the range of activities therein and the reference to the domination of a particular sex is founded on a presumed universality of the mother-child dyad—that all women, regardless of social context, are driven by their biological instincts and carve their lives around their reproductive responsibilities (Moore 1988: 22). A second critique arises from erroneously assuming that in all cultures alike, the activities undertaken in the domestic sphere are seen as inferior. And thirdly, in many societies, the boundaries of domestic/private and public/corporate may be fluid and/or non-existent—both women and men's contributions may be valued equally within relations of production and they both may be given access to and control over resources, and a political voice (Tiano 1988).

These are valid concerns and caution against blindly applying western conceptualisations of gender onto developing societies is certainly justified. Yet, some comment is equally warranted on why the categories of 'public/private' can be employed to analyse women's subordination in the Third World. Regardless of the apparent differences in these societies, most post-colonial, developing countries in the twentieth century (and this is certainly true for India) have instituted political (mostly liberal democratic) and economic structures that produce differential gender access to the state (Simon-Kumar 1999). In many developing societies, particularly in South Asia, the emergence of twentieth century nationhood has not been oblivious of the legacy of administrative, legal and bureaucratic processes laid down by the European colonisers nor a patriarchal classed society that preceded the arrival of the British. In many newly independent post-colonial states, the transition to modern statehood has meant retaining features of the colonial and patriarchal regimes that predated independence (Chhachhi 1991). Moreover, the post-colonial modern state in the Third World has also been committed to capitalist development. The spread of capitalist production was predicated, among other factors, on how the state negotiated relationships between the sexes within the family. Jayawardene (cited in Chhachhi 1991) writing in the context of Sri Lanka, for example, points out that the national objectives of creating a system of "stable, monogamous nuclear families with educated and employable women were associated with capitalist development and bourgeois ideology" along with traditional views of subordinate women as part of nation building. Consequently, there is a tendency, in the transition from pre-state kinship relations to the modern state, to evolve more specific forms of gendered spaces. In the latter case, women tend to increasingly come under the control of men. Staudt (1986: 330) notes that although states have been organised in a variety of ways, "one constancy ... is that women are never central to state power ... [indeed] state formation appears to aggravate or create female subordination."

Despite the parallels, the Third World context is complex and defining women's citizenship reflects the intimate links between society-state ideologies. The feminist political perspectives on women's citizenship in the western state, at best, direct us to broad areas where the Third World and development theory emphasise certain constructions of women—the spaces of the public and private, the dominant images of women in these spaces, and women's relation to production and reproduction. The modern development state, embedded as it is in the history of its own creation as well as in the current of contemporary development thought, presses on women in both contradictory and complementary ways.

Constructing Women's Identity in Development Theory

Notable texts on the conceptual origins of women in development thought point to three dominant constructions of women in development theory (Kabeer 1994; Rathegeber 1990; Razavi and Miller 1995). Before the beginnings of the Women in Development (WID) thought in 1970, women tended to be seen in their 'reproductive roles' as welfare beneficiaries who were not actively involved in productive economic development. Rather, women's main (and often, only) roles revolved around their functions as mother and keeper of the domestic sphere. It was only with the advent of Boserup's critique of this position that women began to assume economic roles in development theory. A tacit definition of 'public' and 'private' spheres within development theory, and women's relationship to them developed within evolving theoretical frameworks. Inherent in the evolving arguments in the 1970s for including women on the development agenda was the unflinching premise that 'development' was ensconced in a space that eluded women's free and fair entry—that they were 'out' and men were 'in.' The modernisation thesis of the time was steeped in the imagery of dichotomy and advocated a move for Third World peoples away from a traditional way of life to a modern one, from the rural to the urban, and from ignorance to skill and technological adeptness (Scott 1996). Modernisation theorists see the public realm as aligned with the symbols of modernity: industrialisation, urbanisation, progress, governance by a state and bureaucracy, and essentially the economic sphere of the market. The private realm is the tradition-bound village, family and household. Not surprisingly, the public realm has been populated by the men who left their villages to participate in the modern life of urbanity (Scott 1996: 9). The earliest WID critiques of development, grounded in a modernisation paradigm (Blumberg 1991; Rogers 1980; Boserup 1970), pointed to the exclusionary potential of capitalist modernisation and technological development for women in the Third World. Women in Development (WID) writing seemed to indicate that these exclusionary tendencies were an aberration, an inadvertent slip of development. Development policy-makers were erroneously 'blind' to the economic and productive contributions of women (Blumberg 1991), resulting in the deterioration of women's economic and social status largely because their labours were not accounted for under the marketed economy of the public realm. Boserup's book (1970), particularly, challenged modernisation theorists' claims that women's rights and status would automatically improve as modernisation proceeded (Jaquette 1990). The emphasis of WID efforts had been (and still is) to justify women's contribution to economic production (Razavi and Miller 1995; Blumberg 1991) and to integrate Third World women better into mainstream development processes as a precursory step to empowerment (Bandarage 1984). Boserup (1970) saw women's participation in economic productivity as resulting in greater association with the public realm and pointed out that women needed to be prepared for this entry, through skill training and education:

> It follows that in the future, when a large proportion of women may have jobs, it becomes an important task to devise new educational and training programmes, which can help to reduce the productivity gap between male and female labour thus fitting women to their new way of life (Boserup 1970: 225).

Women and the 'feminine' as entities in transition from the 'unproductive' private to the 'productive' public are reflected in the shifting constructions of women in the various approaches to WID embraced by developmental institutions. In the pre-WID period, women were solely seen as important in their roles as mothers and caregivers in the private sphere. As their productive 'masculine' relevance was recognised, developmental agencies constructed women as active agents involved in the 'public' development of their communities.[27] Contemporary developmental practitioners and international donor agencies also emphasise economic identity as a step to gaining political recognition. The World Bank's recommendation, for instance, for reducing women's dependency is "to alter the economic environment .... [T]his means that market forces should be allowed to influence the boundaries of culturally acceptable women's activities" (World Bank 1991: xvi). An overwhelming tendency in the WID writings was to equate the 'development process' with the 'productive sphere' wherein active intervention was needed to include women (Rai 2002). The justification for women's presence in this productive/public space was (and to a great degree still continues to be) made either through arguments that economic marginalisation disadvantages women or that development itself suffers from the gender oversight (Moser 1991; Kabeer 1994; Razavi and Miller 1995).[28] Even where critiques of Boserup's thesis were raised (for instance, Beneria and Sen 1981, 1982), there was no questioning the bifurcation of society into the 'productive' and 'reproductive' sphere; if anything, these authors emphasised that women's engagement in the productive (public) was mitigated by their responsibilities in the reproductive space (private) and compromised by their class positions.

Micro-level studies of women's position within the household also give high premium to women's engagement in productive

---

[27] Scholarship on Third World women in development processes identifies the following schools of thought: Women in Development (WID), Women and Development (WAD), Gender and Development (GAD), and the more recent Women, Culture and Development (WCD). For details of the various approaches to WID, see Bhavnani, Foran and Kurian (2003), Goetz (1991), Kabeer (1994), Moser (1993), Rathgeber (1990), and Razavi and Miller (1995).

[28] Arguments for involving women in development ranging from the discrimination to the efficiency hypothesis has been ably covered in several women and development texts and I will not revisit them here.

work *outside* the household. Amartya Sen (1990) emphasises that women's bargaining power within private transactions will be enhanced by the perceived worth of their entitlements. Their entitlements, in turn, would be directly reflected in women's potential to exchange their labour power for earnings outside the household, in the realm of the productive economy. According to Sen (1990: 144), " [o]utside earnings can give the woman in question (1) a better breakdown position (point of an individual's vulnerability)[29], (2) possibly a clearer perception of her individuality and well-being, and (3) a higher 'perceived contribution' to the family's economic position." Sen attributes the lower social status prevailing for female children in north India, where women have traditionally not been part of the dry-cultivation agricultural workforce, to their potential for only lower earning powers (see also Miller 1981). In contrast, women in southern India who have traditionally predominated wet-farming cultivation of crops like rice have better intra-household status. Dyson and Moore's (1983) classic article directly relates female autonomy and reproductive agency with women's ability to be *visible* actors in the agrarian productive sphere (see also Miller 1981). Others (such as Beneria 1982, 1995; Waring 1989) attempted to rationalise why women's work in the reproductive sphere was to be counted as productive sphere activities within macro-economic frameworks. Contemporary developmental practitioners and international donor agencies also recognise a dichotomy that governs women's spaces. The World Bank (1991: xvi), for instance, calls this the ' inside/outside' spaces and postulates that it is through engagement in the 'outside spaces' that women will begin to command a fairer position in society. The Canadian International Development Agency (CIDA), similarly, in its 1992 Interim WID policy set down that one of its objectives was to 'encourage, respond to and support initiatives in and among developing countries in order to *increase women's participation in economic, political and social processes*' (Alexander 1995: 83, emphasis mine). The 'political' and

[29] Sen argues that greater engagement in the productive economy raises break-down positions or the ability for women to lift the levels of their tolerance to vulnerability.

'economic' spheres are not women's natural home; the aim of development is to ensure this parity with men.

What is unmistakable, therefore, is that a traditional body of development literature endorses women's legitimacy in the public sphere—a space defined largely in relation to economic activity.[30] A dominant idea held in development scholarship and practice is that the 'productive' public sphere is, in principle, located in and directed by the 'market' (waged labour market, commodity markets, credit markets, and so on). This definition implies that for women to enhance their position in the state, they must integrate their lives with the productive sphere. By the same token, women's loss of social, economic and political status is linked to the non-integration of women in the productive sphere. Once women, in principle, are fully integrated with the sphere of production, usually through direct participation in the productive economy, their status would be 'restored'. Razavi and Miller (1995), similarly, note that WID /GAD legitimised efforts to influence development policy with a combined argument for 'justice' and 'efficiency.' Further, 'visibility' is a key part of the process of emancipating women. Most WID literature emphasises making women's presence visible in both the public/productive and private sphere. A substantial literature in the 1980s emerged that pointed out that women were the 'invisible' producers (e.g., Byrdon and Chant 1989; Dixon-Mueller and Anker 1988) in an economy—their work was not known, or recorded, and in consequence, their role in economy and society undervalued (Waring 1989). Subsequently, efforts have been on to make recording processes and statistics more gender-sensitive and 'visible.' Beneria and Sen (1981, 1982) recommend making reproductive work more visible, that is, although located in the domestic sphere, such activities as child rearing and child bearing are to be given the recognition of a public sphere/productive activity.

---

[30] It must be noted that this perspective of the public sphere, dominant in early development theory, was a narrow one; it ignored the public sphere as a space of rights that comes from sources other than the productive—the state's legal and political system, for instance, is a key source of rights for women.

The emphasis on encouraging women into 'productive' activity is not without critique. Feminist authors like Maria Mies show that locating women within market processes does not automatically guarantee beneficial political identities; in fact, quite often, it is the market that denudes women of any sense of political empowerment (see Mies 1982, 1994, 1998). Other authors have repeatedly argued that the market system—the sphere of economic productivity—has disempowered women by exploiting their feminine attributes (the stereotype of being docile labourers, agility in certain kinds of tasks, exploiting their roles as primary homemakers) for capitalist development (Elson and Pearson 1981; Pearson 1998). The limits of the market and the use of economic activity as the criteria for defining women's identity are also questioned by critics of the neo-liberal doctrines that have dominated development thinking for over two decades. By the 1980s, although women's economic activity was recognised as crucial to development processes (the argument that they were 'efficient'), it was clear that that identity was used to instrumentalise women for wider development programmes of international aid agencies (Kabeer 1994; Razavi and Miller 1995). Critics of the Structural Adjustment Programmes (SAPs) instituted in developing countries showed that women experienced more hardships than men because their productive activities were exploited to make up for the services that the government was no longer prepared to provide (Afshar and Dennis 1992; Beneria and Feldman 1992; Sparr 1994; Elson 1991, 1992, 1994).

Thus, the relationship between the neo-liberal development state and women's identity is particularly important—if only to point out the contradictory messages it contains for women as citizens. On the one hand, usually propagated by international development agencies and government, there is a strand of thinking that demonstrates that as long as the ideology of the market prevails, empowerment or women's claims to rights clearly lie in participating within the market. The 'natural' allocations of the market would give to each their due of the claims to political rights. The state in its 'minimal' role offers little recompense, especially to women. The dominant ethos in neo-liberalism regarding citizen rights is that the 'new "ordinary" citizen does not make "special" impositional claims on the state based on difference or systemic discrimination because one should be able to take care of oneself' (Brodie 1994 cited in Bakker 1996:5).

Yet, on the other hand, an equally forceful argument is that the market, in reality, is incapable of addressing needs of social justice. It is only the state that can address political rights, quite outside the claims of the market and the advantages of acquiring an economic identity. The logical extension of the argument here is that political rights lie with the state and its active intervention in economic/political life (Bergeron 2001). As Brodie (1994: 55) points out:

> [I]t is clear that the current moment of restructuring can be viewed as a concerted discursive and political struggle around the very meaning of the public and private. The proponents of globalisation seek radically to *shrink the public—the realm of political negotiation—* and at the same time, expand and reassert the autonomy of the private sector and the private sphere (emphasis mine).

It is perhaps not surprising, then, that since the 1990s, scholarship that centres the Third World state as the provider of political rights has proliferated. These writings advocate women's participation in structures of governance as a means to advance their status (Razavi 2000; UNDP 2000). Ostensibly, at least, the debates in development surrounding women's identity appear to be moving from a focus on the economy/productive space to the state/political space.

The foregoing discussion suggests that identity formation for women in the Third World is primarily about constructions in the public sphere, especially the nexus between the economic and the political (the state and the market). From international levels to the grassroots, development ideology is replete with reference to economic production and the market. This is certainly the dominant discourse when defining women's citizenship in a development state: women are projected as either reproductive or productive beings, agents in economic development or passive recipients of development aid. However, merely being labelled 'reproductive' or 'productive' is not the point; what is of significance is what it means to be either reproductive or productive and whether these contribute to a position in the 'contract/charity' polarity. To understand 'meanings' in this way, we must necessarily step outside constraining frames that limit women as caught within a relationship between economics and politics. Instead, it is important to examine how the discourses from juridical, cultural, scientific, political, and bureaucratic arenas bear upon the state's constructions of women in development as well.

Bhavnani, Foran and Kurian (2003) recently put forward an alternative paradigm, the 'Women, Culture and Development Approach (WCD)' as a more inclusive framework to study Third World women's experiences. They argue that development studies' analyses tend to 'be driven by economistic policy considerations, which generally locate women and culture as peripheral to a central project of increasing the gross domestic product of Third World Nations' (Bhavnani, Foran and Kurian 2003: 7). The WCD is an approach that is dynamic and acknowledges the myriad influences on women's lived experiences: history, culture, myth, lore—all of which accrue to embed women in the particular contexts in which they live. Rai (2002) articulates one dimension of this wider context in her analysis of the discourses of post-colonial nationalism and development, illustrating the parallels between the two. Uberoi (1996) draws attention to the historical overlaps between discourses of social reform at the turn of the twentieth century and that of development. Discourses drawn from religion/communalism and nationalism (Kandiyotti 1991; Moghadam 1994, Afshar 1987), images of scientific progress (Subramaniam 2003, Kurian and Munshi 2003), political values of the state structure (as in socialist states, see Moore 1988), war and security (Afshar and Eade 2004) are part of the range of discourses that influence states' gender ideologies. In sum, women's identity in the state draws on an array of meanings that position them in the public sphere—encompassing economic, cultural and political dimensions.

Drawing on this discussion I now turn to the gender ideologies of the Indian State. This profile will, no doubt, be a thumbnail sketch of India's immense and rich gender context. It will nonetheless lay the foundations for building the argument that India's constructions of women's identity in its development policy are the by-product of history and contemporary politics.

The Indian Developmental State

Post-Independence India, with its colonial legacy, was essentially an agglomeration of multiple ethnic, religious and communal identities bound together under a common nationalist umbrella. The nationalist agenda emerged from a common 'enemy'—the colonial rulers—and a common goal: nation-building through economic development. The latter, in particular, was significant in creating images of a unified nation among its citizens (Deshpande 1993) and defining the role of citizens in the newly independent state. Chatterjee (1998:86) notes that the Indian state "was connected to the people-nation not simply through the procedural forms of representative government, it also acquired its representativeness by directing a programme of economic development on behalf of the nation." Chatterjee also points out that the two forms of representativeness and the legitimacy of the state, acquired through the political process and through economic intervention, were likely to be in contradiction of each other. He argued that this was because "[w]hat the people were able to express through the representative mechanisms of the political process as their will was not necessarily what was good for their economic well-being; what the state thought important for the economic development of the nation was not necessarily what would be ratified through the representative mechanisms" (Chatterjee 1998: 87). In the making of a modern, unified India, the political apparatus and the state's economic policies were thus linked in fractured continuity.

To pinpoint a 'gender character' for the Indian State is not easy—the state has a legacy of directly discriminating against women through legislations and policies that exacerbate their often disadvantageous position in society. The state also has a history of indirectly supporting cultural practices that are detrimental to women's equal status in society. Constitutionally, though, the state recognises the equality of women in its Fundamental Rights and acknowledges in its Directive Principles that women are a vulnerable group that requires special rights.[31] Article 14 of the Fundamental Rights provides for the 'equality before the law or the equal protection of the laws' for men and women. Article 15 prohibits, inter alia, discrimination against any citizen on the grounds of sex. Article 15 (3) empowers the State to make special provisions in favour of women. In the Directive Principles, Article 39 directs the State to direct its policy towards ensuring that (a) men and women equally have the right to an adequate means of livelihood and (b) there is equal pay for equal work for men and women. Article 42 of the Directive Principles requires that the State make provisions for ensuring just and humane conditions of work, and for maternity relief. Translating those ideals of equality and protection into the practice of political and social rights, however, has been an arduous struggle. The experience of the Indian state for a majority of women is thus either ambivalent or ridden with contradiction.

A review of the state's responses to landmark legal cases involving women is instructive. The Shah Bano case of the 1980s is a classic and oft-cited example, where the state placed partisan and electoral interests above the welfare of Muslim women in the country. In order to appease conservative Muslims, the government overturned a Supreme Court ruling and withdrew legal provisions that entitled divorced Muslim women to claim for maintenance from their husbands under the Criminal Procedures Code (Engineer 1987; Kumar 1994). The state has also been criticised for its ineffective handling of the 1987 case of *sati*, when a young widow was burnt on her husband's funeral pyre. Although the government passed a Commission of Sati (Prevention) Act, 1987, it is a legal provision that is fraught with problems. While prohibiting the glorification of sati, the Bill treats the act as suicide, placing the onus of responsibility on the victim (Kasturi 1996; Kumar 1994). The state's handling of rape cases has been particularly ineffectual, as with the Mathura case where the Supreme Court acquitted policemen convicted of rape because the 16-year old victim had a boyfriend and was therefore likely to have had consensual sex (Swarup et. al 1994). In the

[31] See Centre for Development and Human Rights (2004) for a summary of the various provisions for women's rights in India.

Bhanwari Devi Sathin case of the late 1990s, the lower courts acquitted men convicted of gang rape because, among other reasons, they were from a respectable caste and were not likely to commit the crime.[32] Similarly, where laws protecting women exist, the enforcement of these laws is weak. Dowry was officially made illegal with the passing of the Dowry Prohibition Act in 1961, but the practice still continues. The recent 'Nisha' phenomenon has highlighted the extent of the dowry industry that the state has deliberately ignored.[33] Kodoth and Eapen's (2005) paper highlights women's growing inferior status in Kerala society, exacerbated through practices like dowry. In response to the widespread abortion of female foetuses, the Pre-Natal Diagnostic Techniques (Regulation and Prevention of Misuses) Act of 1994 (amended twice) was passed which prohibits all genetic counselling facilities, genetic clinics and laboratories from divulging information about the sex of a foetus. Its efficacy still remains to be examined. Agnes (1998) highlights the lacunae in various protective legislations for women that have been passed by the Indian Government in the 1980s.[34] Although, as she argues, the 1980s was a period when the largest number of protective laws were passed, in process and implementation they have not proven to be effective for women.

---

[32] However, in the 1998 rape case of Hanuffa Khatoon, the Supreme Court passed an unprecedented verdict against the accused and in favour of women's rights. The Court noted that, "Rape is a crime not only against the person of a woman, it is a crime against the entire society. It destroys the entire psychology of a woman and pushes her into deep emotional crisis. Rape is therefore the most hated crime. It is a crime against basic human rights and is violative of the victim's most cherished right, namely, right to life which includes right to live with human dignity...." (cited in Nussbaum 2002). Also in 2003, the government enacted an amendment to the Indian Evidence Act stressing that in case of rape a victim cannot be cross-examined about her general character (*The Sunday Express*, October 19, 2003, http://www.indianexpress.com/full_story.php?content_id=33650)

[33] Nisha was a young woman, who in 2003, called the police when her prospective in-laws demanded a dowry in order to go ahead with the marriage. Nisha became an instant symbol across the country in the fight against dowry and dowry-related deaths of women.

[34] See also Kapur and Cossman (1996).

Almost contradictorily, the Indian state has also recognised women's differential status in society and acted to challenge their social and political exclusion. Specific legislative and institutional mechanisms set up by the government seek to ensure the advancement of gender equality in India. The Department of Women and Child Development is a core ministerial portfolio with a Minister of Cabinet rank reporting directly to Parliament. The Government's Five-Year Plans have an organic perspective of women's roles in economic development; the Ninth Five-Year Plan (1997-2002), for example, emphasises women's empowerment and rights. In 1990, the National Commission for Women Act was adopted and the National Commission for Women was set up to advise government on policy matters relating to women. State-level Women's Commissions have been established as well. In 2001, the National Policy for the Empowerment of Women was adopted to eliminate all forms of discrimination against women and to empower women socially and economically. The policy directs Central and State ministries to set time-bound action plans to address women's empowerment (Centre for Reproductive Rights 2004).

In addition, the Panchayati Raj Bill has special provisions for encouraging women's participation in the political process. The Panchayati Raj Bill is an example of 'political creativity' of the Indian government (Nussbaum 2002). In the first local-level elections under the Panchayati Raj, over five million women stood for elections; around one million were elected to posts reserved for women (Kabir c. 2003; Shahid c.2003). Initial evaluations show that women elected to local government bring a unique style of government and focus on issues that tend to be overlooked by their male counterparts (Kabir c. 2003; Shahid c. 2003). Similar legislation is being pursued for national bodies (the Women's Bill), but this is still under debate in parliament following opposition to the Bill from several political parties.

In the case of community-based laws, the rights of Christian women were strengthened in the Supreme Court Mary Roy case in the early 1980s, which conferred equal rights to property for both male and female offspring in the Christian community. In employment-related issues, in 1999, the state set out stringent regulations regarding sexual harassment in the work place. The state also established a proposal to ensure maternity benefits for women labourers who are daily wage earners in the informal sector of the economy (*The Hindu*, March 9, 2000). The Indian Courts also rallied for the cause of women in the Quinacrine Controversy in 1998. Doctors in private practice were sterilising women using quinacrine pellets without proper authorisation or consent. The Supreme Court banned the use of quinacrine as a method of sterilisation. However, when it came to the sale of injectable contraceptives (such as Net-En and Depo-Provera), the Government did not respond favourably to women's groups that asked for these contraceptives to be banned despite sufficient evidence that abuse of the injectables was likely in the context of India.[35]

Understandably, feminist scholars are divided in their opinions regarding the role of the modern Indian state in the lives of its millions of women. Some point out that the state responds in ambivalent ways to the vulnerable conditions in which women live in Indian society, while other scholars present a unidimensional characterisation of the Indian state. Rai (1996a, 1996b), for instance, feels that the Indian state plays no significant role in women's lives. Unlike in many western contexts where the state provides social services of which women are prime recipients, the state in India provides little or no such access for its women. Despite its claims to being interested in social justice, the Indian state's engagement with welfare activities, particularly for women, are restricted by inadequate resources (Rai 1996b: 13). There is also the issue that, at a much deeper level, limits are put upon the claims that citizens, including women, can make on the state (Jayal 1994). In fact, Rai (1996a, 1996b) argues that, with respect to what it offers women, India is a "weak" state. She points out that when the state does intervene in women's lives, it is usually in oppressive and brutal ways. Similarly, Misra (1997) contends that India's liberal democratic polity has played an ambivalent role in women's lives. Political and civil liberties have

[35] The government withdrew its original plan to distribute injectables through its RCH programme. Injectables are available, however, through the private sector.

allowed for the development of an articulate and visible feminist movement, while state action and inaction in individual cases has been less than reflective of an interest in women's well-being. Likewise, long-term structural changes have benefited certain sections of women while pauperising others.

In a more rigid view of the Indian state, Agarwal (1988:14) points out that India, like other South Asian states, perpetuates patriarchal relations with two express intents—to domesticate women and control their sexuality. Kasturi (1996), too, demonstrates in the context of India that the "evolution of a political understanding of the process of development ... [indicated] ... that the development process has actually strengthened patriarchal structures in India" (p.100). Hasan (1994, 2002) points out that contemporary politics in India with its focus on community identities, religious traditions and cultural practices have made women a prime site around which political claims are contested—a politics in which the State is a complicit actor. As Hasan (2002: 270) points out, "the actions of the Indian state suggest that it is interventionist and protectionist in the material sphere, while it remains non-interventionist in the community domain, with the exception of intervention to reform Hindu laws in the 1950s". Rai (1996a, 1996b) and Basu (1998) argue that the state is an inconsistent actor—on many occasions, the state and traditional patriarchy are in binary opposition while in other circumstances, the state *is* the patriarchy that oppresses women. Mary John's (1996: 3075) description of the Indian state takes into account its class constructions; she argues that the state is class and caste-conscious —"[t]he state may thus respond—at times with alacrity—to the claims made upon it by the women's movement, whose spokespersons are invariably middle class and upper caste, and who are also familiar with its structures." According to John (1996), the story is quite different when it comes to implementing policies or laws in favour of a woman of a lower class and caste, especially when it involves opposing those with whom the state identifies. Thus, feminist evaluations of the functioning of the Indian state have highlighted its contradictory nature and its tendency to operate in ambiguous ways. I would conclude from the discussions above that the

Indian state reflects tendencies of a 'post-structuralist' state—it relates to women in unpredictable and uncertain ways. The factors that decide whether the state will act in pro or anti-gender ways is determined by the constructions of women, and the meanings of these constructions. Rai (1996a: 32) quite rightly notes that the Indian state is simultaneously "fractured, oppressive, threatening [and] also providing spaces for struggle and negotiation." These spaces for struggle and negotiation make the need for women to influence discourse and meanings all the more critical.

Women's Identity in the Indian State

Just as the character of the Indian state is not fixed, neither are the elements that create gender identity. In India, women's identity is constituted along two axes (a) their communal and religious identity, and (b) their role in development and nation building. The state's responses to minority women (as in the Shah Bano case mentioned above) are dictated largely by the considerations of the community that the women come from. In these circumstances, the political claims of women are determined by the community's culture of women's rights, rather than of rights provided under a universally accepted notion of citizenship. My interest here, however, is less on the identity constructed by community but rather by the processes of development and economic planning. It is on the construction of this identity of women that the rest of this chapter will focus.

The second axis along which women tend to be constituted within the Indian nation is through their economic identity and role in nation building (Agnihotri and Mazumdar 1995; Chaudhuri 1995; Desai 1986; Kasturi 1996). From pre-independence days, the nationalist movement advocated freedom, dignity, justice and equality as essential attributes for women to participate in nation building (Agnihotri and Mazumdar 1995). In 1938, the Congress party set out to state 'Women's Role in Planned Economy' (WRPE), a document that shaped the foundations of women's role in post-Independence nation building. Chaudhuri's (1995) analysis of the document reveals that there are strong references to women playing equal roles as men in nation building—women's citizenship is affirmed in their capacity as producers and labourers: "... the only social status to be recognised in planned society will be that of the individual worker ... neither motherhood, nor wifehood, nor, *a fortiori*, widowhood matter at all" (cited in Chaudhuri 1995: 219). Every aspect of a woman's life was seen in terms of 'the larger good' that it would contribute to the state. For example, with regard to women's health: "... any steps taken to protect the health of the women workers should not be considered as for their exclusive benefit only, but taken in the interests of the whole nation" (Chaudhuri 1995: 220).

Yet, juxtaposed against this image of citizen is another role that women have to play—as emblems of national (primarily an idealistic image of a 'pure' Hindu woman) culture and tradition. Alongside the image of the socialist worker abstracted from religion and community is another image portrayed by the official channels of the state; the image of a self-sacrificing wife and mother assuming her 'natural' place in the home for the upbringing of India's 'greatest asset'—her children. This opposing image of woman is, in fact, far from secular—it hearkens back to a lost Vedic time and reflects notions of a recovered Hindu Brahminical ideal of woman (Uberoi 1996: xii; Chaudhuri 1995: 223). This was partly the reflection of Gandhi's own conception of women's roles in post-independent India. Gandhi's view was that self-realisation for men and women had to be conducted in separate spheres—for women, it was in the private sphere involving the upbringing and education of children. Kabir (c. 2003) writes:

> While he wanted a vanguard role for women in the freedom movement, Gandhi did not encourage women to compete for power. Rather, he wanted them to enter public life as selfless, devoted social workers to undertake the crucial task of social reconstruction. He wanted women to cleanse politics, to feminise it by bringing in the spirit of selfless sacrifice, rather than compete with men in grabbing power, and thus prove their moral superiority even in the realm of politics. In Gandhi's view ... [w]omen are the embodiment of sacrifice, and their advent to public life should, therefore, result in purifying it, in restraining unbridled ambition and accumulation of property. Gandhi, therefore, created a political space for women within the patriarchal system, projecting the concept of women's role being

complementary to men's, and embodying virtues of sacrifice and suffering.

Chaudhuri, similarly, points out that the WRPE states that a woman's responsibility would equally be to "create a cultural environment in the home for the proper nurture of the children" and "... [not become] a cheap imitation of man or render her useless for the great tasks of motherhood and nation building" (Chaudhuri 1995: 233, 224). In the 1960s, a substantial number of development programmes and policies of the state reflected this role. A typical example was the Community Development programme supported by the USAID. The programme run in rural communities aimed at enhancing women's lives by educating them about better hygiene and nutrition.

In contemporary India these two images of women—as socialised mother and abstract worker—still co-exist and are in tension. Scholars argue that these constructions are reproduced in the state's developmental policies related to women. The political climate of the 1980s and 1990s, in particular, has encouraged reactionary images of women's roles in society. Agnihotri and Mazumdar (1995: 1869), for instance, argue that, "... the mid-eighties have seen an onslaught on even existing rights of women through a harking back to 'tradition' and 'culture' and positing of images which emphasise women's reproductive role as the only natural, historical one." Agarwal (1988: 14) notes that this ideology of gender—the assumption that women are (or should be) primarily housewives and mothers and, secondarily, workers—permeates most policies of modern developing states like India. Women, in most policies related to productive and reproductive functions, land/property holding, and technology control, are located within the context of the nuclear family, thereby assigning primacy to male 'heads of households' (Kelkar 1987). Swaminathan (1991) further argues that the tendency to demarcate certain provisions in the state's Plan Documents as 'women's issues' (especially, those related to reproduction and child care) reinforces gendered assumptions about women's roles in society. Kasturi's (1996) evaluation of three national documents at different historical periods points out that the government has been less inclined to work towards fundamental changes in law and politics. She notes, "over time the political leadership grew away from the promises made to women in the nationalist era ... [and] ... the entire social system and state structure followed a particular path of growth in the course of which the whole gender question was jettisoned" (Kasturi 1996: 141). She asserts that the "Indian state is not gender neutral ... [S]tate and society are influenced by patriarchal values" and that "gender bias, in pernicious forms, unfortunately encouraged by the state in various ways, has weakened the social and economic position of women" (Kasturi 1996: 141).

Since the 1970s, the international literature on women in development has put the spotlight on women's productive roles which is reflected in the Indian Plan documents. Until the end of the Fifth Five-Year Plan (1951/56—1974/1978),[36] women were categorised along with the disabled, aged and destitute within a 'Welfare' Approach. From the Sixth Plan (1980-85), there was a shift in approach as women were positioned as targets of a 'Development' Approach; the Planning processes wanted to ensure that women were beneficiaries of development (health, education and employment) so that they could be partners and participants in the development process (Centre for Development and Human Rights 2003). The Ninth Plan (1997-2002) revised women's role in development as the State embarked on an 'Empowerment' Approach. The aim of the Plan was to "create an enabling environment where women could freely exercise their rights both within and outside the home, as equal partners along with men" (Centre for Development and Human Rights 2004:139).

Yet, in portraying women as productive beings, development policy discourses of the Indian State present multiple images of women's identity—these images can limit or enhance women's capacity to represent themselves as useful citizens of the development state. For instance, there are times when the identities of women are located outside of the dominant developmental discourse, and are either marginalised or excluded. At other times, their subjectivities are represented as

---

[36] The Fifth Five-Year Plan ended in 1978 after only four years when the newly-elected Janata Government took office.

integrally tied in with the main/malestream of development discourses. In her study of the Narmada Dam in India, Kurian (2000) showed how discourses of development—with a strong masculinist interest—made no room for consideration of poor/tribal women's interests in rehabilitation programmes of the state. John (1996), on the other hand, argues that in the emerging discourses of development in the 1990s in India, women—integral to community and other development strategies—were being represented as 'good subjects' who make 'sound economic sense' (John 1996: 3076). The state is a strategic player in constructing identity; where constructions of women challenge the dominant discourses of development, they are marginalised as irrelevant.

How relevant is an analysis of the construction of identity to the kinds of rights that women can access? The aim of any development state, in principle, is to foster a society where all its citizens have equal access to civil, political and social rights. The reality, however, is that the idea of 'rights' sits uneasily within the larger framework of development ideals. Jayal (1994) points out that attaining political 'rights' is not directly a consequence or even a factor in developmental change in India. She points out that the history of developmental intervention in welfare activities in India cannot be seen as akin to the social programmes of a welfare state. The welfare state is motivated by a conceptualisation of rights (both liberal and social rights), which is absent in the case of India. The aim of development intervention was not to maximise welfare or enhance the rights of a collective, but to provide a foundation for the project of modernisation and growth. The outcome of developmental change is directed more towards improving the status of the people so as to ensure some level of parity within the population (especially, in health, education, poverty alleviation and so on). As Jayal (1994) points out:

> The primary purpose of interventionism, and indeed its inspiring and guiding force, was developmentalist. This was not a state that self-consciously and deliberately took on the responsibility of providing for its citizens in clearly defined areas which bore some relationship to the idea of needs, especially basic needs (p. 20).

Therefore, development welfare is not expressed in the language of rights; there are implications that follow this 'oversight.' There is no obligation for the state to provide for development and, likewise, citizens have no foundation other than grounds of morality, to claim for development. The state in a sense becomes a paternal benefactor, and casts its relationship between citizen and state as one of "giver and receiver, benefactor and beneficiary" (Jayal 1994: 23). This exempts the state from direct involvement or liability and makes no reference to access to the state—it is nowhere suggested that development will increase claims to rights for its citizens. However, the state does, through constitutional obligation and a desire for development, undertake the task of providing welfare interventions. Welfare was cast as an economic component of development and was privileged over its social and political aspects (Jayal 1994: 21). Women's development, and the solution to their subordination, was also cast in terms of improving women's contribution to the economy—whether by improving women's access to education and health or removal of inherent barriers within the labour market. Issues of political rewards are, therefore, outside the debate of development; gaining access to the state, say, through visibility of a specific group, is incidental to the intention of the state's intervention in development.

This is where constructions of identities become critical. As Jayal (1994) argues, in market development the resources available for social entitlements are limited, and the state subsidises a reduced 'menu' of services. One consequence of such rethinking is that development welfare will increasingly assume a competitive dimension and resources will be distributed among various groups either on the basis of identity politics or on how the state defines development imperatives. It is in the latter that women's interests and access to the state become significant.

Conclusion

The Indian state is arguably post-structuralist; apart from acting in fragmented ways, its intent in acting for or against women is based on images, meanings, symbolisms and constructions. The state does perpetuate contending constructions of women in either progressive and traditional roles. Both of these constructions find a place in locating women within the contemporary development discourses of the Indian state, steeped as it is within neo-liberal paradigms. Drawing on contemporary theorisations around the idea of the state, and the construction of women's identity within it, I have argued that the state's discourses surrounding gender, influence the nature of developmental policy formulated by the state. The literature cited in this chapter provides a useful ground to begin the task of analysing ideologies within the RCH documents. As a prelude to the deconstruction of ideologies, the following chapter provides a description of the Reproductive and Child Health programme instituted in India as well as in Kerala.

References

Agarwal, B. (1988) "Patriarchy and the 'Modernising State': An Introduction", in B. Agarwal (ed.) *Structures of Patriarchy: The State, the Community and the Household*, Zed Books: London and Kali for Women: New Delhi, pp. 1–28.

Agnes, F. (1998) "Protecting Women against Violence?: Review of a Decade of Legislation, 1980–89" in P. Chatterjee (ed.) *State and Politics in India*, Oxford India Paperbacks: Delhi, India, pp. 521–565.

Agnihotri, I. and Mazumdar, V. (1995) "Changing Terms of Political Discourse: Women's Movement in India, 1970–1990s", *Economic and Political Weekly*, July 22, pp. 1869–1878.

Afshar, H. and Dennis, C. (1992)(eds) *Women and Adjustment Policies in the Third World*, St. Martins Press: New York.

Afshar, H. and Eade, D. (2004) *Development, Women, and War: Feminist Perspectives*, Oxfam: Oxford.

Alexander, R. E. (1995) "Evaluating Experiences : CIDA's Women in Development Policy, 1984–94", *Canadian Journal of Development Studies*, Special Issue, pp. 79–88.

Allen, J. (1990) "Does Feminism Need a Theory of the State?" in S. Watson (ed.) *Playing the State*, Verso: London, pp. 21–37.

Bakker, I (1996) "Introduction" in I. Bakker (ed.) *Rethinking Restructuring: Gender and Change in Canada*, University of Toronto Press: Toronto, pp. 3–25.

Basu, A. (1998) "Appropriating Gender" in P. Jeffrey and A.. Basu (eds) *Appropriating Gender: Women's Activism and Politicised Religion in South Asia*, Routledge: New York and London, pp. 3–14.

Bandarage, A. (1984) "Women in Development: Liberalism, Marxism and Marxist-Feminism", *Development and Change*, Vol. 15, No. 4, pp. 495–515.

Bergeron, S. (2001) "Political economy discourses of globalisation and feminist politics" *Signs*, Vol. 26, Iss. 4, pp. 983–1006.

Beneria, L. (1982) 'Accounting for Women's Work' in L. Beneria (ed.) *Women and Development: The Sexual Division of Labour in Rural Societies*, Praeger: New York.

Beneria, L. (1995) "Towards a Greater Integration of Gender in Economics" *World Development*, Vol. 23, No. 11, pp. 1839–1850.

Beneria, L. and Feldman, S. (1992)(eds) *Unequal Burden: Economic Crises, Persistent Poverty, and Women's Work*, Westview Press: Boulder.

Beneria, L. and Sen, G. (1981) "Accumulation, reproduction, and women's role in economic development: Boserup revisited", *Signs*, Vol. 7, No. 21, pp. 279–298.

Beneria, L. and Sen, G. (1982) "Class and gender inequalities and women's role in economic development: theoretical and practical implications", *Feminist Studies*, Vol. 8, No. 1, pp. 157–176.

Bhavnani, K., Foran, J. and Kurian, P. (2003) (eds) *Feminist Futures: Re-imagining Women, Culture and Development*, Zed Books: London, New York.

Blumberg, R. L. (1991) "Women and the Wealth and Well-being of Nations: Macro-Micro Interrelationships" in J. Huber (ed.) *Macro-Micro Linkages in Sociology*, Sage Publications: Newbury Park, California, pp. 121–140.

Brodie, J. (1994) "Shifting the Boundaries: Gender and the Politics of Restructuring", in I. Bakker (ed.) *The Strategic Silence: Gender and Economic Policy*, Zed Books: London, pp. 46–59.

Brown, W. (1992) "Finding the man in the state", *Feminist Studies*, Vol. 18, No. 1, pp. 7–34.

Boserup, E. (1970) *Women's Role in Economic Development*, George and Allen: London.

Brydon, L. and Chant, S. (1989) *Women in the Third World: Gender Issues in Urban and Rural Areas*, Elgar: Aldershot.

Centre for Development and Human Rights (2004) *The Right to Development: A Primer*, Sage: New Delhi, Thousand Oaks, London.

Centre for Reproductive Rights (2004) "India Chapter" in *Women of the World: Laws and Policies Affecting their Reproductive Lives (South Asia)* found at: http://www.reproductiverights.org/ww_asia_india.html

Charlesworth, H. (1997) "The sex of the state in international law" in N. Naffine and R. J. Owens (eds) *Sexing the Subject of Law*, LBC Information Services: North Ryde, New South Wales, Australia, pp. 251–268.

Chatterjee, P. (1998) "Development Planning and the State" in T. Byres (ed.) *The State, Development Planning and Liberalisation in India*, Oxford India Paperbacks: New Delhi, pp. 36–81.

Chaudhuri, M. (1995) "Citizens, workers and emblems of culture: an analysis of the First Plan document on women", *Contributions to Indian Sociology*, Vol. 29, Nos. 1 and 2, pp. 211–235.

Chhachhi, A. (1991) "Forced identities: The State, Communalism, Fundamentalism and Women in India", in D. Kandiyotti (ed.) *Women, Islam and the State*, Macmillan: London, pp. 144–175.

Connell, R. W. (1990) "The state, gender and sexual politics: theory and appraisal", *Theory and Society*, Vol. 19, pp. 507–544.

Desai, N. (1986) "From Articulation to Accommodation: Women's Movement in India", in L. Dube, E. Leacock and S. Ardener (eds) *Visibility and Power: Essays on Women in Society and Development*, Oxford University Press : New Delhi, pp. 287–299.

Deshpande, S. (1993) "Imagined Economies: Styles of Nation-Building in Twentieth Century India", *Journal of Arts and Ideas*, Numbers 25–26, pp. 5–35, December.

Dixon-Mueller, R. and Anker, R. (1988) *Assessing Women's Economic Contributions to Development*, International Labour Organisation Publications: Geneva.

Dyson, T. and Moore, M. (1983) "On kinship structure, female autonomy and demographic behaviour in India" *Population and Development Review*, vol. 9, iss. 1, pp. 35–60.

Elson, D. and Pearson, R. (1981) 'The Subordination of Women and the Internationalisation of Factory Production' in K. Young et al. (eds) *Of Marriage and Market*, CSE Books: London, pp. 144–166.

Elson, D. (1991) "Structural Adjustment: Its Effect on Women" in T. Wallace with C. March (eds) *Changing Perspectives: Writings on Gender and Development*, Oxfam: Oxford, pp. 39–53

Elson. D. (1992) "Male Bias in Structural Adjustment" in H. Afshar and C. Dennis (eds) *Women and Adjustment Policies in the Third World*, St. Martins Press: New York, pp. 49–68.

Elson, D. (1994) "Micro, Meso, Macro: Gender and Economic Analysis in the Context of Policy Reform", in I. Bakker, (ed.) *The Strategic Silence: Gender and Economic Policy*, Zed Books: London, pp. 33–45.

Engineer, A. (1987) (ed.) *The Shah Bano Controversy*, Orient Longman: Hyderabad, India.

Franzway, S., Court, D., and Connell, R.W. (1989) *Staking a Claim: Feminism, Bureaucracy and the State*, Polity Press: Cambridge.

Fraser, N. (1989) "Talking about Needs: Interpretive Contests as Political Conflicts in Welfare State Societies" in C. R. Sunstein (ed.) *Feminism and Political Theory*, The University of Chicago Press: Chicago and London, pp. 159–181.

Fraser, N. (1991) "What's critical about critical theory? The case of Habermas and Gender" in M. L. Shanley and C. Pateman (eds) *Feminist Interpretations and Political Theory*, Polity Press: Cambridge , pp. 253—276.

Fraser, N. and Gordon, L. (1994a) "Civil citizenship against Social Citizenship? On the ideology of Contract versus Charity" in B. Steenbergen (ed.), *The Condition of Citizenship*, Sage Publications : London, pp. 90–107.

Fraser, N. and Gordon, L. (1994b) "Reclaiming Social Citizenship: Beyond the Ideology of Contract versus Charity" in P. James (ed.) *Critical Politics: From the Personal to the Global*, Arena Publications and Department of Politics, Monash University: Melbourne, pp. 59–75.

Fraser, N. and Gordon, L. (1994c) "'Dependency Demystified': Inscriptions of Power in a Keyword of the Welfare State" *Social Politics*, Spring, pp. 4–31.

Goetz, A. M. (1991) "Feminism and the claim to know: contradictions in feminist approaches to women in development" in R. Grant and K. Newland (eds) *Gender and International Relations*, Open University, Milton Keynes: Suffolk, pp. 133– 157.

Hasan, Z. (1994) "Introduction: Contextualizing Gender and Identity in Contemporary India" in Z. Hasan (ed.) *Forging Identities : Gender, Communities and the State*, Kali for Women: New Delhi, pp. vii–xxiii.

Hasan, Z. (2002) "Religion and Politics in a Secular State: Law, Community and Gender" in Z. Hasan (ed.) *Politics and the State in India*, Sage: New Delhi, Thousand Oaks, London.

Jaquette, J.S. (1990) "Gender and Justice in Economic Development" in I. Tinker (ed.) *Persistent Inequalities*, Oxford University Press: New York, pp. 54–69.

Jayal, N. G. (1994) "The Gentle Leviathan: Welfare and the Indian state", *Social Scientist*, Vol. 22, No.9–12, pp. 18–26.

Jennings, A. (1993) "Public or Private? Institutional Economics and Feminism", in M. Ferber and J. A. Nelson (eds) *Beyond Economic Man: Feminist Theory and Economics,* The University of Chicago Press: Chicago and London.

John, M. (1996) "Gender and Development in India (1970s–1990s): Some Reflection on the Constitutive Role of Contexts", *Economic and Political Weekly*, November 23, pp. 3071–3077.

Kabeer, N. (1994) *Reversed Realities*, Verso: London.

Kabir, F. (c. 2003) "Political Participation of Women in South Asia" found at DAWN website: www.dawn.org.fj/ (accessed 5.8.2003)

Kandiyotti, D. (1991) (ed.) *Women, Islam and the State*, Macmillan: London.

Kapur, R. and Cossman, B. (1996) *Subversive Sites: Feminist Engagement with Law in India*, Sage: New Delhi, Thousand Oaks, London.

Kasturi, L. (1996) "Development, Patriarch and Politics: Indian Women in the Political Process" in V. M. Moghadam (ed.) *Patriachy and Development: Women's Positions at the End of the 20th Century*, Clarendon Press: Oxford, pp. 99– 144.

Kelkar, G. (1987) "Violence against Women: An understanding of Responsibility for their lives" in M. Davies (compiled volume) *Third World, Second Sex*, Zed Books, Ltd.: London and New Jersey, pp. 179–189.

Kingfisher, C. P. (1996) *Women in the American Welfare Trap*, University of Pennsylvania Press: Philadelphia, USA.

Kodoth, P. and Eapen, M. (2005) "Looking Beyond Gender Parity: Gender Inequities of Some Dimensions of Well-Being in Kerala" *Economic and Political Weekly*, July 23, 2005, pp. 3278–3285.

Kumar, R. (1994) "Identity Politics and the Contemporary Indian Feminist Movement" in V. M. Moghadam (ed.) *Identity Politics and Women: Cultural Reassertions and Feminisms in International Perspective*, Westview Press: Boulder, pp. 274–292.

Kurian, P. A. (2000) *Engendering the Environment? Gender in the World Bank's Environmental Policies*, Ashgate Publications: Aldershot, UK.

Kurian, P. A. and Munshi, D. (2003) "Negotiating Human-Nature Boundaries, Cultural Hierarchies and Masculinist Paradigms of Development Studies" in K. Bhavnani, J. Foran, and P. Kurian (eds) *Feminist Futures: Re-imagining Women, Culture and Development*, Zed Books: London, New York, pp. 146–159.

MacKinnon, C. (1982) "Feminism, Marxism, Method and the State: An Agenda for Theory", *Signs*, No. 7, pp. 515–544.

MacKinnon, C. (1983) "Feminism, Marxism, Method and the State: Toward Feminist Jurisprudence", *Signs*, No. 8, pp. 635–638.

MacKinnon, C. (1989) *Towards a Feminist Theory of the State*, Harvard University Press : Cambridge, MA.

Marshall, B. (1994) *Engendering Modernity: Feminism, Social Theory and Social Change*, Polity Press: Cambridge.

Marshall, G. (1994) *The Concise Oxford Dictionary of Sociology*, Oxford University Press: Oxford, New York.

Marshall, T.H. (1950) *Citizenship and Social Class*, Cambridge University Press: Cambridge.

Moghadam, V. (1994)(ed.) *Identity Politics and Women: Cultural Re-assertions and Feminism in International Perspective*, Westview Press: Boulder.

Mies, M. (1982) *The Lace Makers of Narsapur: Indian Housewives Produce for the World Market*, Zed Books: London.

Mies, M. (1994) "'Gender' and Global Capitalism", in L. Sklair (ed.) *Capitalism and Development*, Routledge: London and New York, pp. 107–122.

Mies, M. (1998) *Patriarchy and Accummulation on a World Scale: Women in the International Division of Labour*, Zed Books: London.

Miller, B. (1981) *The Endangered Sex: Neglect of Female Children in Rural North India*, Cornell University Press: Ithaca.

Misra, K. (1997) "Indian Feminism and the Post Colonial State", *Women and Politics*, Vol. 17, No. 4, pp. 25–45.

Moore, H. (1988) *Feminism and Anthropology*, Polity Press: Oxford.

Moser, C.O.N. (1991) "Gender Planning in the Third World: Meeting Practical and Strategic Needs" in R. Grant and K. Newland (eds) *Gender and International Relations*, Suffolk: Open University, Milton Keynes, pp. 83–122.

Moser, C. (1993) *Gender, planning and development: theory, practice and training*, Routledge: London and New York.

Nelson, B. (1990) "The Origins of the Two-Channel Welfare State: Workmen's Compensation and Mother's Aid" in L. Gordon (ed.) *Women, the State and Welfare*, University of Wisconsin: Madison, pp. 123–149.

Nussbaum, M. C. (2002) "Sex, laws, and inequality: What India can teach the United States" *Daedalus*, Wntr, vol. 131, iss.1, pp. 95–107.

Pateman, C. (1988) *The Sexual Contract*, Stanford University Press: Stanford, California.

Pateman, C. (1989) *The Disorder of Women: Democracy, Feminism and Political Theory*, Polity Press: Cambridge.

Pearson, R. (1998) "'Nimble fingers' re-visited: reflections on women and Third World industrialisation in the late twentieth century" in C. Jackson and R. Pearson (eds) *Feminist Visions of Development: Gender Analysis and Policy*, Routledge: New York and London, pp. 171–188.

Petiteville, F. (1998) "Three Mythical Representations of the State in Development Theory", *International Social Science Journal*, vol 50, Iss. 155, pp. 115–124.

Pringle, R. and Watson, S. (1992) "'Women's Interests' and the Post-Structuralist State", in M. Barrett and A. Phillips (eds), *Destabilizing Theory: Contemporary Feminist Debates*, Polity Press: Cambridge, pp. 53–73.

Pringle, R. and Watson, S. (1996) "Feminist Theory and the State: Needs, Rights and Interests" in B. Sullivan and G. Whitehouse (eds) *Gender, Politics and Citizenship in the 1990s*, University of New South Wales Press: Australia, pp. 64–80.

Rai, S. (1996a) "Women and the State in the Third World", in H. Afshar (ed.) *Women and Politics in the Third World*, Routledge, London and New York, pp. 25–39.

Rai, S. (1996b) "Women and the State in the Third World: Some Issues for Debate", in S. Rai and G. Lievesley (eds) *Women and the State: International Perspectives*, Taylor and Francis: London, pp. 5–23.

Rai, S. (2002) *Gender and Political Economy of Development*, Polity Press: Cambridge, UK.

Rathgeber, E.M. (1990) "WID, WAD, GAD: Trends in Research and Practice", *The Journal of Developing Areas*, Vol. 24, pp. 489–502.

Razavi, S. (2000) *Women in Contemporary Democratization*, UNRISD: Geneva.

Razavi, S. and Miller, C. (1995) *From WID to GAD: Conceptual Shifts in the Women and Development Discourse*, Occasional Paper No. 1, UNRISD: Geneva.

Rhode, D. (1994) "Feminism and the state", *Harvard Law Review*, Vol. 107, No. 6, 1181–1209.

Rogers, B. (1980) *The Domestication of Women*, Tavistock: London.

Sarvasy, W. (1992) "Beyond the Difference versus Equality Policy Debate: Post Suffrage Feminisms, Citizenship and the Quest for a Feminist Welfare State", *Signs*, Vol. 17, No. 2, pp. 329–362.

Sen, A. (1990) "Gender and Co-operative Conflicts", in I. Tinker (ed.) *Persistent Inequalities,* Oxford University Press: Oxford, pp. 123–149.

Scott, C. (1996) *Gender and Development: Rethinking Modernization and Dependency Theory*, Lynne Rienner Publishers : Boulder.

Shahid, F. (c. 2003) "Politics and Power: A Gendered Perspective from South Asia" found at DAWN website www.dawn.org.fj/ (accessed 9.8.2003)

Simon-Kumar, R. (1999) 'The meanings of the public sphere: negotiating women's social rights in development contexts', paper read at the Southern Regional Conference of the International Geographical Union Commission on Gender, Gendered Sites, Human Rights, Gendered Sights, Human Rites, Dunedin, New Zealand, February.

Sparr, P. (1994) (ed.) *Mortgaging Women's Lives: Feminist Critiques of Structural Adjustment*, Zed Books: London and New Jersey.

Staudt, K. (1986) "Women, Development and the State: On the Theoretical Impasse" *Development and Change*, Vol. 17, pp. 325–333.

Subramaniam, B. (2003) "Imagining India: Religious Nationalism in the Age of Science and Development" in K. Bhavnani, J. Foran, and P. Kurian (eds) *Feminist Futures: Re-imagining Women, Culture and Development*, Zed Books: London, New York, pp. 160–177.

Swaminathan, P. (1991) "Gender in Indian Planning: A Critique" in S. L. Raj (ed.) *Quest for Gender Justice*, Satya Nilayam Publications: Madras, India, pp. 53–68.

Swarup, H., Sinha, N., Ghosh, C. and Rajput, P. (1994) "Women's Political Engagements in India: Some Critical Issues" in B. J. Nelson and N. Chowdhury (eds) *Women and Politics WorldWide,* Yale University Press: New Haven and London, pp. 361–379.

Tiano, S. (1988) "Women's Work in the Public and Private Spheres: A Critique and Reformulation" in M.F. Abraham and P.S. Abraham (eds) Women, Development and Change: The Third World Experience, Wyndham and Hall: Bristol, USA, pp. 18–44.

Thornton, M. (1995) "The Cartography of the Public and Private", in M. Thornton (ed.) *Public and Private: Feminist Legal Debates*, Oxford University Press: Melbourne, pp. 2–16.

Uberoi, P. (1996) "Introduction: Problematizing Social Reform, Engaging Sexuality, Interrogating the State" in P. Uberoi (ed.) *Social Reform, Sexuality and the State*, Sage Publications India Pvt.: New Delhi, pp. ix–xxvi.

UNDP (2000) *Women's Political Participation and Good Governance: 21st Century Challenges,* UNDP: New York.

Waring, M. (1989) *If Women Counted: A New Feminist Economics,* Macmillan: London.

Watson, S. (1990) (ed.) *Playing the State*, Verso: London.

Watson, S. (1992) "Femocratic Feminism" in M. Savage and A. Witz (eds) *Gender and Bureaucracy*, Blackwell: Oxford. pp.186–204 .

Witz, A. and Savage, M. (1992) "The gender of organizations" in M. Savage and A. Witz (eds) *Gender and Bureaucracy*, Blackwell Publishers/*The Sociological Review* : Oxford, pp. 3–62.

World Bank (1991) *Gender and Poverty in India: A World Bank Country Study*, World Bank: Washington.

Yuval-Davis, N. and Anthias, F. (1989) *Woman-Nation-State*, MacMillan: London.

4

The Reproductive and Child Health Programme in India

An Overview

In this chapter, I present an overview of the RCH programme, focusing on the historical, demographical and institutional contexts in which the programme is being instituted. The RCH claims to offer a population programme that is perceptibly different from programmes pursued in the past by the state. In emphasising its uniqueness, I aim, first, to briefly trace the historical development of population programmes in India since the mid-1950s. Second, and more central to this book, I shall describe the various aspects of the RCH programme; in particular, I will examine the steps proposed, and already undertaken, by the Government of India (GoI) and the Government of Kerala (GoK) to implement the RCH programme.

Population Programmes in India: A Brief Historical Overview

Although population control became an official subject of interest in India with the initiation of the Family Planning Programme in 1951, the role of the programme within development policy—in terms of budgetary and planning commitment—was prioritised only in the Third Five Year Plan (1961–66). For instance, only Rs. 6.5 million were allocated to family planning in the First Five Year Plan (1951–56), compared with Rs. 50 million in the Second Plan, and Rs. 250 million in the Third Plan (IIPS 1995). When first initiated, the family planning programme was designed with a Clinical Approach, which largely meant that people desiring information or methods of contraception approached a clinic-based family planning unit. The main emphasis of the programme was the promotion of the rhythm method of contraception. The operational focus of the programme was restricted to the provision of advice in government hospitals and rural medical centres. There was also a focus on gathering information on the motivational aspects of family planning (Jolly 1986). By the Second Plan (1956–61), it was clear that population growth had far exceeded the government's expectation and that more stringent measures to control population were needed. In 1955, Frank Notestein, a well-known demographer and Leona Baumgartner, New York Health Commissioner, visited India and recommended an interdisciplinary population programme emphasising a public health approach which included the use of contraceptives with strong demographic support from the centre (Karkal 1998). Sterilisation as a method for permanent contraception was introduced in 1959. Family planning clinics were increased from 147 to 4167, and the number of sterilisations conducted from 1956–1960 totalled 152,677 (Jolly 1986). At the end of the second plan, serious shortcomings were identified with the clinical approach—it had a medical and middle-class bias and operated in a setting that was insensitive to the culture of the local population (Karkal 1998).

During the Third Plan, the clinical approach was replaced by the Family Planning Extension Education Approach, which was initiated in 1963, when intensive educational measures were introduced to motivate the population to adopt family planning methods. This approach involved active outreach strategies to the masses—a key tool employed by the MoHFW was the Information, Education and Communication schemes (IEC). The IEC basically were messages, related to family planning, propagated through a variety of means ranging from mass media (like television, radio, newspapers and magazines) to door-to-door campaigning by health workers. The IEC messages contained information on a range of issues, from norms of ideal family sizes, appropriate methods of childcare to birth control methods. The idea of the 'Small Family Norm' was introduced in the 1960s; the ideal family size of two children was promoted. In 1962, the government introduced 'out-of-pocket' expenses for people coming in for sterilisations (Karkal 1998). Besides sterilisation and natural methods, the Lippes Loop (an Intra Uterine Device) and the contraceptive pill were introduced on a large scale in 1965.[37] Despite the initial enthusiasm and high acceptance of the Loop by women, subsequent side-effects led to negative propaganda and acceptance levels dropped considerably. Continuation rates for the Loop were about two years and, for the Pill, even lower.

The Third Plan also set, for the first time, numerical demographic goals that were to be achieved within a specific period.[38] During the period from January 1961 to March 1966, the 'performance' of the family planning programme had increased substantially; 1.37 million sterilisations were performed and 0.81million IUDs were inserted (Jolly 1986). Despite these efforts, by the end of the Third Plan, birth rates were still inordinately high at 41 per 1000. Knowledge, Attitudes and Practice (KAP) Studies showed that, although individual family planning decisions corresponded to the small family norm, this did not, however, translate into demographic results at the national level. Consequently, following the Second Plan, there was a clear shift from a welfare approach to population control (Karkal 1998).

---

[37] Since the 1960s, three considerations seem to influence the government's decisions to make available select contraceptive methods: (a) high reported rates of efficiency (b) compatibility for mass use and (c) cost effectiveness. Sterilizations, apart from their efficiency, were a one-time operation. Condoms could be made available for mass use at little cost and needed no medical supervision. The IUD was introduced with the expectation that it would comply with these criteria. In addition, IUDs could be inserted by auxiliary medical staff, thereby not requiring the presence of physicians (Kumar 1997).

[38] In 1962, the demographic goal was to reduce crude birth rates (CBR) to 25 per 1000 population by 1973. This goal could not be achieved and by 1968, the goal was to reduce CBR to 23 per 1000 population by 1978-79. As this second goal could not be achieved either, yet another goal was set. In all, between 1962 and 1992, demographic goals were set at least 11 times (Reddy 1998).

The Inter-Plan Period (1966–69) saw an emphasis on the development of family planning infrastructure. In 1966, the Department of Family Planning was formally set up. The practice of fixing annual 'targets' decided by the central government was initiated during this period. In 1968, the Social Marketing Programme was made operational which aimed to promote and distribute at affordable prices contraceptives through a wide range of private outlets. The scheme sought to endorse specific brands of contraceptives, so that people would automatically associate a name with a product. The scheme was first used to market condoms, under which the brand 'Nirodh' was popularised and made available at a highly subsidised price.[39] The total expenditure on family planning at this time had gone up to Rs. 705 million, a budget increase of nearly three times the Third Plan. The mid-1960s was also the time when the state expanded (and experimented) with a broader range of contraceptives. The emphasis on the rhythm method, which characterised the earlier stages of the programme, was increasingly being replaced by 'modern' contraceptive methods—the Lippes Loop, the diaphragm and the contraceptive jelly (see Cassen 1978).[40]

In the Fourth Plan (1969–1974), the extension education approach was substituted with the Integrated Approach; the essential component of this shift was a merging of the family

[39] According to figures from Operations Research Group and Family Health International, condoms distributed through the social marketing programme represent one-third of all condoms distributed annually in India. Approximately 525,000 outlets including pharmacies, general stores, grocers, paan-bidi shops and bakeries are involved in the programme. Finally, annual sales for condoms grew from less than 16 million condoms in 1968-69 to 320 million in 1990-91 (Verzosa and Kakkar 1996).

[40] Most of these earlier modern contraceptive methods were later withdrawn from the government's programme for a variety of reasons. Officials felt that women did not know how to use the diaphragm or the jelly appropriately, and they proved to be logistically unsuitable. The IUD, after initial enthusiasm, declined in acceptance (Cassen 1978). Women's groups in the 1990s are seeking to make the diaphragm available in the public health system as it is a contraceptive for women that does not require dependence on male partners or service providers.

planning services with the maternal and child health services being run by the Ministry of Health. It was felt that family planning services would be better accepted if presented in the context of maternal health. In 1970, vaginal tubectomy was introduced, and this meant that women could undergo sterilisation even outside the post-partum period (Karkal 1998). The Medical Termination of Pregnancy Act (MTP), 1971, came into force in 1972. Although the MTP was intended to allow for abortion for the health and safety of women (risk to the woman's life, grave physical and mental injury to the woman, and substantial impairment to the child), it is also widely recognised that abortion can be accessed in cases of contraceptive failure.[41] Also during the early 1970s, the 'camp' approach was adopted; that is, family planning services were taken out to local people. Camps were short duration (a day to a few days) temporary, mobile units that went from place to place advertising and delivering contraceptive services. Surgical methods of contraception, in particular, vasectomy, was promoted through camps. Camps were popular and attracted large numbers of contraceptive acceptors, not least because of the larger financial incentives that were given to those who were sterilised.[42] The camp approach was abused during the Emergency Period of 1975–77, involving cases of forced vasectomies, among other problems. There was a sudden increase in the number of steri-lisations carried out from 2.67 million in 1975–76 to 8.26 million in 1976–77 (IIPS 1995). Following elections in 1978, in a move to distance itself from the legacy of the Emergency, the new Janata government re-emphasised the voluntary nature of the family planning programme and its commitment to community welfare. The Family Planning Programme was renamed the Family Welfare Programme and focused on maternal and child health services.

An army of health personnel, meanwhile, was being built up alongside the development of the family planning programme to

[41] Estimates show that as of 1995-96, about 566, 500 abortions were conducted in India (Centre for Reproductive Rights 2004).

[42] The District Collector of Ernakulam, S. Krishnakumar, was an ardent supporter of the camp approach and promoted it widely. In July 1971, he conducted the largest camp where 626, 913 men underwent vasectomy.

motivate and deliver the contraceptive services. In the early 1970s, the idea of the 'multi-purpose' worker was promoted. The multi-purpose workers were expected to provide a range of family planning, maternal and child health, and public health services. During the Seventh Five Year Plan (1985–90) the Government envisaged a three-tiered outreach health system. Family Welfare sub-centres formed the lowest rung of the ladder; they were staffed by one male and one female multipurpose worker/auxiliary nurse midwife (MPW/ ANM) and were expected to serve populations of 5000 (or 3000 in particularly undeveloped, tribal, or hilly areas). On the next level was the Primary Health Centre (or PHC), which serves a population of 30,000 and was staffed by a medical officer, staff in supervisory positions and multipurpose workers. At the top was the Community Health Centre (CHC) covering a population of about 100,000 (the area of a community development block) and staffed by specialists in paediatrics, surgery, and obstetrics and gynaecology. CHCs serve as 'first referral units' (FRUs) that provide essential obstetric care, including caesarean sections and blood transfusions (World Bank 1996: 71–72).

There is also some level of provision of family welfare services through a range of NGOs and private sector bodies. A recent study notes that the Department of Family Welfare funds about 97 large NGOs and 800 smaller ones in the states. It is estimated that about one percent of contraceptive users approach NGOs for their contraception (Centre for Reproductive Rights 2004). The private health sector is also involved in maternal and child health delivery but this tends to be in the area of curative health (and some contraceptive retail sales) rather than educational or preventive public health.

The National Health Policy (NHP) was drawn up in 1983. The Policy document that laid down the long-term demographic goals aimed to achieve a Net Reproduction Rate (NRR) of 1 by 2000.[43] For this the Family Welfare (FW) Programme set a birth rate goal of 21 per thousand, death rate of 9 per thousand, natural growth rate of 1.2, infant mortality rates below 60 per thousand

[43] The introduction of the NRR was significant in that the indicator basically reflects that one mother should give birth to one daughter or , in other words, that child-bearers in a set population are controlled.

live births and couple protection rate (number of sexually active people using contraception) of 60 percent.[44] The NHP also laid down maternal and child health goals of reducing the maternal mortality ratio to 200 maternal deaths per 100,000 live births, supplying 100 percent of pregnant women with tetanus toxoid immunisation and antenatal care, and ensuring that trained personnel attend 100 percent of deliveries. In 1985, the Universal Immunisation Programme (UIP) was launched with the aim of universal coverage of vaccinations to pregnant women and children. A programme of social marketing of oral pills began in 1987. The 1980s was also the time when 'modern' innovative methods of female sterilisation such as, the laparoscopic method and tubal ligation were introduced into the programme.

A major goal in the Eighth Five-Year Plan (1992–97) was to strengthen child health services. In 1992, the Child Survival and Safe Motherhood Programme (CSSM) was started to strengthen the achievements under the UIP and ensure that the maternal and child health goals listed in the NHP were fulfilled (World Bank 1996). The CSSM is designed to address major causes of morbidity and mortality in women and children; the achievements under UIP were sought to be strengthened along with providing better facilities for safe motherhood. The latter included measures to prevent anaemia, provision for safe delivery kits, training of traditional birth attendants or *dais* to conduct delivery, and measures to strengthen referral services for pregnancy-related complications.

Present Population Framework

The National Population Policy, 2000, forms the current framework of population policy in India. The immediate objectives of the NPP 2000 is to address the unmet needs for contraception, health care infrastructure, and health personnel,

[44] The Seventh Plan Document (1985-90) admitted that to expect the country to achieve this goal in the specified time was unrealistic. To quote the document," [i]n the light of the progress made in the initial period of the Sixth Plan, the health policy targeted a net reproduction rate of one by the year 2000 AD; a review, however, indicates that this goal would be reached only by 2006-2011" (Planning Commission 1985: 281 cited in Reddy, 1998).

and to provide integrated service delivery for basic reproductive and child health care. The policy aims to achieve a medium-term goal of bringing TFR to replacement levels by 2010. There are fourteen key goals that the NPP 2000 has set to achieve by 2010 and include:

1. reducing infant mortality rate to below 30 per 1000 live births
2. reducing maternal mortality ratio to below 100 per 100,000 live births
3. Promoting delayed marriage for girls, not earlier than age 18 and preferably after 20 years
4. Achieving universal access to information/counselling and services for fertility regulation and contraception with a wide basket of choices
5. Containing the spread of Acquired Immune-Deficiency Syndrome (AIDS) and promoting greater integration between the management of reproductive tract infections (RTI) and sexually transmitted infections (STI) and the National AIDS Control Organisation
6. Bringing about convergence in implementation of related social sector programmes so that family welfare becomes a people-centred programme.[45]

The NPP 2000 also recommended the setting up of a National Commission on Population to oversee its implementation. A Commission was established in 2000 headed by the Prime Minister and comprised of Chief Ministers of the various states, Minister for the Department of Family Welfare, government officials, demographers and NGOs.

In addition, the National Health Policy, 2002, and the Tenth Five Year Plan (2002–2007) stresses the need to improve public health infrastructure so as to be accessible to all social groups. The NHP, 2002, recognises that women as a social group have discriminatory access to health care. Under the policy, Central Government funding is to give top priority funding to programmes targeted at women's health (Centre for Reproductive Rights 2004).

---

[45] National Population Policy, online document at http://populationcommission.nic.in

A key goal of the Tenth Five Year Plan is to increase the utilisation of public health facilities from less that 20 percent to more than 75 percent by 2010. The Tenth Five Year Plan also recognises the importance of introducing "quality control tools and concepts ... into every aspect of health care in order to ensure that the population and system benefit from institutionalised norms, accountability and responsibility" (Centre for Reproductive Rights 2004: 77). A National AIDS Prevention and Control Policy and National Blood Policy was introduced, with the aim to reduce HIV infection transmissions to zero rate by 2007 and create socio-economic environments that help prevent HIV/AIDS.

Contraceptives and Legislation in India

The Indian legal code with regard to contraceptives is not a comprehensive body of law, but instead comprises jurisdictions scattered throughout various codes, policy statements, and fields of law (such as criminal or penal codes, public health codes, press laws, and consumer laws). As such, there is no specific statute in India governing or controlling the manufacturing, advertisement, sale or use of contraceptives, their standards, or quality in any direct or exclusive way. All regulating guidelines in national law relate primarily to the approval of contraceptives as drugs. The key central statutes are the Drug and Cosmetics Act (1940) and the Drug Control Act (1947). Provisions in these Acts are administered by the Ministry of Health and Family Welfare. Testing and trial introductions of new drugs are conducted by the Indian Council of Medical Research (ICMR) (see Centre for Reproductive Law and Policy 1995).

In the same way, there are no specific statutes governing the dissemination of information, advertisement, publicity, promotion or packaging of contraceptives. These are covered primarily by media and penal laws. These gaps in law can potentially open avenues for exploitative advertising. Ravindran (1993), for instance, notes that misleading information is provided on the packaging of the popular oral contraceptive, Mala–D. Another oral contraceptive, Centchroman, marketed under the brand name 'Saheli' as the revolutionary once–a-week pill was advertised in the marketing brochure as "free from side effects" (Kumar 1997).

There are also no central statutes that explicitly set forth universal principles of informed consent, non-discrimination, confidentiality and right to humane treatment in family welfare. With regard to patient rights, patients can claim compensation under the 1872 Indian Contract Act, Indian Penal Code if death has occurred by a doctor's negligence; the Law of Torts if medical negligence has occurred; and the 1986 Consumer Protection Law, which seeks to protect consumers from faulty or hazardous products and negligence for a paid commodity or service. Under the Medical Council Act, complaints can be laid against doctor misconduct. The introduction of these safeguards for clients has generated a risk-averse mentality among medical practitioners. Doctors at rural clinics tend to be more hesitant to undertake risky treatment and preferred instead to refer patients to the larger hospitals. The delay in treatment could potentially affect the outcome of the patients' illness, yet doctors now preferred to avoid taking responsibility for such cases, for fear of inviting lawsuits against them.[46]

The RCH Programme: A Background

In October 1997, the GoI formally launched the Reproductive and Child Health Programme. The RCH, initiated against a backdrop of the ICPD, was the Government of India's initiative to replace the existing Family Welfare Programme. In comparison to the Family Welfare Programme, the RCH aimed to be gender sensitive, that is, grounded in the realities of overall health needs of women and children, implementation needs of health workers, and local demographic needs and conditions. In lieu of the target-motivated programme, which primarily emphasised fertility reduction, the RCH service provision has alternate purposes. These are to increase service coverage, so as to make accessible health facilities to the population, to focus on reducing unmet

---

[46] The Centre for Reproductive Rights (2004) covers reproductive laws and policies in considerable detail.

needs,[47] and to improve the quality of services, defined according to specific standards (Government of India 1997a). It is expected that these goals could be achieved through increasing community participation in decision-making around reproductive health issues, and improved institutional management in programme delivery. The RCH is also intended to institute services that were earlier neglected, such as counselling and a better referral system. Another new introduction was the greater interdependence with the NGO and private sector, so as to fill gaps in public health sector services (Visaria and Visaria 1999). The World Bank's (Measham and Heaver 1996) appraisal of the GoI's efforts is that new signals usher in the new programme (see Table 4.1 below).

The impetus to initiate the recent round of changes to the population programme in India came from both external and internal sources. A key external motivation for the government to review its population policy was the tangible shift in international ethos following the ICPD, 1994. For the Indian government what this meant was that there was pressure from donor organisations to review the institutional structure of the population policy; the move towards the RCH was thus, undeniably, donor driven. Alongside, there were also domestic catalysts that set the stage for the government's acceptance of a policy change. Since the 1990s, there has been growing discontent within the Ministry of Family Welfare that the Family Welfare Programme does not reach its desired population goals. In January 1992, the MoHFW issued the *Action Plan for Revamping the Family Welfare Programme* in India, a document which identified several weaknesses in the existing programme (Merrick 1996). The Action Plan recommended a twelve-point strategy for improving the effectiveness of the Family Welfare Programme. Some of these recommendations included (a) generating a national consensus and policies for the Family Welfare Programme, (b) improving the quality and outreach of family welfare services, (c) implementing special initiatives for ninety

[47] Unmet needs refer to services for couples who do not want to have any more children or who wish to space their next child but are not currently practicing contraception.

'backward' districts, (d) modifying the system of targets and incentives, and devolving more responsibility to the states, (e) upgrading and improving the performance of immunisation and maternal and child health services, (f) revitalising training for staff, especially field level workers, (g) involving non-governmental organisations, and (h) strengthening inter-sectoral co-ordination between the FWP and other relevant government agencies (Merrick 1996).

In order to address the shortcomings identified in the report, the government set up two independent committees to review the population situation and to advise it on policy changes. The second committee, in particular, comprising largely of experts in the field of demography and planning, was headed by Dr. M.S. Swaminathan. In May 1994, the Swaminathan Committee submitted to the MoHFW a draft report with recommendations for a new population policy. The report proposed establishing population and social development committees at the national, state, district and local levels of government to promote a participatory political environment and community involvement in addressing family welfare issues (Merrick 1996). It also recommended withdrawal of the target approach, empowering women by increasing their opportunities to participate in paid work, and shifting the emphasis of the programme from national goals to helping couples achieve their reproductive goals (Khan and Townsend 1999). Among the suggestions for implementing the new population policy was establishing a Population and Social Development Fund to replace the Department of Family Welfare (Merrick 1996). Critical appraisals suggest that the government has not wholly accepted the recommendations of this committee and many aspects are still "under discussion" (Merrick 1996: 15; see also Visaria and Visaria 1999).

A tangible result of these revisionary discussions was the decision in 1995 to eliminate the state's practice of enforcing numerical targets, popularly called the Target Free Approach or the TFA. The system of targets in India was adopted in the mid-1960s, and was largely an incentive scheme for acceptors of specific family planning methods (mostly, sterilisations and IUDs) and field workers in order to motivate greater acceptance rates of contraceptives. The numerical targets for each state were fixed by the central government (usually arbitrarily), and these were passed on to the state governments, districts, and community level centres to be achieved within an annual period. The central and state governments religiously adhered to the target system for decades because "it was quantitative, easy to monitor and because it was expected to have a direct link with reduction in fertility" (Khan and Townsend 1999: 44). The system of numerical targets have been criticised widely on human rights grounds (see, among others, Freedman and Isaacs 1993). The incentive system is widely seen as a key factor in encouraging poor service provision by health providers (Khan and Townsend 1999). This was supported by the statements of providers who were participants in my research. A senior official in the Department of Family Welfare in Kerala, admitted that, "to achieve that figure often we have had to compromise the quality of the services. For example, there have been instances of Copper-T (an intra-uterine device) [being] introduced, removed and re-introduced in the same beneficiary. A lady in her 43rd year of life [was] brought for sterilisation. People who [are] ... well past their productivity ... those who are in the 50 or 60 year olds also used to be brought for vasectomy, male sterilisation." The TFA was introduced on an experimental basis in one or two districts of Kerala and Tamil Nadu in India in 1995. A year later, in April 1996, the government declared the entire country as target free. The target free approach generated mixed responses in various groups. Women's groups welcomed the government's shift away from the target-oriented system while demographers argued that the removal of targets would be ineffective. In informal conversations with representatives of the Population Foundation of India, I was told that the overall feeling was that it was premature to remove targets; it was first necessary to ensure that all eligible couples, and adolescent boys and girls were educated about modern contraceptive methods.

The target-free approach was also responsible for dismantling prevailing practices of work performance by health workers. For instance, apart from abolishing method-specific targets for field workers, the government has also scrapped the practice of provider and motivator incentive for IUDs and sterilisation and giving motivator certificates for achieving targets set for staff.[48] As one policy document notes, the change in approach will now be reflected, for example, "in how workers interact with clients, how communities participate in the identification and monitoring of service delivery, and how workers' performance is measured" (Government of India 1997a). In the absence of targets, field workers' performance was to be assessed using indicators of quality. For instance, the registration of pregnant women would be measured not in the numbers registered but the numbers registered before 16 weeks of pregnancy (Government of India, n.d.).

In the years immediately following the removal of targets, the 1996–97 performance indicators for acceptance of sterilisations, condoms and IUDs registered a sharp decline. In 1997–98, the declining trend appeared to be reversing—the proportion of people accepting these methods had increased over the 1996–97 figures, but was still lower than in the pre-TFA period. These figures, and the concern that field level staff were misinterpreting the removal of targets to mean that they need not promote contraceptives anymore, compelled the MoHFW to review its TFA policy.[49] The government shifted from a TFA approach to a Decentralised Participatory Planning (DPP) approach for population programmes (Government of India 1996).[50] In the

---

[48] The earlier practice was to reward health personnel (both the ANM and medical doctor) for every IUD that was inserted or sterilization conducted.

[49] Recent published statistics indicate that female sterilizations in all major states have increased from 1997-1999, from as much as 17.6% in Assam, 4.9% in Punjab and 12.5% in Uttar Pradesh (Centre for Reproductive Rights 2004).

[50] Mavalankar (c. 2000) notes that the introduction of the TFA led to inconsistent practice in the various states. Aspects of the TFA, such as quality of care, community participation and encouragement of spacing between births, did not appear to have become part of the programme. Moreover, in the field, the processes for monitoring and reporting had become complicated for the health staff. Consequently, there was some revisioning of the TFA and a new "Community Needs Assessment Approach" was introduced in 1998.

latter, the targets were brought back; the only difference was that unlike pre-TFA times, instead of the Central Government fixing targets, this would be done by communities themselves and relayed to the state. The DPP was emphasised as a *bottom-up* approach to population planning, involving the community in the setting of goals. In the bottom-up planning approach, the health worker or the ANM will determine her own work load on the basis of the "felt needs" of the community, and the 'service needs', as determined by the number of pregnancies and births in her area, rather than fulfil the targets set by the central government and state authorities. Plans formulated at the sub-centre and the PHC level will be integrated to form a District Action Plan. The State Action Plan will, in turn, be an aggregation of the District Action Plans. The National Plan that will be the All-India programme of action in reproductive health will be a consolidation of State Action Plans.

A RCH approach provides a package of reproductive and child health (RCH) services. Building on the success of the UIP and the CSSM programmes, the RCH expects to cover all aspects of women's reproductive health across their reproductive cycle, from puberty to menopause (Government of India n.d.). The RCH also emphasises accentuating community participation in planning for services and prioritising needs and strategies (Government of India n.d.). Under the RCH, the government plans to disband the erstwhile approach of top-down planning and substitute in its place a bottom-up planning approach; that is, it will move from a target-based activity to a client-centred and demand-driven quality services programme (Government of India 1997a). The participatory approach to family planning requires a strong partnership and communication network between the PHC health workers and other village level functionaries like representatives of the panchayats, non-governmental organisations, pradhans, primary school teachers, and practitioners of traditional systems of medicine, to name a few. To prepare ANMs for these additional organisational tasks, the state governments embarked on a state-wide training programme, that has as its focus participatory methods of needs appraisal of the local community (field interviews; Government of India 1997c).

The RCH was also founded on providing good quality care to the users of the programme. Quality of care is assessed along various dimensions, particularly, service delivery (such as, promoting informed choices and follow up care), interpersonal communication, technical quality (in the competence of the providers and equipment) and social relevance of programmes (as in encouraging male participation, and increasing role of women in the programme).

This chapter, thus far, has attempted to provide a general historical overview of the evolution of the Reproductive and Child Health programme, its objectives and philosophies. The following

Table 4.1 *Changing the Signals (Reproductive and Child Health)*

	Old Signals	**New Signals**
Primary goal	Reach two child family size norm	While still encouraging smaller families, help clients meet their own health and family planning goals
Priority services	Family Planning especially female sterilisation, immunisation	Full range of MCH services
Performance measures	Number of cases	Quality of care, client satisfaction, coverage measures
Management approach	Top down and target driven Male driven	Decentralised and client needs-driven Gender Sensitive
Attitude to client	Motivate and persuade	Listen, assess needs, and Inform
Accountability	To the bureaucracy	To the client and community, plus health and family welfare staff

Source: Measham and Heaver (1996), p. 5

sections focus on the government's strategies for implementation, especially specific areas of the programme, namely, programme design, services, funding, and monitoring that have been proposed.

The RCH and Implementation

This section highlights some of the key features of the programme. The descriptions that follow are meant to be an overview of various relevant aspects, rather than an exhaustive account of the government's implementation of the RCH.

Programme Design

The RCH programme is centrally-funded by the Government of India. Its implementation was planned to be spread over two phases, RCH-I and RCH-II. The first phase of the programme commenced in 1997/98 for a five-year period culminating in 2001/02. The implementation strategy of RCH- I had three components. First, in terms of service provision, the programme had essentially two parts—a national-level strategy and another restricted to specific districts. The first and larger part, was to be implemented in all districts. Interventions such as child survival and safe motherhood, facility for safe abortions, building up physical infrastructure, enhanced community participation, adolescent health and reproductive hygiene, were to be offered in all districts. This was to be implemented in a phased manner with 178 districts being covered in the first year, 202 districts being covered in the second year, and an additional 127 districts being covered in the third year (field interviews). The second part of the programme was restricted to specific districts with interventions like screening for RTI (Reproductive Tract Infections)/ STI (Sexually Transmitted Infections), improved delivery services and emergency obstetric care to be offered only in these selected districts. In addition, the World Bank also funded the development of reproductive health projects in certain districts, called the District Project Implementation Plan (DPIP). All states were to prepare State Implementation Plans (SIP) indicating the interventions to be taken up in various districts. In Phase I, 24 project plans in districts have been proposed by state governments, and have been approved by the

World Bank. More districts were to be covered by the World Bank subsequently in Phase II. The World Bank project was intended to assist the GoI to "improve management performance... and to strengthen institutional structures for timely, co-ordinated utilisation of project resources" (World Bank 1997: 2).

Service Provision

The services that were proposed to be offered under the RCH were not entirely new; most of the 'package' was an extension of services already being provided under the government's family welfare programmes. The government added newer services intended to address reproductive morbidity and sexual health. As one RCH policy document points out : "RCH is equivalent to Family Planning + CSSM + prevention of RTI/STD and AIDS + client approach to providing FW and Health Care Services" (Government of India 1997e:3). The MoHFW distinguishes between two kinds of service packages, an 'essential package' and a 'special package' of services. The essential package includes services related to (a) prevention and management of unwanted pregnancy, (b) maternity care, including prenatal services (registration at the health centre, at least three pre-natal check ups, folic acid tablets, and tetanus toxide injections), delivery services, and post-partum services (breast feeding support, early identification of post natal sepsis, nutrition counselling, neonatal problems, etc.), and (c) child survival care, such as immunisation, detection of high-risk cases as in low birth weight, etc. Special interventions relate to emergency obstetric care (in case of complicated pregnancy cases), and special programmes that have been sanctioned by the government for specific populations, like urban slums, tribal populations, and adolescents.

Not all the services provided by the government would be uniformly available throughout the country. Allocation of services is determined by two criteria. The first consideration is the *site of provision*, whether the point of service delivery is a sub-centre, PHC, CHC or district hospital. Not all the services available at the level of PHC would be available at the sub-centre, and not all services provided at the CHC/FRU would be provided at the

PHC, and so on. For instance, tubal ligations, vasectomies, and medical terminations of pregnancies upto 8 weeks, would be available at the PHC level, but not at the sub-centre. Medical termination of pregnancies up to 20 weeks, on the other hand, would be provided only at district hospitals. The second consideration pertained to the characteristics of the population in which the health centre is located. For this, the government categorised all districts in the country into 3 types—A, B, and C. This distinction has been made on the basis of crude birth rate and female literacy rate, which according to one policy document "reasonably reflects the RCH status of the districts" (Government of India 1997b: 4). In 'C' category districts, the status of RCH is poor, and is accompanied by low awareness, low education status and, often, low economic status as well. The infrastructure, roads and access to electricity are also generally poor in these districts (Government of India 1997b). A and B level districts have better statistics to begin with and may not need the same kind of interventions that are proposed for C level districts. For instance, referral transport for women with complications in delivery, and belonging to indigent families has been proposed for C category districts (Government of India 1997b: 16). Women in these districts are likely to belong to lower income households and are at risk as they are likely to be assisted in delivery by untrained persons. There are some services such as consultant gynaecologists that would be made available to all the three category districts (World Bank 1996b). In all, there were 58 'A' category districts, 184 'B' category districts and 265 'C' category districts.

In sum, the state's provision of services encompasses a wide range of interventions that cover medical, social, organisational and management needs identified within the existing family welfare programme.

Financing the RCH[51]

The RCH is part of the overall Family Welfare Programme of the GoI, which is a centrally-sponsored programme. The financial

[51] These figures in this section are based on the documents I have cited and reflect currency conversion rates prevalent at the time in 1996-97.

commitment for the RCH programme during the first phase was Rs. 5112.53 crores. In addition, the sub-projects funded by the World Bank were expected to cost approximately Rs. 547.50 crores out of which Rs. 283.88 crores would be disbursed for projects in the first phase, and the remaining funds by the second phase period (Government of India 1997d). The central government's programme was to be funded with external assistance from major international donor agencies. The major funding bodies for the RCH are the World Bank (total funds US$ 480 million in Phase I till 2002 and US$ 240 million in Phase II), European Commission (ECU 200 million), UNFPA (US$ 50 million), UNICEF (US$ 150 million), ODA- UK (US$ 21.1 million) and DANIDA (US$ 9.00 million). The World Bank (WB) is the largest external funder of the RCH. Kerala was to receive approximately Rs. 49.9658 crore (approximately US$ 120,000) in the first phase of the RCH sub-project. Agencies such as the ODA, DANIDA, UNFPA and UNICEF will support a limited number of budget items, mainly training, institutional development, vaccines and selected equipment. The WB funds are proposed to be used for orientation workshops on RCH, institutional development through training, modified management information systems, local capacity enhancement, some operational costs and IEC activity (World Bank 1996b).

The funding scheme under the RCH must be critically evaluated against gaps and needs in the existing programme. Ravishankar (1996) points out the following shortcomings in the Indian Family Welfare programmes: (a) per capita expenditure on family welfare services in India is low by international standards, and has declined in real terms since 1991; (b) physical and human infrastructural ratios fall far short of prescribed norms, and operational costs such as fuel, drugs, and maintenance do not receive adequate funding; and (c) the most critical needs are for capital enhancement, mostly construction works. Ravishankar goes on to argue that funding for the RCH must be developed keeping in mind these weaknesses in the existing structure, and the proposed shift in emphasis of the programme. For instance, the move by the RCH towards quality-oriented reproductive health will require greater contact between health providers and the community. This would then entail greater mobility for the providers. The government would then have to consider provision of vehicles as a necessary part of the programme. In Ravishankar's estimate, the funding for the RCH currently allocated will need to be supplemented with private sector services to fully address reproductive health requirements in the country.

Institutional Development

The institutional context in which the RCH is implemented is significant on three counts. First, as a programme of the MoHFW, the RCH is a new creation within the Ministry, and builds on new and existing organisational and institutional structures within the MoHFW and other government departments. A key aim of the RCH is to integrate the various programmes that are functioning alongside to achieve the same objectives in the field. An integrated health service is being seen as a primary institutional objective of the programme. In this regard, the MoHFW seeks the involvement of the Ministries of Welfare, Urban Development, Rural Development, Departments of Health, Women and Child Development and Education. For instance, the MoHFW proposes to co-ordinate its programmes with the District Literacy Programme, headed by the District Magistrate, to link its messages of RCH and population control with the Total Literacy Campaign (Government of India 1997d: 14). New institutions are also proposed to be set up for the operationalisation of the RCH. For instance, the government plans to set up a Procurement Support Agency (PSA) at the national and state level to ensure supply of goods (equipment, medicines etc.) and services (of consultants, trainers, etc.) (Government of India 1997f; World Bank 1996b). A state-level society called the State Committees on Voluntary Action (SCOVA) with the Chief Secretary as Chairman and State Health Secretary as Vice Chairman for the disbursement of funds will also be activated under the programme. The SCOVA will consider applications from the voluntary sector in urban and rural areas for projects in the area of maternal and child health, and family welfare. On another level, relationships between existing institutions are being reviewed and reworked. At the district level, the RCH is being implemented at a time when the Panchayati Raj or local self government is also being operationalised, calling for closer ties between the health centres and local administration. Under the new system of self-government, the health centre administration and funding is a local community or panchayat concern. As a government document points out, the "...panchayati raj system will have a greater role in planning, implementation, and assessment of client satisfaction" (Government of India 1997b, p. 4). Field interviews suggested that the new system meant greater authority of locally-based leaders to influence the day-to-day functioning of the doctors in PHCs, a situation which raised resentment among the medical staff, and a fractious relationship between the health system and local administration.

Alongside these social and political liaisons, the government, under the umbrella of the RCH, also proposes to enhance networking with local non-governmental organisations (NGOs), especially women's organisations and the private sector of health provision, especially those that provide Indian Systems of Medicine (ISMs). With regard to NGOs, the RCH documents note that the government system and the NGO functioning are actually "complementary in nature" (Government of India 1997b: 34). The government proposes to capitalise on the NGOs' flexibility and rapport with the local community to attempt to set in place innovative programmes which may not be successful if undertaken by the state. At the village level, the RCH envisages small, grassroots NGOs being utilised for advocacy of RCH/family welfare practices. 'Mother NGOs' or umbrella organisations for the smaller agencies are expected to provide training for grassroots NGO staff, so as to be more effective counsellors for family welfare. At the national level, the RCH sees a limited number of NGOs assisting the MoHFW in select programmes, such as running a baby-friendly project in hospitals. Similarly, these NGOs could help in enforcing the Pre-Natal Diagnostic Technique Act, which bans the sex determination of foetuses through amniocentosis. Finally, a limited number of NGOs may be mobilised for mobile clinics offering contraception (Government of India 1997b).

The government also proposes to have closer liaison with the private non-voluntary health sector, both in western and traditional forms of medicine. The government proposes to capitalise on this advantage that the private sector has, and provide only those services that cannot be offered by the private sector. Similarly, the government seeks to create closer ties with indigenous systems of medicine, providing funding for research, and development of plantations of medicinal plants in wastelands, and denuded forests (Government of India 1997b: 24).

Monitoring and Evaluation

One of the most important changes with the shift to a reproductive health programme has been the need to find appropriate methods to monitor and evaluate the programme, especially its quality-oriented aspects. The family welfare programme has a tradition of recording elaborate statistics in various registers; under the RCH an attempt is being made to integrate related information into one report (Murthy 1999). The government constituted a committee to study and recommend appropriate measures that could be used to evaluate performance and service quality. The committee evolved a new monitoring and evaluation system, which has three main components (Pathak et al. 1999):

1. Monthly activity reports from the sub-centre, primary health care centre, and first referral unit: The monthly activity reports record information on a range of activities, including antenatal, natal and postnatal care, childhood diseases, maternal deaths, immunisation, communicable diseases, etc. Alongside these conventional indicators, some new ones had also been added, such as complicated deliveries referred to the FRUs, RTIs/STIs detected, adverse reactions to immunisation, interactions with panchayat health committee, anganwadis, mahila sanghs, and the community.
2. Technical assessment of sub-centre level services by a female health visitor: A woman health inspector was expected to conduct a technical assessment of sub-centre level services. This inspector would check, for instance, the accuracy of ANM records, the technical skills of the ANM, availability of equipment and supplies, and clients'

knowledge and perceptions of service delivery. This information would also feed into ANM training.

3. Rapid household surveys and facility surveys by independent agencies: The government intended to undertake household surveys in 50 percent of the districts each year. The sample for the survey consisted of about 1000 households in each district. Two sets of questionnaires were to be used. The first would examine service coverage and quality of public health services, and would be targeted at married women in the reproductive age group, and women who have given birth in the previous three years. In addition, a second set of questions would explore clients' perceptions about the government's services and questions on awareness about RTIs, STIs, and HIV/AIDS. This second questionnaire would include male respondents as well, regardless of marital status. These surveys were expected to provide not only managerially useful information, but also give the clients an opportunity to express their views about the reproductive health services.

Assessments of these monitoring indicators have, by and large, been seen as a step in the right direction (Murthy 1999; Pathak et al. 1999; Townsend and Khan 1996). It is expected that with the various levels of evaluative data that is collected, individual states can chart their own priorities and modify their services in an appropriate way.[52]

Design of the RCH Programme in Kerala

The RCH programme is administered in Kerala under the Department of Family Welfare, and the Directorate of Health Services (DHS) of the Kerala government. One of the primary activities under the RCH (at the time of my field visits in 1997–98) was the state-wide training of trainers and ANMs in the TFA

[52] At least two rounds of evaluation surveys have been carried out since the start of the RCH. Specially designed questionnaires called the Household Questionnaire, Woman's Questionnaire, Husband's Questionnaire, Village Questionnaire and Health and Nutritional Questionnaire were used in the surveys (Raju et al. c. 2003).

and RCH programmes. Given Kerala's achievement in the population field, it is not surprising that in the district categorisation schema used by the GoI, Kerala has 12 out of its 14 districts in the 'A' category, while the remaining two are 'B' category districts.[53] This categorisation reflects the high levels of health and low levels of mortality and morbidity that prevail in the state. My interviews in the selected districts indicated that the RCH was seen as an important introduction that would benefit the existing health system. As Kerala had already achieved most of the goals the GoI had set for the country to achieve by 2000, the officials in the state saw the RCH as facilitating the "extension" of these existing indicators. As a consequence, the aim of the RCH in Kerala is, purportedly, focused on improving the quality of health services. Some of the following comments from ministry officials underscore this view:[54]

> I#7: Of course, we have attained a lot of the parameters that are expected to be covered by 2000 A.D. But whatever things we have achieved, we have to sustain that achievement and not only that we have to go for a research set up so that more areas [are] to be addressed.
>
> I#4: I see it [the shift to the RCH] as providing an opportunity for the state to make a kind of transition which is dictated by the present state of development of health provision in the state.

The "present state of development of health provision" that the official refers to is indicative of the widespread view amongst providers that the RCH, with its emphases on child and maternal health, is more relevant for the less developed areas elsewhere in India than for Kerala, where population indicators were relatively better. The RCH was seen as an opportunity to focus on the improvement of the quality of the services provided, rather than strive to meet the basic requirements of a health system prescribed by the GoI.

In 1996–7, the implementation of the RCH programme in Kerala was being undertaken as two projects, one funded by the

---

[53] Both the health centre sites that I had chosen for grassroots interviews were located in 'A' category districts.

[54] In order to maintain anonymity, the interviewees have been assigned numbers. A profile of the participants in the interviews is provided in the Appendix.

UNFPA and the other by the World Bank. The World Bank project in Kerala had two components: (a) a State-wide Implementation Plan (SIP), and (b) two districts, Palaghat and Kozhikode were selected under the World Bank-RCH project in India. The funding proposal submitted by the Government of Kerala to the World Bank totalled Rs. 35 crores, with Rs. 18 crores meant for Palagat District, Rs. 12 crores for Kozhikode, and the rest for the SIP.[55] The SIP submitted to the World Bank was prepared along strict guidelines set out by the World Bank in conjunction with the GoI. I was told by respondents that the Government of Kerala had little flexibility over the items and agenda that had been set as priority areas for improvement. The SIP contains proposals for improving infrastructure, training, IEC activities and equipment purchases.

The UNFPA project in Kerala also has two sub-projects. The first, which was the implementation of a Reproductive Health project in the 'B' category district of Malappuram, was already underway at the time of my fieldwork in 1997. Under the Malappuram project, the UNFPA had sanctioned around Rs. 2.6 crores for the Kerala Government to carry out an approved programme in the selected district. In addition, the UNFPA also sanctioned a sum of Rs. 24 crores to the Kerala government for the implementation of Integrated Population and Development (IPD) projects during 1998–2001. The IPD projects covered Kasargod, Wynad, and Kannur districts (Government of Kerala 1997). The IPD projects consisted of two kinds of intervention, the first of which was a 'reproductive health intervention' (for which 75 percent of funds would be set aside). This would be supported by sectoral interventions in population education, information, communication, advocacy, gender equality, equity and women's empowerment and youth, for which 25 percent of funds would be used.

The approach to designing a reproductive health intervention is different in the WB and UNFPA projects. The WB project is a norm-based one (in that the project design follows strict pre-

[55] These statistics are based on information provided to me in 1997-98. The actual amounts subsequently sanctioned by the World Bank are not available.

determined guidelines and objectives), and the UNFPA project follows a need-based assessment (Interview I#2). In the need-based assessment approach, rather than work with pre-set norms, the UNFPA constituted a team of experts that included reproductive health, gender, and educational consultants. The UNFPA team conducted a situational analysis, namely, they assessed the needs of communities through visits, interviews and consultations in various parts of the state, and used these assessments as the basis for planning interventions in the state.

The UNFPA-RCH schemes formulated for Kerala strive to give representation to women's reproductive health needs. The World Bank project constituted a District Reproductive and Child Health Society (DRCHS) that included a representative each from a developmental NGO and a women's organisation (World Bank 1996b). The UNFPA project gives attention especially to issues of gender equality and equity. Their interventions include programmes for empowering women for increased participation in decision-making within the community and family (Government of Kerala 1997). These programmes (in the proposed format) aim to contain elements of personality building to increase women's self-assurance and self-esteem, provision of information on their rights, government social and economic schemes, and special schemes for adolescent girls (Government of Kerala 1997).

Respondents in my study generally felt that the new programmes had benefits for women as well as the health system. The removal of the regime of targets was seen as a great relief for the grassroots providers—as one middle-level policy-maker in the DFW commented:

> I#1: They seem to understand that some burden has been taken from their shoulder. That element of compulsion—they used to be punished earlier. If their achievements were low, if it was below 29 percent, they used to get punishment transfers. The best performing persons would receive State or District level awards ...the removal of that element is a big relief.

I also asked participants about the obstacles that would be faced in implementing the RCH in Kerala. Most of the responses reflected intra-organisational issues as crucial to the successful implementation of the programme. There were those who felt that personnel shortages were the most pressing need in Kerala and unless vacancies in the various organisational levels were filled, it was unlikely that the implementation would be absolutely successful (Interview I#2). Other responses suggested that the attitudes of ANMs to the new work ethos was likely to be met in the initial stages with resistance—in the immediate context, their workload had increased, and they had to adopt interactive relationships with individuals which they have not been used to in the past. There was also the fear that now elaborating on the disadvantages of contraceptive methods (when earlier they had deliberately not educated local people about these adverse reactions) could raise ill feelings in the community towards them.

The RCH in 2001

In an informal follow-up interview that I had with a senior level bureaucrat in April 2001, I learnt of the state's activities since 1997 under the RCH. The World Bank's RCH project, I was told, was particularly beneficial to the DFW's services. The WB funding for the project was a flexible one, allowing the state-level DFW to utilise grants for needs that the state identifies. Under this project, the state was able to improve obstetric services in the PHCs in the peripheral areas so as to reduce the load on larger hospitals. The DFW was also able to institute a hospital level monitoring strategy (thus far, any monitoring of health services had been done at the district level). Under the UNFPA funded projects, a gender specialist had been appointed at the Kerala Institute for Local Administration (KILA) to train local leaders in gender issues as part of the state-wide Panchayat or local government training programmes. The State Women's Commission had also been commissioned by the DFW to conduct around five studies on various gender issues such as violence, legal frameworks, etc. As part of the Life Cycle approach, a cervical screening programme for women over 45 years of age is being instituted. Under the European Commission's grants to the state, there has been a focus on health sector reforms particularly an evaluation of the tasks undertaken by the various functionaries of the state.

Conclusion

This chapter presented an overview of the family planning programme in India, in particular, the Reproductive and Child Health programme. Aspects related to services, budget, training, and institutional change were examined. The chapter also attempted to examine some of the salient features of the programme as it is being instituted in Kerala. The following chapters are 'analytical'—they present the results of the deconstruction of the dominant discourses found within the text of the RCH documents and interviews with policy-makers. The next chapter focuses on the various manifestations of a neo-liberal discourse in reproductive health policy.

References

Cassen, R. (1978) *India: Population, Economy and Society* Macmillan Press: London.

Centre for Reproductive Law and Policy (1995) *Women of the World: Formal Laws and Policies affecting their Reproductive Lives*, The International Programme: New York.

Centre for Reproductive Rights (2004) "India Chapter" in Women of the World: Laws and Policies Affecting their Reproductive Lives (South Asia) found at: http://www.reproductiverights.org/ww_asia_india.html (accessed 4.9.2004)

Freedman, L. and Isaacs, S. (1993) "Human Rights and Reproductive Choice" *Studies in Family Planning*, Vol. 24, No. 1, Jan/Feb., pp. 18–30.

Government of India (n.d.) *Reproductive and Child Health Programme*, Department of Family Welfare, Ministry of Health and Family Welfare, New Delhi.

Government of India (1994) *India: A Country Statement*, Report Presented at the ICPD, Cairo, Ministry of Health and Family Welfare, New Delhi.

Government of India (1996) *In-Service Training under Family Welfare Programme: Guidelines for Developing in-service training plan at district level*, Ministry of Health and Family Welfare, New Delhi

Government of India (1997a) *Decentralised Participatory Planning in Family Welfare Programme under Target Free Approach*, Ministry of Health and Family Welfare, New Delhi

Government of India (1997b) *Reproductive and Child Health Programme: Schemes for Implementation,* Ministry of Health and Family Welfare, New Delhi.

Government of India (1997c) *Training of Auxiliary Nurse Midwives (ANMs) for "Building Effective Community Partnerships for Implementing the Reproductive and Child Health Programme (RCH)",* Ministry of Health and Family Welfare, New Delhi, [goi.tm.1]

Government of India (1997e) *Manual on Target Free Approach in F.W.P,* Ministry of Health and Family Welfare, New Delhi.

Government of India (1997f), *Untitled Report of Financial Status under RCH marked official No, M. 15012/3/96—UIP (B& A),* Ministry of Health and Family Welfare, New Delhi.

Government of Kerala (1997) *State and District Project Formulation Exercise : Kerala, Directorate of Health Services,* Trivandrum, Kerala [gok.obp.9].

Indian Institute for Population Sciences (IIPS) (1995*), National family health survey : MCH and family planning : India, 1992–93,* IIPS: Bombay.

Jolly, K. G. (1986) *Family Planning in India, 1969–1984: A District Level Study,* Hindustan Publishing Corporation: India.

Karkal, M. (1998) "Family Planning and the Reproductive Rights of Women", in L. Lingam (ed.), *Understanding Women's Health Issues: A Reader,* Kali for Women: New Delhi.

Khan, M.E. and Townsend, J.W. (1999) "Target-Free Approach: Emerging Evidence", in S. Pachauri (ed.) *Implementing a Reproductive Health Agenda in India: The Beginning,* Population Council: New Delhi, pp. 41–75.

Kumar, R. (1997) *Reproductive Rights as Human Rights: Studies in the Asian Context,* monograph published by the Asian Forum for Human Rights and Development (FORUM-ASIA): Bangkok, Thailand.

Mavalankar, D. (c. 2000) "Paradigm Shift in India's Family Welfare Programme: A Review of Target-Free Approach in Family Planning". *International Council on Management of Population Programmes.* Found at: http://www.icomp.org.my/Country/inno75.html (accessed 20.06. 2005)

Measham, A.R. and Heaver, R. A. (1996) *India's Family Welfare Program: Moving to a Reproductive and Child Health Approach,* World Bank, The International Bank for Reconstruction and Development: Washington, D.C.

Merrick, T.M. (1996) "Family Welfare Policy Issues" in A. R. Measham and R. A. Heaver (eds) *Supplement to India's Family Welfare*

Program: Moving to a Reproductive and Child Health Approach, The World Bank: Washington, pp.13–23.

Murthy, N. (1999) "Decentralised Participative Planning and Monitoring" in S. Pachauri (ed.) *Implementing a Reproductive Health Agenda in India: The Beginning*, Population Council: New Delhi, pp.123–145.

Pathak, K.B., Ram, F. and Verma, R. K. (1999) "Monitoring and Evaluating New Systems" in S. Pachauri (ed.) *Implementing a Reproductive Health Agenda in India: The Beginning,* Population Council: New Delhi, pp. 147–160.

Raju, K.N.M. et al. (c. 2003) "Reproductive and Child Health Project: Rapid Household Surveys in Karnataka, Kerala and Goa". Found at http://www.isec.ac.in/project10-2005.pdf (accessed 20.06.2005)

Ravindran, T.K.S. (1993) "Women and the politics of population and development in India" *Reproductive Health Matters*, Number 1, May, pp. 26–43.

Ravishankar, V.J. (1996) "Financing Requirements of India's Reproductive and Child Health Program", in A. R. Measham and R. A. Heaver (eds) *Supplement to India's Family Welfare Program: Moving to a Reproductive and Child Health Approach*, The World Bank: Washington D.C., pp. 94–107.

Reddy, P. H. (1998) "Population Programme in Ninth Plan", *Economic and Political Weekly*, January 31, pp. 239–244.

Verzosa, C. C. and Kakkar, P. (1996) "Information, Education, and Communication Efforts and Social Marketing" in A. R. Measham and R. A. Heaver (eds) *Supplement to India's Family Welfare Program: Moving to a Reproductive and Child Health Approach*, The World Bank: Washington, pp. 60–71.

Visaria, L. and Visaria, P. (1999) "Field-Level Reflections of Policy Change", in S. Pachauri (ed.) *Implementing a Reproductive Health Agenda in India: The Beginning,* Population Council: New Delhi, pp. 77–121.

World Bank (1996a) *Improving Women's Health in India*, World Bank: Washington.

World Bank (1996b) *India: RCH project—Criteria for Appraisal of District/ City Proposal and Guidelines to prepare State Implementation Plans under WB supported RCH Project.* World Bank, South Asia Region.

World Bank (1997) *Project Appraisal Document: India, Reproductive and Child Health Project, Population and Human Resources Operations Division, Country Department II,* World Bank, South Asia Region.

5

Tracing Neo-liberal Rhetoric in the Reproductive and Child Health Programme

Constructing State and Citizen within Market Paradigms

There is nothing in the RCH documents to overtly suggest that the paradigmatic shift to a reproductive health framework was a concomitant move to embrace the ideology of neo-liberalism. The services and institutional arrangements outlined in the previous chapter reflect a standard implementation and service delivery plan for a large-scale programme devoid, one may argue, of an ideological drive apart from the logic of development policy management. Yet, it is in the subtleties of context and practice, revealed in discourse, that the neo-liberal ideology of the RCH emerges. Norman Fairclough points to this subtlety in his notion of 'commodification' of language, i.e., "the process whereby social domains and institutions, whose concern is not producing commodities in the narrower economic sense of goods for sale, come nevertheless to be organised and conceptualised in terms of commodity production, distribution and consumption" (Fairclough 1992: 207). As he notes, in contemporary society, it is not uncommon for areas like arts, education and theatre to be referred to as 'industries', with tasks of producing, marketing and selling cultural commodities. The manifestations of the neo-liberal discourse embrace various forms including constructions of consumerism, the language of management and marketing, economic rationales, assumptions of social worth, and so on. Thus, it is with some interest in the wider ideological context that I regard the statement of the Union Minister for Health and Family Welfare, Mr Thakur, in 2000 that the National Population Policy 2000 envisaged a "paradigm shift in programme management and implementation." For undertaking such a gigantic task, the Minister *sought the participation of the corporate sector* (*The Hindustan Times*, Wednesday July 12, 2000)—an indication that family planning was slipping into private and market influenced arenas.

This chapter begins the task of deconstructing[56] the ideological content of the RCH policy documents and interviews (see footnote for an explanation of document referencing)[57] to explore traces of neo-liberal discourses in the RCH policy. I use empirical evidence to demonstrate that the so-called 'paradigmatic' shift of the Indian Family Welfare Policy to a Reproductive and Child Health programme is bounded by the language of commerce and the discourse of neo-liberalism. As the language of the market

---

[56] The methodology used for the "deconstruction" of ideology was discourse analysis, with a focus on both manifest and latent themes in the text (Berg 1998). I looked for: (a) rhetorical terms and keywords that were repeatedly used in the documents and interviews, (b) thematic clusters, and (c) the social context in which themes and terms were used. Interviews and documents were coded manually and descriptive codes were used.

[57] A brief note on the method used to reference the RCH documents for the analyses in the present and the following chapters. An indexing scheme involving three sets of characters was used. The first two sets of characters were letters while the last was a numerical marker. The logic was as follows. The collected documents were first sorted according to the place of origin – 'goi' meant that the document originated from the Government of India and 'gok' meant that the document originated from the Government of Kerala. The second set of characters denoted the kind of communication that the document was – 'obp' indicated an 'official background paper', 'oc' was an 'official communication', 'tm' referred to 'training materials', and 'om' was an 'official meeting'. The last set of characters was a number and was randomly attached to a document of a particular kind that I happened to sort. Thus, 'goi.oc.3' referred to the third GoI document that was an official communication. A list of the documents used and their codes are given in the Appendix.

dominates policy, the state critically re-evaluates the individual user's role in relation to public health services and, eventually, itself. The neo-liberal discourse is revealed in the way the state seeks to set up the health system as a market operation in which it (the state) is a provider. Traces of the market are reflected primarily along two discursive locations in the policy, namely, (a) in discussions of what the role of the state is as provider of family welfare services, and (b) in the construction of users of the programme. A perusal of the RCH's stated aims sets the stage for this analysis. Significantly, what emerges is that a complex form of contractual relationship is being instituted between individual and state contrary to what was an earlier patrimonial one (Yeatman 1997). This chapter argues that reinventing the state-individual relationship evokes contradictory dichotomies: individualised vs. social health care, democratisation vs. commodification of citizenship, and autonomous vs. dependent persons. What is important is that both dimensions reflect strategies of the state to extend particular notions of obligations and rights of citizens, or in other words, a particular brand of governance that is consonant with market development.

The Intent of the Programme

The RCH documents indicate that the government's reproductive health policy is informed in its programme objectives and strategies by two kinds of rationales: one drawn from a systematic assessment of the earlier programme shortcomings and another from a concern with the satisfaction of the programme's users. As noted in Chapter 4, the RCH programme aims to provide a range of both relevant and quality services to the users of the state's programme; to develop community-level structures for participation in the planning and implementation of programmes; and, finally, to improve the efficiency of the programme delivery system. These objectives (as stated in the RCH documents) were derived from the observation that there were specific lacunae in the existing programme that needed to be addressed. First, there is a concern that people "have not availed family welfare services to the desired extent" (goi.nd), a testimony to the poor quality of services that have been proffered by the government. Second, there is also concern that "deficiencies in the implementation of the maternal and child health services have been responsible for a high incidence of maternal mortality and child/infant mortality and low health status of women and children" (goi.oc.5:1–2). This concern, statistically supported, has ramifications for the number of children that are likely to be desired by families, and ultimately, birth rates for the country as a whole. A third lacuna cited in the policy documents reflects deficiencies in the family welfare delivery system. Documents note that over the years several programmes co-existed with similar objectives but were being run simultaneously under different identities, either by the same government body or various agencies, tending to diffuse the efforts of the state and its agencies in the specific area of family welfare (e.g., goi.oc.3; goi.oc.5). As the document goi.oc.5:1 notes, "[w]hile ... these programmes did have a beneficial impact ... the separate identity for each programme was causing problems in its effective management and ... was also reducing somewhat the outcomes." What the RCH recognises as a pertinent need is the integration of these several programmes for efficient management and optimum outcomes. Most of the programmes introduced under the CSSM, for this reason, had resulted in "indifferent success" (goi.tm.2:2). Further, the documents note that an "integrated RCH would help in reducing the cost of inputs to some extent because overlapping of expenditure would no longer be necessary and integrated implementation would optimise outcomes at the field level" (goi.oc.3:2). Specific weaknesses in the existing programme are seen especially in the area of neonatal care, reproductive tract infections/sexually transmitted diseases, obstetric care, MTP, delivery of services to urban slums and tribal areas and inadequate promotion of traditional systems of medicine.

A fourth shortcoming identified in the policy documents is the "inadequacy of the investment made for Family Welfare" (goi.oc.5:2). This has severe implications when considering that, "in almost all respects, the health care system needs up-gradation and it needs to reach out to many more people" (goi.oc.5: 2). The Approach Paper to the Ninth Plan, the RCH documents note, highlight that there is a severe inadequacy of investment in the family welfare sector in comparison to the 7th and 8th Plans (goi.oc.3: 4) and is likely to hinder the government's objective of "reducing the unmet need, increasing service coverage and ensuring quality of care" in its programmes (goi.tm.2:1).

These 'rationale' that preface the RCH is juxtaposed, it would seem, between two imperatives of the state. On the one hand, the state acknowledges that *user-satisfaction* and needs are central, and that the state must be responsive to those needs. On the other, the state recognises *system-specific weaknesses* that need to be addressed through institutional reform. The concern with strengthening the institutional base of family welfare services is not dissimilar to the language of health sector reforms that are being implemented around the world. Against a backdrop of structural adjustment or restructuring since the 1980s, the health sector in countries of the North and South has been subject to debates about financing, resource allocation and efficient management. What is increasingly recognised is that these reforms are not merely organisational or structural but involve redefining relationships between sets of institutional actors in the arena of health delivery such as, the state, service providers, other health bodies and users. Standing (1999, 2000), for example, notes that there are two distinctly independent agendas in Health Sector Reforms: the first, the regulation of health expenditure, is an outcome of economic expediency, whereas a second, specific issue of institutional reform, reflects deeper concerns with the role of the state and public governance.

The intent evident in the RCH documents to reform the health and family welfare system is motivated by the objectives resonant of market conditions: quality improvement, efficiency outputs and optimum results. However, the improvement of the family welfare delivery system is also substantially dependent on reworking the relationship between the state and individual in the provision of public goods, i.e., family welfare services. The documents, for instance, point out the various kinds of institutional arrangements that will ensure success of the RCH, such as *gaining support* for the policy through interventions by local leaders, *increasing accountability* of health workers to citizens, and increasing inter-sectoral collaboration with other government departments that are involved in *improving literacy* and economic conditions of the population (see goi.oc.5: 3, for example).[58] The face of the health sector reforms demands considerable re-writing of the conventional relationships of the public health service with its users, especially with respect to devolution of rights and increasing accountability to citizens.

As the RCH adopts the languages central to reform and restructuring, there is a clear shifting of discursive locations for the individual users of family welfare services—who they are, their role, their rights (including the limits of their rights), and their obligations. It is these shifts that I explore in detail in this chapter. In the following section, I examine the manner in which users of the family welfare programmes in the policy are referred to. Arguing that these references reflect a particular positioning of the user, I unpack the implications and expectations of this positioning.

The RCH and Construction of Individuals

The RCH policy documents tend to refer to users of family welfare services as 'individuals', 'beneficiaries', 'citizens', and 'consumers.' But most dominantly, the documents refer to users as 'clients.' The policy documents, for instance, emphasise that the RCH programme is "need based, *client-centred*, demand driven, high quality and integrated" (goi.oc.5:3) and that the family welfare system will take a "*client-centred* approach to service provision" (goi.n.d.). A World Bank report evaluating the RCH in India pointed out that India's Family Welfare Programme aims to carry out the commitment given at Cairo "to implement a *client-centred* approach that responds more effectively to the reproductive health and family planning needs of women and men in India" (Measham and Heaver 1996:1). Further, the Target Free Approach emphasises:

- Bottom-up planning from sub-centre to national level with a focus on *client choice* and high quality service

[58] Unless otherwise stated, all emphases of document and interview texts are my own addition.

- A *participatory two-way interaction between workers and clients* to assess the "felt needs" of clients
- *Helping clients* meet their needs on the basis of existing services, and
- Improving the quality of services to meet *client needs* both on a priority and long term basis (goi.tm.3:2)

The use of the term "client" to refer to users is an innovation within development/welfare policies in India where targets of programmes have been conventionally referred to in the Government system as "recipients" or "beneficiaries," underscoring an unequal if altruistic relationship between the state and the individual (Jayal 1994). In contrast, the use of a client-provider relationship is typical of the language of reform, especially in restructuring public services (McGuire 1997), where altruism has given way to the rhetoric of contractualism.

The incorporation of the term "client" in the Indian family welfare service is not merely a cosmetic shift in the semantics of officialese. It is apparent from the RCH policy that the entire approach to programme management in the family welfare services is built on assumptions of client behaviour, client needs, and services that will satisfy clients. The user is recognised as the key person in the planning process (evident in a senior official's comment that "... they [users] are also planners for the providers"). In addition, one policy document also notes that, "... the shift in the philosophy of the programme calls for community participation for planning, implementing and monitoring" so as to make it a "*people's programme*" (goi.tm.1:1). On paper, there are clear indications that the state is keen to develop participatory mechanisms that customise public service to the needs that clients identify.

In the context of the RCH programme in India, the use of the terms 'consumer' and 'client' appears to be a deliberate *step-up* for the users of the family welfare services. The shift in construction of users from mere 'beneficiaries' to 'clients' is one that is resonant with the notion of rights in terms of decision-making and participation in the programme design. For instance, I asked a senior medical officer at the Department of Family Welfare about the predilection for the use of the term 'client' instead of 'beneficiary'. His response was that:

> I# 4: Beneficiary means charity, we are not charity. This is not charity ... they are not beneficiaries. They are getting the results of what they are paying for. And they have a right to [it]... they have a right to decide what kind of services they get.

I asked similar questions to middle-level bureaucrats within the DFW and DHS to understand their interpretation of the construction of the notion of the "client" in the family welfare services in Kerala. Their responses (reproduced below) suggest that the kind of relationship that was expected between the State and the user in the new set-up was distinctly different from the one that had prevailed prior to the institution of the RCH. For instance, some middle-level bureaucrats told me:

> I#2: Now it is emphasised that it should be quality services, and it should be client-centred approach. We should know the needs of the clients ... *the decision should be from the clients' side*. It shouldn't be that we make the decisions for them. All they need is help to make the decisions—that is the attitude.
>
> I # 7: *[The] decision is taken by the clients themselves.* It is a client-centred one. You just help them, you just make them aware these are the services we are giving them. They decide which one is suitable. That kind of change has come.
>
> I#6: Quality service should be given to the acceptors of the family welfare programme. And the Government of India has already discussed and [has made it] in the Plan discussion that *the client should be given the quality service* to the maximum possible level at their door step or to the institution where they prefer to conduct that ...

The policy-makers construct the position of the "client" as that of an individual who has agency within the production and implementation of policy. The client was the centre of the policy, and the satisfaction of the client was projected as the key objective of the RCH. Even when policy-makers referred to users as "beneficiaries", it was to denote an unusual sense of empowerment among the users of the services. There was a distinct positioning of users as the ones who direct the course of action in the programme.

> I#1: Now [after the RCH] *the decision-maker is the beneficiary* himself or herself. It is the recipient. Whoever is coming to receive it [contraceptive methods] is the decision-maker. It is not ours. We [just] tell them all the methods....

> I#12: So it is aimed towards people, towards *the beneficiary* ... how well a service [can] be given to them.

Interestingly, it wasn't only the policy-makers in the government sector who used the term 'client'. The representative of a non-governmental women's health group, whom I interviewed used similar language to refer to users. For instance:

> I#5: ... we also wanted, through dialogues and discussion... to understand ... how things have changed for both *the providers and the clients.*

In one instance, an official referred to the users as "consumers". I clarified the usage of consumers and its relationship to the oft-used term 'clients:'

> I#4: We are using this opportunity to move away from a provider-oriented provision of services towards something *where the consumer* has at least a slightly more important role than what he has right now.
>
> *Q: Is that how you see your clients—as consumers?*
>
> You know, consumer... means anyone in any economic transaction—you are the person who provides and you are the person who consumes. And now these persons are consumers.

The client, for all practical purposes, has been made the pivotal figure on which the policy's strategic interventions have been rationalised. In this set-up, the state is positioned as a provider who is not an "outsider" who imposes a set of rulings about how people should organise their reproductive lives but as an agency that works with the users to satisfy their well-being. The state's role is to guide and help, but never to make decisions for the clients. The policy asserts that the "thrust of the programme *will be to satisfy* the communities served by the health facilities" (goi.tm.2: 1). As the RCH document states,

> ... [i]n the final analysis, *what people want is the same as [what] the health administrators*, health providers and reproductive health researchers want, 'a happy and healthy life for men and women without fear of disease and unwanted pregnancy'" (goi.obp.1: 37).

From planning *with* individual clients, the RCH reveals, the state also works *with* communities for their well-being. The above excerpts from the documents suggest that a particular focus of the newly-instituted reproductive health programme is to involve communities in developing people-friendly and relevant policy. Interview transcripts with officials also reveal a strong sense of partnership between the state and citizens, and increased grassroots participation and community involvement in 'need-identification' and satisfaction.

> I# 8: [The community's] representatives would have discussed their needs with them. *So we should try and do according to that...* Now there is much importance for community involvement...
>
> (*I ask the interviewee to define community involvement*)
>
> [Earlier] ... according to the government, suppose you have to do an ORT (Oral Rehydration Therapy) programme ... so the ORT programme will be done. We did not enquire into their needs. It is not like that now. When we say community involvement — community leaders, voluntary organisations, local bodies, etc. will draw up a plan of action.

> I# 11: Now there is more community participation. I think there will be more benefits because of it.

> I#3: ... because the RCH is being implemented under the target-free approach, one hopes that there will be much more community involvement. I mean the plans are made from the sub-centre, then it goes up to the district level. What is to be achieved is set at the state level and the district level. So that way it is quite different. *We're supposed to [involve] the NGOs and people in the community and make the plans at the sub-centre.*

All these transcripts demonstrate a shift in language (and concomitantly, one would hope, in attitude and practice as well) from 'what the state wants' to focusing on what the 'community needs'. This shift, seen amongst health workers at the grassroots in Kerala, appears to correspond to what the RCH documents have indicated to be the institutional paradigm shift—from a top-down to a bottom-up approach. In making this shift, the policy-makers unwittingly assigned specific attributes and roles to the main actors: the state and the users. Note the words that accompany the use of the term client, on the one hand—"decision-maker", "right", "payers"—and those which describe the state's role, on the other—"help", "we do according to their needs", "decisions are not ours", "find out their needs."

At first reading, the erasure of the arcane State-Individual relationship of altruism/charity is striking. In its place, a client-provider relationship denotes a non-hierarchical professionalism. It also lays down the ground rules for the kind of claims that the individual can make on the state. The excerpts indicate that the user as consumer/client has the right to expect goods and services from the state. The user has the freedom to determine the shape and form of his or her needs. The user also has the right to demand the kind of services s/he expects. And finally, s/he has the right to expect that the goods/services s/he receives will address her/his specific needs. The RCH depicts the true spirit of participatory development; they are co-producers of policy/programmes with the state. Recall the words of respondent I#4: "… they [the clients] are also *planners* for the providers."

Two significant analytical insights can be drawn from the reference to and positioning of users as clients/consumers. First, a predominant trend is the tendency to draw on market/neo-classical economic frames of references to construct users. The 'client' is akin to the idealised consumer of the market place, an individual who by virtue of her/his paying capabilities has the right to set the rules for the kind of goods s/he needs. All the attendant terms associated with the use of the term 'client,' such as quality services, rights, and needs, ground the user as an actor/agent in a market-operated context. Further, by the continuous invoking of the imagery of consumer/client, the state situates the citizen within a broader framework of contractual relationships that are typically associated with neo-liberalism (Hindess 1997). From the comments of the official I#4, "… [t]hey have a right as people who paid for it. They have a right to decide what kind of services they should get," it would seem that the fundamental criteria for entering into this contractual relationship with the state is the ability to participate in monetary transactions with the state.

A second insight reflects the tendency of RCH documents to move between the terms 'clients' and 'citizens,' collapsing the rights of the client with that of the citizen—"[i]t is the legitimate *right of the citizens* to be able to experience sound Reproductive and Child Health..." (goi.oc.5:3). The notion of "*rights*" in this context marks a fluid terrain that portrays users as consumers/clients and citizens; as citizens, they have the right to reproductive health, and as consumer/clients within a market paradigm, they have the right to the services they demand. The public space of citizen's rights, therefore, becomes merged with the market place of consumer tastes.

The complexity of client rights under the RCH will be unpacked in following sections, but first I review some literature that examines client/citizen-State relationships under market paradigms.

Market Rhetoric and Citizens As 'Clients': An Overview

The use of a market analogy to redefine the state's social services in the wake of economic restructuring in both the North and the South, especially in health and education, has been an increasingly common strategy since the early 1980s (McGuire 1997; Whitty 1998). The strategy imposes market or economic criteria on resource allocation decisions and public accessibility conditions, and tends to focus on efficiency and effectiveness of outcomes of services provided by the state (Standing 1999). The language and strategies of corporate management have filtered liberally into public service administration. Cost recovery, increased linkages with the private sector, and the institution of insurance schemes, for instance, are among the strategies that have become familiar in economies that have restructured their health services.

Locating the user has been an especially important part of this process. The positioning of users of public services as 'clients' has had ambivalent connotations in the context of western societies. Since the 1990s, changing the culture of public access to a client-oriented one has been widespread (McGuire 1997). As consumers of the state's restructured user-payee services, 'clients' are revered as investors of a growing enterprise. Hence, the state has often enough propagated the 'empowerment' of clients by offering them 'choices' and the benefits of competition.

By the same token, 'clients' also refer to people who are dependent on the government for social welfare provisions. Fraser (1989: 152) examined the US social welfare system and found that social welfare claimants get positioned either as "purchasing consumers" or "dependent clients." Fraser points out that although both these subject positions are disempowering, the latter, i.e., dependent clients, is considered to be an inferior position. In the case of purchasing consumers—who incidentally are predominantly male—they are assessed for benefits on the basis of their monetary contributions as workers and, hence, their claims upon the state are rights bearing or they are seen as 'possessive individuals,' people who possess the resources to make claims on the state. Dependent clients who are assessed in terms of their ascriptive status (as mothers or spouse) are—in Fraser's words—"negatives of possessive individuals" (1989: 152). Both these subject positions tend not to empower recipients, largely because these constructions do not construct them as active co-participants involved in shaping their life conditions. Instead, bureaucracy imposes administrative definitions, hindering opportunity for individuals to define their own conditions, and thereby, needs. In contrast to the construction of the rights bearing 'client/consumer' of the market-state, there is a repressive aspect to the relationship between clients and bureaucracy. The derogatory status of welfare 'clients' has worsened under the discourse of the market and Reagonomics, and the deterioration of the welfare state. Individuals unable to be workers or producers in the economy are considered as unfit citizens (Hindess 1997).

Despite the allure of 'improved' quality of services, researchers critique the imposition of market standards on public goods because it re-orients state-citizen relationships in ways that are problematic for the exercise of rights of individuals as citizens. McGuire (1997), for instance, argues that in projecting citizens as clients, the state rescinds its obligation to citizens to pursue goals of social justice. McGuire notes that the function of public services is not to produce efficient outcomes but to enhance social justice and facilitate collective consumption, namely, that efficiency is subsumed to equity (McGuire 1997). By detracting an objective of equity from public services, the gap between the 'haves' and 'have-nots' in society can only be aggravated. Imposing the criterion of purchasing power for public services restricts accessibility to the state's public goods, just as the dictum of economic independence from the state, positions welfare recipients within a forced and unequal bargaining relationship as citizens within the state (Hindess 1997). Often, beneath purportedly gender-neutral norms, the marketised health systems have disproportionate impacts on women and other disadvantaged groups (Whitty 1998). Standing (1999) points out that in developing country contexts, where health sector reforms have aimed at efficiency, there have been specific gendered impacts. For example, she notes that when cost recovery through institution of user charges were effected in Nigeria, maternal deaths in the Zaria region rose by 56 percent along with a decline of 46 percent in the number of deliveries in the main hospitals. Similarly, the reduction of preventive services (as opposed to paid curative services) is likely to have more implications for women. Examining the 'rights' to efficient services of the 'client' should be within a framework that considers these larger determining factors (Standing 1999).

Similarly, McGuire (1997) also questions the politics of positioning users of public services as 'clients.' She argues that the relationship between consumer, customer (who purchases services), client (who co-produces) and provider (who delivers) is more complex in a public service than in the private sector. In the latter, the customer pays for the services that the firm produces. In public services, there are multiple stakeholders and each of them has multiple identities simultaneously. For example, as citizens, individuals want equitable access to public services. As taxpayers, they have the right to expect efficient outcomes for the investment they make into services (as tax). As the 'consumer/client', they would expect reliability and quality as outcomes of services. Given these multiple interests of citizen/individuals, it is not easy to separate one set of needs or privilege one identity of the citizen/individual. In projecting the citizen as primarily a consumer, the state narrows the concept of citizen and citizen-needs to a limited set of issues.

This exercise of evaluating how various institutional actors use the term 'client' indicates at the very least that users of public services can have multiple subject positions with very different implications. The initial excerpts that I examined above seemed to give a broad range of decision-making abilities to the client in the RCH programme. Nonetheless, they are bound within the terms of a consumer/client/citizen contract. What exactly are the terms of the 'contract' that the clients of the reproductive health programme in India are bound by? In an attempt to understand the deeper layers of the client-state relationship, I unpack the notion of 'client' as it has been used in the RCH documents and as interpreted by policy-makers within the family welfare system in Kerala.

Unpacking the 'Client' in the RCH

The RCH policy's 'client' holds a unique discursive space in the ideology of the state and eventually, in the material form of policy. In this section, I demonstrate the ways in which policy documents and interviews construct the 'client's' agency, and facilitate (or limit) the opportunity for the citizen/user to behave as a purchasing consumer. I examine the characterisation of the client with respect to four attributes: (a) freedom to represent individual needs, (b) endowment of rational behaviour, (c) potential to have access to health, and, finally, (d) ability to identify needs.

Freedom: individual needs versus national needs

The policy documents are clear that the RCH has been instituted to fulfil specific national goals set down as priorities by the Government of India. The policy reiterates that the government's fundamental focus on fertility reduction remains a central concern, and continues to be a major consideration in the design and promotion of family welfare programmes. One document points out that "the main objective of the Family Welfare Programme for the country has been to stabilise population at a level consistent with the needs of national development" (goi.oc.5:1). Similarly, another Government of India document categorically underscores that the "objective of the Family Planning Programme is to *reduce the birth rate*" (goi.tfa.1). The RCH programme's primary objective is informed by this national need:

> the RCH Programme intends to integrate fertility regulation, Maternal and Child Health with reproductive health services such as screening, diagnosis and treatment of Reproductive Tract Infections (RTIs) and Sexually Transmitted Infections (STIs), *with the aim to reduce infant and maternal mortality and morbidity and unwanted fertility, thereby, eventually contributing to stabilisation of population growth* and improv[ing] the health status of women and children" (goi.oc.1:1).

A similar objective is also evident elsewhere: "...[t]he Approach Paper to the Ninth Plan brought out by the Planning Commission has identified reduction in infant mortality, [and] maternal mortality *for bringing about reduction in the desired level of fertility as one of the most important objectives during the Ninth Plan.* It has identified the RCH at the Primary Health Care (PHC) level as part of the strategy for achieving health goals in the Ninth plan" (goi.oc.3: 4). So also, another core policy document of the RCH notes that the fundamental obligation of the Indian Government is to the state's national goals:

> ... the RCH Programme will seek to provide relevant services for assuring Reproductive and Child Health to all citizens. However, RCH is even more relevant for obtaining the objective of stable population for the country. The overall objective since the beginning has been that the population of the country should be stabilised at a level consistent with the requirement of national development (goi.oc.5: 3).

The state's commitment to re-organising the state-individual relationship and centring the 'client' is mitigated, as seen above, by the overriding concern with population control and national development. Against the above emphasis of the state, the government's statement that "the overall strategy of the Government of India (Department of Family Welfare) is to *simultaneously* strive for obtaining Reproductive and Child Health arrangements for the whole of the country *and* to promote and make available contraceptive/terminal methods for desirous couples" (goi.oc.5: 3) must be deconstructed using the lens of 'rights' within a reproductive health paradigm—the right to make informed reproductive decisions. The simultaneous emphasis on the dual focus of enhancing individual freedoms and reaching state goals can result in an inherent contradiction in the state's commitments. Its commitment to individual interests, for instance, can potentially be at odds with its national needs, while enforcement, of any kind, of national goals is in direct opposition to individual freedoms which form the foundation for individuals to exercise their legitimate rights as citizens. The quotes above from goi.oc.5, in particular, clearly indicate the potential for conflict in the policy; the 'legitimate right' of the citizen only partially justifies the functional significance of the RCH. In the final analysis, the RCH gains validity because it is 'even more relevant' for obtaining the objectives of fertility control and, eventually, national development and economic growth. There is a subtle tension in the policy, and an undeniable privileging of national needs over individual needs.

My interviews mirrored this prioritisation of national over individual needs. Some of the comments made by senior and middle-level officials in Kerala are reproduced below:

> I #6: *Two-family* norm is a Government of India policy. Limit the family size. So whatever it is, whatever policy we have addressing [to the] family identities, it is always addressing the limitation of the family. That has not been changed. But we are changing the service-provider point of view and the client service—that is, [providing] quality service.
> I#1: Fertility control certainly is an objective but then we differ because we assess the need, you explain whatever fertility control methods are available to the beneficiary, to the eligible couples. You present them the whole different methods, maybe temporary or permanent. You present all this to them and you allow them to choose the method they want to adopt.

It is interesting that upon clarification, the initial enthusiasm for the idea that "clients are decision-makers" appears muted. The officials above, confronted with the need to situate individual rights in the context of the state's agenda of fertility control, interpret "freedom" within the broader commitment of conformity to the state's priorities. The individual/citizen's freedom to exercise her/his rights was posed as the state's ability to try to be sensitive to consumer needs. In this case, it becomes an issue of service delivery—client "rights" become an issue of improvement in the way public service is produced, distributed and accepted.

The question that becomes pertinent at this point is whether as the citizen evolves into a consumer, the right to well-being is enhanced or limited by the imperatives of the market? The comments by the policy-makers in the excerpts above would suggest that the client does not control the terms of the market discourse, but can operate with some freedom within its parameters. In the language of contractualism, the relationship between the state and individual established discursively is less underwritten by the presumption of the autonomy of individuals, than it is by the assumption that populations need to abide by the terms of the market contract. In the context of reproductive health, the terms of the contract are explicitly in favour of population control and economic stabilisation rather than the development of individual autonomy.

The following excerpt from my interview with a senior-level officer underscores the state's limited interpretation of individual freedom. As the official points out, where fertility levels are not a huge worry, there is greater scope for individuals to exercise their 'freedoms'. Where it is a concern, the state holds greater control over the kind of decisions (and forecloses the opportunity for the exercise of individual rights) that people make. Note the following excerpt:

> I#4: As far as Kerala is concerned, what we believe is that it [*fertility decision-making*] is an option that can safely be left with women ... the earlier style of advocacy and persuasion is prescribed only for two districts—that's Malappuram and Kasargode. In the rest of the place, all that we will do in the new RCH is to have the information available to them. Let them make the choices. But in *Malappuram and in Kasargode* <u>*where we believe*</u> *that fertility rates are unnaturally high, the advocacy would still go on.*

The official's response shows the conditional "freedom" permitted to the client. The official points out that in Kerala (the reference is to the generally low levels of fertility prevalent in the state), birth control was an option "that could safely be left with women." But, in the same breath, the official adds a caveat: where fertility rates were considered high in Kerala (Malappuram and Kasargode), "advocacy" or persuasive tactics in promoting fertility control were still likely to continue. Thus, to the policy-makers, the notion of individual freedom prevails only as long as it does not counteract the government's programme of population control. While advocacy or persuasion does not denote the excessive kinds of coercive tactics that the Government has used in the past, there is a strong suggestion that the state can still regulate the opportunities for people's reproductive freedoms. Whilst these regulative strategies go directly against the idealised norms of freedom in the market, they are implicitly written in the sub-text of regulative behaviour that underlies the manifest ideology of neo-liberalist 'freedoms.'

Perhaps the instances where state priority and individual choices are most vividly in conflict, are in the series of population control policies introduced since the mid-1990s. Almost at the same time that the RCH was introduced in 1996/97, the propaganda slogan 'One is Fun' was popularised by the Ministry of Family Welfare as an encouragement for families to have only one child. By 1997, several state governments (Haryana, Andhra Pradesh, Madhya Pradesh, Uttar Pradesh and Maharashtra) had begun to release their own state-level population policies either in final or draft form. These policies advocated the two-family norm emphatically and proposed a range of incentives and disincentives (including, being barred from public office in panchayats) for people who had over three children. Despite a public interest litigation petition, the Supreme Court in 2003 upheld the two-family norm of the Haryana Government.

Amongst my respondents, at least, there seemed to be no obvious recognition that there were two potentially incompatible discourses at play here. Even for those who claimed expertise in gender issues—one of my interviewees was a gender researcher for the Government of India at New Delhi and had contributed to the development of the RCH—the contradiction between individual interests and state goals was not satisfactorily resolved. In response to my questions, the consultant suggested that the idea of population control was not inimical to individual rights—that these are not discourses in conflict or in opposition to each other, but rather, ideas that co-existed in a hierarchy. Individual rights were always (from the start of the ICPD) subsumed within the umbrella of population control. Her comments are below:

> I#3: No, I don't think that even the ICPD talks about pushing *it* [population control] down under the carpet. It talked about approaching *it* [population control] in a broader context rather than with a narrow focus. The ICPD definitely talks about improving the quality of life of men and women and helping them to make their own decisions.

The response of the researcher reinforces the argument made by Amalric and Banuri (1994: 702) that the "apparent contradiction between the two main principles of the draft [ICPD] document—to stabilise world population and to respect people's rights—is never acknowledged." As long as that contradiction is not addressed (or is left ambiguous), national governments and local providers can interpret it in a way that suits their purposes. In the Indian context, individual rights are subsumed within the discourse of population control.

In general, then, the state never sees the client as having sweeping powers to determine the shape of its services. The client's participation as a planner is limited as is her/his ability to manipulate the circumstances of her/his well-being. This is most evident in contexts of *conflict*; interviews reveal that policy-makers are clear, should there be a divergence of individual and state interests, that the state's inherent priorities will prevail. For instance, in my interview with a senior-level official at the DFW, he made it clear that the provider's needs "may not coincide with the viewpoint of the consumer per se ..." (see below). As a provider, the policy-maker, then, will have a "real dilemma"—of not knowing whether to provide what the people want or to provide what is important from the national point of view. The full excerpt from which I have drawn these comments is given below:

> I# 4: The real problem [there] is—unlike the normal consumer—where *he has freedom in the market* [59] – here there is a question of 'merit good' coming in. Now from the national point of view or from past experiences of providing health services, the service planners have emphasis on certain items, which may not coincide with the

[59] Though not central to the analysis in this chapter, it is worth pointing out that the "normal consumer" is a "he."

> view-point of the consumer per se. Options which are found to be more cost effective may not be accepted by the consumer because he might want a costlier option ... Now as a planner who claims to stand at a distance, you believe that need and demand do not coincide. *Now where do you strike a balance? Do you have the right to decide that this is your need—you shall get this. Or do you want to respond to the demand and provide what is there?*

The excerpt clearly points out that the client of the family welfare service in India is not a "normal" consumer who has "freedom" in the market—the client's freedoms are obviously more limited. Therefore, in the event that "needs" and "demand" do not coincide, the implicit preference would be to privilege the state's priority. That is why "merit good" has to be applied to the needs expressed by a client. The merit good is likely to be an evaluation by the policy-makers of the general benefit that accrues to several actors in the family planning field by fulfilling a particular need. The benchmark for this criterion is drawn from "national objectives" and "cost effectiveness," both very likely to contradict individual interests. What emanates from a perusal of these excerpts is that only a limited opportunity is offered by the state to determine the course of the policy based on the clients' needs structure. In the end, as one of the bureaucrats pointed out, it is like saying "the consumer can have a car of any colour so long as the choice of his colour is black" (I#4).

The problem for the state, then, is to reconcile the apparent contradiction in its own discourse of user-centred policy. In a bid to resolve the tension between individual needs and national goals, the state has had to employ two key strategies. First, it questions the capacity of individuals to make 'rational, objective' decisions. Second, it re-invents its relationship with the individual in a way that suggests devolution of rights to the individual while retaining core decision-making facilities—especially as to what is permissible reproductive behaviour—for itself. The analysis of the interviews below details these points.

Rationality: capabilities of the client

The tendency to question the capacity of the client to act in a rational fashion is a strategy that is used by policy-makers to establish the pre-eminence of the state's objectives. 'Rationality', by implication, appears to be the capacity of the individual to converge her or his own sense of well-being with that of the state. Documents that paid lip service to individual interests as the priority of the RCH programme simultaneously also expressed a 'concern' about the long-term effect of permitting individuals to make decisions about the number of children they should have. In a Government of India document (goi.oc.6:1), it is pointed out that:

> ...while there are no two opinions about the need to remove *numerical targets* for the sake of quality of service, *there is a concern* that such a move, when taken country-wide, may lead to decline in *performance* [acceptance of contraceptives by users] initially.

The reference to a 'concern' is also reflected in interviews; the 'experts' of the state, in some form or the other, expressed an unease about how individuals would carry through the expectations of informed reproductive and sexual decisions in the new policy environment of 'freedom' and self-determination. The gender researcher, for instance, notes:

> I#3: ...well, the government talks about that too ... not to pressurise to accept family planning. That's what they tell their health workers too. But *there is this concern* ... I don't think that the population control crisis is forgotten ...

The success of the target-free approach, especially, relied heavily on the 'responsible' fertility behaviour of couples, given that an ANM's strategy for 'recruiting' volunteers for contraceptive acceptance was to change drastically. Several studies (e.g., Health Watch 1999) have shown that in the initial years following the introduction of the TFA, grassroots workers in the field interpreted the absence of numerical quotas as an indication that they need not do outreach 'motivational' work promoting contraceptives. Instead, the ANM's role was to attend to clients who actively sought reproductive health services. For the contraceptive acceptance levels to be maintained, the implicit expectation was that individuals and couples would make 'responsible' reproductive decisions.

I questioned the interviewees about this—the assumption about the average person's ability to make judicious fertility decisions (such as, the size of the family and spacing). The responses suggest that officials fall into one of two camps, those who believed in the ability of individuals to act rationally, and those who did not. The basis for these constructions in both these camps is worth analysing in some detail.

> Do you think that people are actually capable of making these decisions—what is most appropriate for them?
> I#7: Actually, they are much capable of making the decisions. We thought previously they are not in a position to come to a decision. But now we find that they are very much capable of making a decision especially in Kerala because most of them are educated and about 86% literacy is there.
> I#12: In Kerala, especially in these parts, I think that people have a good awareness, they have a consciousness, they have the awareness. As for the small-family norm, they have already adopted it.

Both the above respondents believe in individuals' "capability," the "consciousness" and the "awareness" to act 'rationally.' What is interesting about these comments is that in both instances, individual capability was shaped by people's "awareness" to adopt the small family norm. 'Capability' corresponded with the state's drive to control the population. In the case of the first quote, although not explicitly stated, the association with education and literacy clearly shows that the official is drawing on conventional development wisdom that increases in literacy and inclination to use contraception go hand in hand. The ability to behave in a responsible fashion was not innate; if it exists, it is largely as a result of the externally-imposed educational process. 'Awareness' was exhibited in people's choice of small families; the corollary would be that any decision not to have a small or two-child family is an expression of 'irrationality.'

Another group of interviewees strongly doubted that Indian users had the necessary capability to act responsibly when making reproductive decisions. For instance:

> You said that you are going to leave decision-making completely to the client. In this situation, do you think that our women or couples are capable of making such responsible decisions?

> I# 1: ... we are still in the experimental stage. Or as you call it, this will be the running in period. For a year or so. So we can only say in a year or two how successful we are.
> I#2: That time—for it to come—it will take some time. When the Panchayat Raj itself came, we gave them the decision-making capacity ... the people have not come to that stage yet. But they will come there gradually. If we never give them (the chance), they will never reach that stage. Like that, even here, in the beginning there may be problems—that may be why some achievements are going down. That we are expecting in this stage.
> I#11: ... that depends on the area. For example, in city areas there are mostly highly educated people—they know well. But in our rural places, we have to insist. For example, this is not completely a city area ...of that, a proportion at least will come only if we insist...
> ...but still, I think we still have to give a little push, I don't think that people will come along voluntarily (for family planning methods).

One gets the sense that the participant officials in this research were reticent in constructing the average individual/couple as capable of making rational reproductive decisions. The inherent desire of the 'client' to restrict the number of children s/he has is suspect—the state still had to "push" or "insist." A truly target-free approach could be, according to the interviewees, adjudged successful only if the outcomes matched the projections of the state (especially with regard to stabilisation of population). That correspondence was likely to come "gradually," and the present programme was in that sense only "experimental." Only those people who were "educated" or who lived in urban areas (and unwittingly, imbibed the values of development) could comprehend the significance of a two-family norm. Although the average Keralite, perhaps, was a shade ahead of her/his counterparts in other parts of the country (or even, 'backward' districts like Malappuram and Kasargode in the state itself), the state's acceptance of the 'client' as a responsible citizen was conditional.

There is an interesting point of similarity in both the camps (those who believed in user capabilities and those who didn't)—the arguments are grounded in almost similar considerations of ability to 'control' births. What both sets of responses indicate is that policy-makers' interpretation of rationality is tied to the idea of low levels of fertility. Rationality, within a development policy framework, is influenced by the neo-Malthusian logic—one that promotes smaller family sizes. The following comment by an official within a non-governmental population agency well exemplifies the construction of rational behaviour:

> I#17: Yes it is a woman's decision but you see, if we go that way, it becomes philosophy. You see, I want to commit suicide. It is my right ...a woman who wants to have 10 children ...we don't find that she is very normal *(Why do you say that?)* Because in that concept, having that many children will have many problems. But if you want to have all that you can't be normal. We went to one place and there was a woman there with 6 children. She told us, " it is an asset to me."

From the official's 'modernist' conception of normality, anyone who wants to have large families falls outside parameters of rational behaviour. His assumption prevails contrary to his experiences with real people; his own example of the woman with six children illustrates that people do have alternative values about the worth of children—"... it is an asset to me." But this clearly does not alter the dominant perception that associates fewer numbers of children with the rational individual.

My emphasis in this analysis is not to support large families, but instead to show how this perception of rationality acts as a constraining factor for the 'consumer/client' to participate as an equal member in market exchanges. It reflects an inherent fear of the nature of choices that may be made by an individual and thus fundamentally compromises the potential for meaningful democratic participation. The dominance of one view of reproductive practices forecloses alternative ways of thinking, and if anything, compromises freedom of informed choices. The implications of such a construction are seen in the quote above where policy-makers are given the right to overrule the individual "client's" interests. This is justified because the policy-makers are more capable of seeing objectively, given that they are capable of "standing at a distance". The client/user (unless educated and 'buys-in' to the development framework that prioritises economic growth) is never quite on par with the policy-makers.

Accessibility: purchasing power in the health market

A third dimension for assessing the characteristics of the 'client' is to examine how the user fits the requirement of a purchasing customer/consumer. In the analysis above, I already established that the ability to pay for services is implicitly woven into the discourse of being constructed as a consumer-client. Non-paying clients, on the other hand, do not necessarily pay for services and, often in public service parlance, are recipients or dependents who meet eligibility criteria (Fraser 1989; McGuire 1997). Further, I also showed that the shift in the discourse to user charges is gaining currency within the public health care and family welfare services in India. In this sub-section, I explore the implications of the discourse of purchasing power for accessibility to reproductive health care.

In India, the user of the family welfare services is not yet a paying client. All family welfare services in the public sector are provided free of charge. Any payment is only indirect, through the taxation process. And, according to Indian tax laws, there are many segments of society that are exempted from taxation—the poor (defined as people who fall below a certain income level) and those whose main income source is from agriculture, are among them. It is usually this segment of the population—the rural population and poor, incidentally, that is dependent on the government's services. Therefore, a majority of the users cannot claim the status of purchasing consumers, in the strictest sense. The senior bureaucrat I spoke with at the DFW acknowledged this point although he had earlier pointed out that users were "consumers", and that "... they are getting the results of what they are paying for ...." When I asked explicitly what proportion of people using FW services actually pays for it, the response was:

> I#4: No, they pay for it in the sense, when you look at the public finance angle—ultimately, this comes out of the state exchequer. And ... frankly—there is no direct payment—no direct payment involved. But ultimately the tab is borne by everybody, the tax payer.

The official's perception of who has the right to be a purchasing customer is aptly put. It is true that there is no direct payment to the family welfare programme for its services. So, although the tab is to be borne by "everybody," in reality, it is primarily the "tax payer" who funds the state's programme. The family welfare service, then, is not a *purchased commodity* but rather a *subsidised one*. The tab is not, unlike the interviewee's response, borne by everyone. It is actually borne only by a few, and it is only they who can claim to be purchasers of the service. The rest can either be 'citizens', exercising their right to health, or 'beneficiaries' of a service that the state finds important to provide.

The distinction between 'right-bearing citizen' and 'welfare-beneficiary' of the state in health services is an issue that will clearly arise in the wake of the state government's interest to effect cost recovery under health sector reforms. Although, as of 1998 when I was interviewing in the field, user payee health care was not introduced in the state's health system, there was strong support for it in the government sector and in non-governmental organisations providing family planning services (Interview I#17). In fact, reproductive health was being debated in the same arena as cost savings in the family welfare programme. The 1997 World Bank's *Project Appraisal Document (India: Reproductive and Child Health Project)* makes detailed references to cost-effectiveness and user payees in the reproductive health programme:

> [t]he new family welfare approach being implemented by GOI will result in some *savings* within the current budget. Real expenditures on the free distribution of contraceptives, as well as compensation for sterilisation and health guides, are already being reduced and will be reduced further during the project period....[T]he financial implications of going beyond these measures and charging for a proportion of the costs of medical services, drugs and vaccines have been calculated as part of project preparation. The opportunity to charge for activities which require universal coverage for effectiveness such as immunisations, and which help implement the right of every woman to have safe deliveries, is limited. However, cost recovery is being piloted....[T]his may escalate and result in the recovery of a small share of the costs of reproductive health drugs (wb.2: 17 emphasis in original).

With an emphasis on cost recovery, the state (and the non-state funders that support the programme) is seeking to find all possible avenues to raise income from investment into the reproductive health programme. The excerpt above indicates a dilemma that faces the state—how to maintain a commitment to reproductive well-being while being in a position to charge for services. For instance, the World Bank excerpt above notes that "*the opportunity to charge for activities which require universal coverage for effectiveness such as immunisations, and which help implement the right of every woman to have safe deliveries, is limited.*" Evidence from the field has demonstrated that where user charges have been implemented, use of services and health conditions has deteriorated (see for instance, Sparr 1994). Anecdotal evidence suggests that where health benefits depend on a social wage, vulnerable groups in society, especially the poor and women, tend to lose out. In developing countries, where household health expenditure is, as a rule, disproportionately allocated to women, the adverse implications of financial stratifications in access to public health care is likely to have more damaging implications (Standing 1999).

In a bid to resolve the conflict between cost recovery and maintaining conditions of reproductive well-being, the state appears to be moving to a context where health services are envisioned as being *stratified*. According to the strategy of stratification, all citizens are entitled to some basic services from the state. However, the citizen can access more advanced or sophisticated care only if s/he has the purchasing power to do so. For instance, the senior health official in the following extract describes a hypothetical situation of user payee health care and underscores what the woman client has the right to demand from the state under the current context of prudent servicing of health care:

> At the PHC level, what does this mean for a woman user? Would the state system be free at all at any level?
> I#4: We believe that any woman should have an access to free family welfare services—totally free....[c]ertain things like a delivery—an ante-natal check up should be free for her. But going from there, if she wants to have an ultrasound done... that is not part of the basic antenatal care. This is something that will give us an opportunity to charge... And since safe delivery is a first priority—in RCH, this (ultrasound) will become part of trying to provide those services...But

> since it will not form part of the basic services and because it will mean certain investment in terms of maintenance—in terms of hiring personnel—the cost of that we'd like to come from ultrasound. So we will be charging for that.

The divergence between the 'client/consumer' and the 'client/ citizen', in the marketised health care system, is vividly seen in this excerpt. The individual who can access a technologically sophisticated health system is the one who can purchase it. The 'right' to health, which the client-citizen is entitled to, is clearly different from what a client-customer in the state's services is capable of accessing. The woman in the example given by the official above will have to pay for advanced care, whereas basic care will be made free. *Uniform* health care is, therefore, not envisaged as a universal right of all citizens elevated to the status of clients. There are apparent income-linked differentials among citizens that the state not only accepts but also *needs to encourage* if its investment in health is to be financially viable. In the following excerpt, the senior official notes that:

> I#4: But I am just trying to show you the distinction between the primary care, which will be his *(the client)* right—which he will get free. And something—primary care plus—which he will be paying for.

In effect, two points can be emphasised. First, the evolution of the state into a marketised public health care provider is implicitly built on the assumption of differentiation within the population. The state will serve different segments of society differently, and will tailor its services in the same way. At a fundamental level, some services will be deemed 'core' and free, while others will be classified 'secondary' and to be purchased. Interestingly, it is at points where the state's interests coincide with individual needs that the state does not propose to withhold free health services. For instance, fertility regulation or contraceptive methods and immunisation are expected to be offered free (Interview I#4).

Accessibility to these latter services will be restricted and contingent on the purchasing ability of citizens rather than their entitlements as citizens of a state. Within this stratification, the state as market sets criteria as to what comprises basic and what comprises secondary care. A further point is that health-care, even reproductive health-care, is increasingly individualised. Apart from the few areas where the state will ensure that certain objectives are achieved, the discursive shift towards constructing the 'client' is also a shift towards devolving responsibility of health care onto the individual her/himself. As a market provider, the state is bound to *provide* reproductive health services, not *ensure* that all citizens can access them.

Articulations: constituting user needs

A fourth point around which I unpack the idea of the client is in the ability of the user to formulate and articulate her/his own construction of needs independent of the intervention of the state, which could then become the basis for service provision. However, the RCH document reveals, the client does not occupy a space outside of the state's ideological framework. The documents indicate that the state will *constitute* the clients' needs as much as it seeks to satisfy them. A typical example is in the use of the term *felt need*. In doing away with the target oriented scheme, the current policy has replaced work strategies of grassroots workers. ANMs are no longer concerned with targets, quotas and incentives; rather, according to the RCH, ANMs are instructed to use as guiding principles concepts such as— "requirement of the area" and "felt need." The "requirement of the area" for a particular service is a complete coverage of services offered by a PHC (including prenatal care and contraceptive distribution) whereas the "felt need" is the actual use or demand for services at a particular time (goi.oc.6: 12). The "felt need" may often fall far short of the service requirement. It is the task of the grassroots workers to ensure that clients' "felt needs" are increased through motivational tactics of the IEC programmes. The excerpts below come from doctors at a local level PHC and the last from a middle-level bureaucrat at the Department of Family Welfare, respectively.

> I#12: The approach right now is that we should not insist and force things on people. Apart from that, the beneficiary should have that feeling ...it is their need, it is their issue, on that basis they have to be made to feel that it is <u>their</u> felt need. That should be made clear in our

other activities, of course in motivating them and in making things clear to them. We have to create awareness and make felt need and give that service. And then we have to offer that service.

I # 7: We are increasing the felt need by awareness and other factors and once it becomes 100 percent, it also becomes [a service requirement]. That is the aim of the RCH...there is no need to push it [contraception]. You just give awareness...so that means by giving awareness to people, more and more Information, Education and Communication facilities, naturally more and more people will come forward and it can be successful.

I # 11: When you talk of motivation, anyway there will be some group somewhere who won't have it. No matter how you try—it is hard. But through this [RCH], we should be able to bring in some more—a lot more people, for sure.

The use of the idea of 'needs' is a tricky one; comments of the policy-makers in the upper rungs of the institutional hierarchy and of health providers at the local level demonstrate that *creating a need* is as much a part of the policy's objective as *satisfying the need* is. Often, these needs are less an individual's subjective requirement than a carefully posed norm that the individual finds herself or himself needing to meet. Family planning services have always aimed to alter the behaviour of individuals with respect to their reproductive behaviour. The present system suggests the same requirement: that state structures should strive to meld state needs with that of individuals. Once again, there is a contradiction here between what constitutes free, informed expression of reproductive needs and a construction of needs as regulated by the state. A senior official at the DFW seemed to sense this discrepancy as he explained to me what a felt need was. The essence of the description is given below:

I#6: Actually now the felt need is *addressing their...* "felt needs" means the service *which we are giving* or the acceptor desires to get from the provider. So suppose in an area—100 people ...are available and [only 60 or 70] come in for the service from the provider. That is actually—put in terms of the "felt needs"—that is not the real service. If you are providing the quality service, of course, the unmet need also will be taken care of. Naturally as the quality of service increases, the felt need will also be getting increased. It is a misnomer—felt need. It has to be changed.

The official starts out by explaining "felt needs" from the point of the user but then shifts the description to the provider's point of view—from "addressing their…" to "the service we are giving." It is only after the shift to a provider's perspective of "felt needs" that the conceptualisation of a need as a service issue is followed through. To this official, too, "felt needs" is something that should be "increased" in individuals, rather than understood or responded to by the health provider. For this official, explaining the term "felt needs" raised inconsistencies. First, the official seems to have realised that there is a discrepancy in the use of the term "felt needs" to depict a value that is imposed on individuals. Second, the term "felt needs" suggests that the family welfare programme merely responds to the clients' needs, not regulate them. To do so would be to accede control to the client. However, the state's conception of services is not only about being responsive to individual's demands for services (as the official puts it, if only 60-70 people out of a 100 people come for services from the provider "that is actually—put in terms of the "felt needs"—that is *not* the real service") but about being responsive to the state targets. He ends by saying that "it is a misnomer—felt need. It has to be changed."

Other officials linked increasing "felt needs" through IEC work. The IEC is the MoHFW's mass media organ and the main source of propaganda about the state's ideas on contraceptive use and reproductive behaviour. The official below equates increase in mass media work with identifying "felt needs." For instance:

> I#8: And…but according to the target free approach, we are giving much importance to the felt need of the community. And these "felt needs" can be identified only through IEC work.
> I#6: We will be giving them awareness. And giving some increases in the IEC activities.

Despite what the official in the first excerpt says, IEC is not so much to identify "felt needs" as it is to "give them awareness." This comment raises the question: What is the primary objective of IEC? Is it to communicate to the population at large the state's current philosophy of birth control?

What we see, therefore, is not the informed, bargaining relationship that is supposed to take place ideally in a marketplace but a subtle inscription of state power in subtle forms. One possible and relevant, reading of the state's aim to constitute individual needs can be drawn from the Foucaultian perspective of governmentality. Foucault (cited in Burchell 1996) describes the art of government as the "conduct of conduct," of shaping, guiding, correcting and modifying behaviour of individuals and the way they conduct themselves so that it converges with the ideologies (or, in Foucault's words, political rationalities) of the state. Rose (1996:43) argues that the power of the state is in the ability to translate political programmes articulated, for example, as national efficiency, democracy, and equality from a central point into diverse localised points—it is in a sense, the "ability to govern at a distance." The successful art of governmentality is not one that imposes itself on individuals—"it's not a matter of imposing laws on men, but rather ... to arrange things in such a way that, through a certain number of means, such and such ends may be achieved" (Foucault 1979: 13). For this to happen the state organises "... forces (legal, architectural, professional, administrative, financial, judgmental), techniques (notation, computation, calculation, examination, evaluation), devices (surveys and charts, systems of training, building forms) ..." that would regulate the decisions and actions of individuals and groups (Rose 1996:42). What this entails is the translation of the techniques of domination into techniques of the self, viz., the state establishes its domination when the individual no longer recognises that the values and ideologies that form the basis for her/his actions are anything but her/his own.

There appear to be echoes of Foucaultian governmentality in the way the RCH is promoting its rights-based programme for its clients. Increasingly, the strategy of the MoHFW is to make individuals feel that the state's needs are their own, thereby effacing the distinction between *acts of compliance* and *acts of empowerment.* A singular advantage of this tactic is that the chances of resistance to external ideology will be minimal.

Overall, in summing up the four attributes given to the 'client' in the RCH, one can argue that the citizen/user/consumer in the market place of family welfare is situated in a complex ideological terrain. This is not unlike the findings from other international critiques of health sector discourse. Grace (1991), for example, analysed health promotion discourses in New Zealand and showed how an overt commitment to 'empowerment' of consumers veiled an equally strong objective to *plan, change and control* individuals' perception of health. Grace notes that the object of the discourse, i.e., the consumer, is seemingly positioned as being in control while the health provider is simultaneously positioned as controller. Whitty's (1998) analysis of the National Health Service policy in the United Kingdom found similar strands of market ideology ingrained within the broader overt objectives of "empowerment" and "participation." She quotes critiques of so called participatory planning in the National Health Service in the United Kingdom by pointing out that mere transformation of "I" into "we" does not entail empowerment (Whitty 1998: 145). If anything, it can "easily mask subtle forms of control" (Whitty 1998: 145). Goltz and Bruni (1995) similarly analyse the knowledge underlying Australia's health promotion approach. They analyse nursing texts and show that the main aim of nursing practices is to increase social control in the name of increasing individual responsibility to one's own health. The danger in the use of neo-liberal discourses is that they alienate the possibility of a radical social change accompanying access and rights to health.

Conclusion

This chapter attempted to trace neo-liberal ideology in the RCH. What emerges from the analysis is that the outcome of the adoption of the market analogy in family welfare services in India may have implications that have little to do with serving citizen interest or enhancing the structures of democratisation. From the evidence provided above, the state as market-provider stratifies health services, distinguishes between paying and non-paying clients, and seeks to control the process of articulation of citizen needs. Further, in redefining the role of the state and user under the framework of the market, a tacit contract that limits the scope of the state's intervention in universal public health emerges. Alongside, the invocation of the analogy of the market asserts that individuals have only limited legitimacy for claims upon the state. As the citizen metamorphosises into a consumer, the citizen has less access to the public space of political debate. The state also recharts its intervention into the lives of its people; through adoption of the market metaphor, the state considers systems-improvement its priority, marginalising issues like equity, justice, access, rights and so on.

Needham's (2003) critique of New Labour's conception of citizenship in the United Kingdom in terms of customer/consumer models highlights the costs to democracy: the consumer is encouraged to act out of self-regard rather than public good and the state tends to focus on experiences of policies and services rather than the political questions behind them. Models of democratic citizenship based on community, co-production and voluntarism, in Needham's opinion, are compromised in the commodification of the relationship between the state and the citizen.

Given the analysis and discussion of data above, it would seem inappropriate to equate the client/citizen depicted in the RCH policy with the purchasing consumer of the market place. What I have tried to show is that the subject-position granted to users of the family welfare services is not, despite the use of similar language, consonant with the fundamental characteristics of a consumer in the market place. Though not quite a candidate for charity, the client, nonetheless, does not have the bargaining capacities of a customer. The status of the client is simultaneously contradictory: s/he controls/and is controlled, s/he decides/and has decisions made, s/he plans/and is constituted by the programme. The 'client' in the Indian Reproductive Health programme, in effect, holds a rather fluid, uncertain relationship with a state service that is, as Whitty (1998) comments in the context of the UK, a 'hybrid' of both public/private and state/market. The acknowledgment of a rights-discourse (inherent in a feminist discourse on reproductive health) is questionable within this hybrid space. This examination of the ideology of the consumer supports the analysis in the next chapter where I examine specific ideologies around gender that proliferate in the RCH policy.

References

Amalric, F. and Banuri, T. (1994) "Population: malady or symptom?" *Third World Quarterly*, Volume 15 (4): 691–706.

Berg, B. L. (1998) *Qualitative Research Methods for the Social Sciences*, Boston, London: Allyn and Bacon.

Fairclough, N. (1992) *Discourse and Social Change*, Polity Press: Cambridge.

Foucault, Michel (1979) "Governmentality", *Ideology and Consciousness*, Vol. 6: 5–21.

Fraser, Nancy (1989) *Unruly Practices: Power, Discourse and Gender in Contemporary Social Theory*, Oxford: Polity Press.

Goltz, K. and Bruni, N. (1995) "Health Promotion discourse: language of change?" pp. 510—549 in H. Gardner (ed.) *The Politics of Health: The Australian Experience* (2nd Edition), Churchill Livingstone: Melbourne.

Grace, V. (1991) "The marketing of Empowerment and the Construction of the Health Consumer: A critique of Health Promotion' *International Journal of Health Services*, Volume 21 (2): 329–343.

Hindess, B. (1997) "A Society Governed by Contract?' in G. Davis, B. Sullivan and A. Yeatman (eds) *The New Contractualism*, Macmillan Education Australia Pty Ltd: Melbourne pp. 14–26.

Jayal, N. G. (1994) "The Gentle Leviathan: Welfare and the Indian State", *Social Scientist*, Vol. 22, No.9–12, pp. 18–26.

Measham, A.R. and Heaver, R. A. (1996) *India's Family Welfare Program: Moving to a Reproductive and Child Health Approach*, The International Bank for Reconstruction and Development: World Bank, Washington, D.C.

McGuire, L. (1997) "Service Delivery Contracts: Quality for Customers, Clients and Citizens", in G. Davis, B. Sullivan and A. Yeatman (eds) *The New Contractualism*, Macmillan Education Australia Pty Ltd: Melbourne, pp. 102–118.

Needham, C. (2003) *Citizen-Consumers: New Labour's Marketplace Democracy*, Catalyst Working paper, available at: http://www.catalystforum.org.uk/pubs/ (accessed 10 September 2005).

Rao, M. (2004) *From Population Control to Reproductive Health: Malthusian Arithmetic,* Sage Books: New Delhi.

Rose, N. (1996) "Governing 'advanced' liberal democracies" pp. 37–64 in Andrew Barry, T. Osborne and N. Rose (eds) *Foucault and Political Reason*, UCL Press Limited: London.

Sparr, P. (1994) (ed.) *Mortgaging Women's Lives: Feminist Critiques of Structural Adjustment*, Zed Books: London and New Jersey:

Standing, H. (1999) "Frameworks for Understanding Gender Inequalities and Health Sector Reforms: An Analysis and Review of Policy Issues", paper prepared under the Global Health Equity Initiative Project on 'Gender and Health Equity' based at the Harvard Centre for Population and Development, website: http://www.hsph.harvard.edu/grhf/Hupapers/gender/standing.html

Standing, H. (2000) "Gender Impacts of Health Reforms—The Current State of Policy and Implementation", paper presented at the ALAMES meeting, Havana, Cuba, 3–7 July.

World Bank (1997) *Project Appraisal Document: India, Reproductive and Child Health Project,* Population and Human Resources Operations Division, Country Department II, South Asia Region.

Whitty, N. (1998) "In a Perfect World: Feminism and Health Care Resource Allocation", pp. 135–153 in S. Sheldon and M. Thomson (eds) *Feminist Perspectives on Health Care Law,* Cavendish Publishing Limited: London, Sydney:

Yeatman, A. (1997) "Contract, Status and Personhood" in G. Davis, B. Sullivan and A. Yeatman (eds) *The New Contractualism,* Macmillan Education Australia Pty Ltd.: Melbourne, pp. 39–56.

6

Gender Sensitivity

The Ideology of Gender in the Reproductive and Child Health Programme[60]

> But is there such a thing as women's point of view? Who speaks from it? How can it emerge validly self-reflective from an invalid condition? How can it be identified? How distinguished from delusion? How can anything any woman thinks be false in a theory that purports to validate all women's experience? If every woman's views are true, regardless of content, how is feminism to criticize the content and process of women's determination, much less change it?
>
> Regardless of the weight or place accorded to daily life or women's insight, feminist theory probes hidden meanings in ordinariness and proceeds as if the truth of women's condition is accessible to women's collective inquiry. The pursuit of the truth of women's reality is the process of consciousness ...
>
> MacKinnon 1989, p. 39

A second predominant set of discourses in the RCH pertains to the idea of 'gender' and 'gender sensitivity.' As noted in Chapter 4, gender sensitivity is at the heart of what the RCH calls its 'paradigm shift,' and hopes to deliver a package of services that draw on and contribute to women's overall status. This chapter outlines the key themes that emerge when these notions are put to the test; what does the policy mean by gender sensitivity? In unpacking the way the term 'gender' is used, the state's ideologies of gender will become more apparent.

---

[60] A revised version of this chapter was published in the *Economic and Political Weekly*, Vol. XXXVII, No 32, pp. 3369-3377, 2002.

The term *gender* has a legacy of being open to multiple interpretations[61]. The widespread consensus in scholarship is that gender encompasses, among other things, issues of body differences, social roles and relations, sexual and gender identity, gender divisions of labour and gendered symbolisms. Society manifests multiple dimensions of gender distinctions; gender-sensitivity is an active effort to endorse gender equity. Effective ways to engender state policy have been on feminist agendas for decades. By and large, feminists have been critical of exercises that focus on a technical approach to assimilating 'gender' within programme and institutional contexts, undermining the relevance of addressing issues of power that contribute to women's subordination (see, for instance, Baden and Goetz 1997; Kabeer 1994; Koczberski 1998). Developmental organisations often assume that gender issues can be effectively tackled through carefully crafted 'gender-sensitive' programme design without substantially questioning the dynamics of power and inequity in society. What needs to be critically examined are the fundamental understandings about gender that these gender-sensitive policies propagate—their 'ideologies of gender'—and if these values can indeed be mobilised for the emancipation of women.

The RCH has claimed, by and large, to provide services that are gender-sensitive. This claim is an important one, for the bulk of the programme is directed at women's health and seeks to enhance women's ability to make appropriate reproductive decisions. For this analysis, some of the questions that I set out to ask in the exploration of gender ideologies in the RCH were: How does the state construct gender and women in the programme? How have women's interests been developed within the context of reproductive health? Is the state's emphasis on gender issues a sign of its commitment to equality and equity for women? And finally, what can women hope to gain from the Indian state's reproductive health programme? As in the earlier

---

[61] The term 'gender' itself has been defined differently by different feminist authors. For a review of this literature, see Hawkesworth (1997), Nicholson (1994) and Kurian (2000).

chapter, the data corpus for this analysis is drawn from government documents and interviews.

The chapter is divided into three sections. The first offers an overview of the policy's description of gender sensitivity. The second section analyses four persistent discursive themes about 'gender' and 'women' in the RCH, and discusses the implications of these discourses. The third and final section evaluates the interpretation of gender-sensitivity in the RCH and its implications for a gender-sensitive discourse on reproductive health.

Gender Sensitivity and the RCH Policy

In keeping with the resolutions of the ICPD, 1994, the Government of India gives special consideration to the provision of gender-sensitive services under the RCH programme. Gender sensitivity, which is seen as integral to the provision of good quality services, is defined as being "responsive to the needs of women" in planning and implementation (goi.nd). Interestingly, the concept of gender-sensitivity appears to have gained currency in the documents in the wake of the ICPD. There is, for instance, no mention of providing 'gender-sensitive' services in the *India: Country Statement* that was presented at the ICPD in Cairo, in 1994 (goi.obp.1).[62] By 1996, however, the documents emanating from the MoHFW, the DFW in Kerala, and the major funding agencies of the RCH programme in India elaborate plans to provide services that are gender-sensitive (see goi.nd).

Widely-acknowledged facts about women's physical, social and economic constraints in obtaining health and family welfare services in India have prompted the need for gender sensitivity in designing reproductive health policy. Chatterjee (1996: 30) identifies some of these:

- Women bear their health problems in a 'culture of silence' and do not seek timely health care;
- They often cannot travel beyond the area of their normal activities to obtain services;

[62] This is not to suggest that there was no mention of women or women-specific programmes in the document. Rather, a coherent, well-defined strategy of gender-sensitivity had not been articulated at that point by the government.

- They cannot usually approach male health providers; and
- In general, families, including women themselves, spend less time, effort, and money seeking health care for women and girls than for men.

Chatterjee goes on to argue that the Department of Family Welfare's concern with meeting targets had, thus far, resulted in a delivery system that views women primarily as *reproducers* rather than as *producers* in the economy. According to Chatterjee, this construction of women has had two implications for women: (a) the health delivery system tended to ignore the provision of general health care for women, and (b) the system tended to overlook those women who did not fall into the category of the typical reproducer in society, such as, adolescent girls, unmarried women, post-menopausal women and infertile women. Chatterjee (1996) points out that with the recognition of the needs of these women, there should be considerable improvement in the supply side of reproductive health services. Similarly, argues Chatterjee, other areas where there are gender imbalances in access and provision of services relate to:

- the focus in the earlier programmes on female sterilisation as the main form of contraception;
- inadequate number of female health personnel whom women can approach, insufficient support for existing female workers; and
- the need to emphasise male involvement in the programme.

Recognising these shortcomings, efforts have been made to address gender-specific issues in the RCH. The inclusion of gender-sensitive components in the policy is interesting for the various dimensions along which the state addresses this issue. Conceptually, the policy's efforts to be gender-sensitive are located simultaneously within women's rights to reproductive health care, and the broader context of women's social development. The RCH draws on the philosophies of the ICPD and defines the reproductive health approach as, "... people [having] the ability to reproduce and regulate their fertility, women [being] able to go through pregnancy and child birth safely, and the outcome of pregnancies [being] successful in terms of maternal and child survival and well-being, and couples [being] able to have sexual relations free of pregnancy and of contracting diseases" (goi.oc.5: 2). Alongside, the documents recognise that the knowledge and use of reproductive health services is inextricably tied to the level of social development within a community and, therefore, gives importance to issues of women's empowerment, especially through education. For instance, document goi.oc.5: 2 notes that "...while there is steady improvement due to economic development, spread of education/literacy and empowerment of citizens, substantial problems in regard to education/literacy ... and particularly in regard to empowerment particularly of women, remain." A key activity proposed by the state under the RCH is better collaboration with other government departments that deal with women's affairs. At the level of the state in Kerala as well, issues around gender and development have been recognised as critical to the success of the programme. In its proposals submitted to its major funders, the World Bank and the UNFPA, the Government of Kerala makes specific mention of the relevance of pursuing activities such as women's empowerment within the ambit of the programme. For instance, the Integrated Population and Development (IPD) project of the UNFPA for Kerala notes that, "[t]he major focus would be on education of girls, the health of the women, the survival of infants and young children, and, in general, the empowerment of women" and that "areas of concern which are to be addressed in this context are education, especially of girls, and *gender equity and equality*" (unfpa.obp.2: 1). Approximately 25 percent of the UNFPA's funds to Kerala are expected to be set aside for the implementation of gender-related activities of "equity, equality and women's empowerment" (gok.obp.9: 2 and Interview I#2).

Strategically, too, the programmes' interventions are founded on principles that can be viewed as sensitive to the needs of women. First, the government takes a life-cycle approach to women's health in the RCH programme; that is, the state aims to provide health services that address women's health across their life cycle, from childhood to adulthood (goi.nd). The documents recognise that "[g]ood health is cyclical in nature. In a woman's lifetime, her health status during any phase of life impinges upon the next phase" (goi.nd). The life cycle approach includes the health of the girl child right from birth through the reproductive years and into menopause and geriatric health. As one senior official in the Kerala DFW commented, the RCH programme intended to provide health care from "womb to the tomb" (Interview I#1). Secondly, the programme recognises that, thus far, the Indian family welfare programmes have focused on women in reproduction to the exclusion of male responsibility. Therefore, a key project under the programme has been to 'engender' the reproduction process; that is, it seeks to make men visible in the process of reproductive decision-making and contraceptive use.

At the level of the programme, the RCH provides services that are critical to women's reproductive well-being. The programme has extended its services from family planning and maternal health to include the treatment of women-specific diseases like Reproductive Tract Infections (RTIs). The provision of a universal essential obstetric care package and the crisis interventions proposed under emergency obstetric care would be important for preventing maternal mortality. There is also a special emphasis on providing counselling services for women and men (Interviews I#7, I#3). It is proposed that the PHC should be equipped to handle round-the-clock delivery services (goi.oc.5: 15). Further, the state will also cover transport charges for referral obstetric cases for women from indigent families to first referral units (FRUs) (goi.oc.5: 17). The MoHFW also plans to improve the facilities for medical termination of pregnancy (MTP) at the level of PHCs, by deputing a medical doctor weekly or fortnightly to PHCs to perform MTPs (goi.oc.5: 18-19).

Over and above this provision, under the scheme for 'decentralised participatory planning,' there is an emphasis on enhancing the processes of participation between ANMs and individuals and the community, respectively. ANMs will spend more time with clients so as to understand their needs. An adolescent programme is also envisaged under the RCH—education for young girls about sexuality, menstrual hygiene, contraception, safe sex, pregnancies and infection would be offered to the community (Interviews I#2). In addition to services, the RCH also recognises the importance of providing facilities, such as privacy during counselling and treatment, as a key aspect of gender-sensitive care.

The state also recognises that gender sensitivity is reflected through changes at the organisational level. The state has made provision to appoint women doctors to attend to RTI/STI cases in the PHCs (goi.oc.5: 21) and the appointment of a gynecologist in every PHC is being considered (Interview I#16). There is also integration of gender-sensitive components in the training of grassroots workers, such as sensitising them to the importance of privacy during interviews, listening to clients, being patient, using a friendly tone of voice, and readily clarifying questions that may be asked (goi.tm.3: 3). As one respondent noted, women would have a better option of exercising their own free choices.

> If you say we have this new policy, what would it mean for women in the villages?
>
> I #3: What it means is that at least there is no more coercion. We hope that with better counselling she's being given a chance to decide on what she should use, whether she should control her fertility. If she decides to do so, what is the method she should use. It is not that an ANM tells her—go and use an IUD. She makes the choice.

The state also recognises logistical inconveniences in its female staff's work pattern; for instance, the state is willing to financially support the purchase of mopeds (light motor vehicles) for ANMs so as to be able to increase the reach within their coverage area (goi.oc.5: 12–13). Finally, the state, in the effort to ensure representation of women's voices within the community, plans to network with, and work alongside women's organisations and local NGOs to mobilise the community's support for the planned projects under the RCH (Interviews I#4, I#6).

The responses to my interview questions, as with the documents, also drew out similar ideas of gender sensitivity in the RCH. One of my interviewees, a representative of a women's organisation, identified the institutional problems of the ANM staff as important to providing a gender-sensitive service.

> You said the key areas in which it (RCH) could be gender-sensitive—could you elaborate a little bit?

> I#6: One of these areas where we have addressed the issue is that the female health workers ... once the programme becomes target free ... she should be much more concerned about women's health needs [and] help women articulate their health needs ... so we have done all these series of ways in which a health worker can provide better services to women. So that women won't run away from her, women are able to confide in her. We also touched on this issue of health care providers vis-à-vis her supervisors and the higher level authorities as to how she can be empowered ... in order to be able to take her clients to the referral centres and where she would be heard also and in turn provide better services to women.

This particular respondent has drawn attention to the role of the ANM in providing a gender-sensitive reproductive health services, mostly with regard to helping women articulate their needs better and giving the ANM autonomy to make decisions about her patients. As such, the recognition in the RCH policy that the ANM is the linchpin for the success of the programme may contribute to allowing greater autonomy in their work. For instance, a government of India document notes that, "the success of the new approach will depend greatly on the ANM, the backbone of the health programmes in the rural areas of our country" (goi.tm.1:1).

Yet another senior bureaucrat at the DFW, when asked about the benefits of the programme (especially to women), said:

> I #4: One thing is that providing information itself will have a certain beneficial impact. And the second one is that ...the reality as of now, as things in Kerala [stand] is that the sterilisation or the temporary methods have become the responsibility of the woman. Now given that situation—improvement of the quality of services will be to her interest to a certain extent.

The official picks up two other dimensions of the RCH that will prove particularly useful to women. The first is the provision of information in the programme, which would make a tremendous difference to women's capabilities to make informed reproductive decisions. A second factor that he points to is the improvement in the quality of service given, which has been considered under the general upgradation of the services of the state, and will nonetheless benefit women more than men, because they primarily use the state's services more intensively than men.[63]

In sum, some of the strategies aimed at providing gender-sensitive quality services are:

- Focusing on women's health problems such as reproductive tract infections
- Encouraging male participation in family planning
- Keeping clinics open at times suitable to women
- Training in gender sensitivity for service providers
- Getting women's feedback in monitoring
- Encouraging involvement of panchayats that now have thirty percent women members (goi.nd)

From the accounts reproduced above, there are certainly strong elements of 'gender sensitivity' in the programme, viz., women's needs as a distinct set of requirements, and the various aspects that could enhance the benefits for women have been considered in the RCH. It must also be noted that the MoHFW/DFW's efforts at making the programme gender-sensitive are fairly broad; they are inclusive of measures to improve the health delivery system, enhance women's personal and social autonomy, and address women's health needs. However, the social meanings around gender or the discursive context (i.e., the state's understanding of roles of women within society and the development process) influence the construction of needs around women, and subsequently, policy outcomes for the RCH. The following section analyses the state's gender ideologies.

'Gender' Themes in the RCH

The analysis of underlying discourses revealed four intersecting value structures that inform policy-makers' constructions of women and gender. The themes that emerged showed a strong propensity for policy-makers to construct women in 'instrumental' ways, i.e., an improvement in women's well-being was promoted as being a benefit in achieving ends other than for women

---

[63] The linking of quality services with gender-sensitivity is important, as I argue later, because it is a key point where market ideology is integrated with feminist discourse.

themselves. Two instrumental constructions, were prominent: the instrumental construction of women, first, as mothers, and second, as vehicles for development objectives. In the latter construction, the policy indicated a focus on women's health because of the larger implications for society and the population. A third theme centred around the idea of 'equality' for women with respect to men. And finally, a fourth theme explored the discourses around the construction of the notion of gender in 'sex-neutral' rather than 'sex-specific' ways. These discursive themes are pivotal in positioning women in particular ways within reproductive health policy and, ultimately, question the concept of gender-sensitivity itself.

Women as Mothers

The centrality of the 'mother-child' dyad as the 'natural' role of women in reproduction, and the relevance of this nexus appeared to be a strongly underlying ideology that influenced policy-makers' and practitioners, understanding of the RCH. As the various excerpts below show, the respondents drew heavily on an essentialist maternal imagery (of altruism, sacrifice and selflessness) in their constructs of women. That the RCH was built on this principle seemed only 'natural.'[64] Some of the instances in which the 'mother-child' unit was expressed are given below. Of the responses, the first was made by a senior official in Kerala while the others are comments of medical officers located in PHCs.

> I#1: ... the emphasis is always on the *mother and child*. There may be some reason for the planners for deciding or taking such a decision considering this mother and child as a unit. So the role played by the *mother in the family, in the society and probably in the nation*. So that is how it goes.
>
> I#12: Only a *strong mother can have a strong child*. That way, a strong child when brought up like that [healthily] when it has its own

---

[64] This portrayal of women has been pointed out about pre-WID development policies as well. For example, development policies in the sixties defined 'womanhood' in terms of 'motherhood', and positioned women as recipients of welfare programmes (Kabeer 1994).

child or is married, can have healthy children. So, we should think very fundamentally and we should begin at a basic level.
I#11: Mainly, [the programme is meant] for women's health...that is, there should be a healthy mother. Only then, we will have healthy children. Mainly women will benefit more from it. All these programmes will *first benefit women, then from that children will get it* ... Our aim is to improve maternal and child health, that is the final aim.
I#9: Content [of the RCH]? ... it's that right now the family welfare programme is concentrated more to the women and child health. Health (services?) should be more concentrated upon the care of maternal and child health care ...[so that] the *population that is born should be healthier*...

Further excerpts reinforce that the construction of woman-as-mothers was not an artifact of the policy machinery. Rather, the state was reflecting what was portrayed as natural by society and by women users themselves. One of my interviewees, a middle-level woman policy-maker, characterised women in Kerala as perceiving no identity for themselves outside of their roles as mothers:

> I#2: But, our women have a problem—not just ours, but all over India—if we tell them to do something for the mother, they are indifferent but if we tell them that it is for the child as well, they will do it. That is a peculiarity of our women ... if we give them iron tablets, many women do not eat them because they think that the children will become dark. Even if they know that it has benefits for the mother, there are those who do not eat it because the child will become dark. So also, when we insist that they take TT [tetanus toxoide] immunisation, they are interested only if we tell them that even the child will not get sick because of this. So they are interested that the child gets more care than the mother.

The primary focus on women as mothers, according to this official, is not one that is imposed by the state or state's policy. Women's responses to the state's health programme indicated that women identified their role as mothers as their primary identity; the state in turn tailored its policies making the implicit assumption that programme efforts would be accepted if the benefits to children were emphasised. Women's interest in medical care is contingent upon the benefits that will reflect on their children. For women, "they are interested that the child gets more care than the mother".[65]

The comments above reflect the dominant role that women in Indian society are traditionally constructed in—as mothers. It also reveals the fundamental social 'unit' that the RCH is premised upon—the mother and child. While there are no surprises in these constructions, there are, however, likely policy implications. The focus on the mother and child is a deviation from the various fundamental social categories that have been identified internationally as central to population programmes. Since the 1950s, at international population conferences, the international community has toyed with various 'units' that population programmes should be targeted towards. Broadly, the language of the conferences has moved from policies meant for 'families,' 'parents,' and 'eligible couples' to 'individuals' (Freedman and Isaacs 1993; Dixon-Mueller 1993). The ICPD, 1994, adhered to the categories of 'couples and individuals' in its Programme of Action. However, from the comments of health workers in India, the 'mother-child' unit seems to be the basis for the development of a reproductive health programme. Chatterjee's (1996) critique of mainstream population policy notwithstanding, one would argue that women continue to be cast as biological and social reproducers. This normative bias appears to influence what policy-makers consider as priorities in the RCH. As the excerpt below indicates, the primary objective of the RCH—from a gamut of reproductive well-being possibilities—is focused around child survival and safe nutrition.

> I#1: The primary objective is child survival and safe motherhood is the most important component. So anything which comes in between. Anything which is an impediment to child survival, or for safe motherhood or for the health of the mother … remove those obstacles. It may be RTIs, STDs, AIDs, [or] infertility, for example. So anything—any diseases or disorder or any problem which prevents the mother or child from surviving—gaining good health. That is our primary aim.

---

[65] Note that this is a policy-maker's construction of women, which may or may not be a 'true' representation of women's identity.

I#3: But you've got to admit the Ministry of Health's focus [on reproductive health] would be purely on stuff related to health. So therefore it boils down to safe motherhood and family welfare and RTIs and STIs.

I#4: And since safe delivery is a first priority—in RCH, this [ultrasound checks] will become part of trying to provide those services.

The comments above disclose the state's philosophy of reproductive health—that it is about "any problem that prevents the mother or child from surviving and gaining good health." The official's comments suggest that women's health is significant to the extent that it supports "safe motherhood" and "safe delivery." The instrumentalist construction of women is revealed in the programme's objectives—*safe delivery is a first priority* (Interview I#4). For all practical purposes, the maternal and child health service is the strongest component of the RCH. The emphasis on antenatal check-ups, ensuring provision of tetanus shots and iron and folic acid tablets in the RCH training programmes (Interview I#9) reflect the state's keen interest in the physical health of mothers.

Critics, however, raise arguments in favour of and against an emphasis on maternal health. While there is considerable validity in emphasising the role that women play as mothers in most societies (and this representation is particularly strong in the Indian society), there is also some disquiet in compressing women's diverse roles into a singular characterisation with motherhood. Critical views argue that often this emphasis on motherhood conceals rather than highlights women's health issues—reproductive health becomes conflated with maternal health. Beall (1997) and Bang and Bang (1989) have pointed out that despite the label of MCH, the 'M' in the 'MCH' tends to be ignored in reproductive health service provision (Beall 1997; Bang and Bang 1989). Maternal health is relevant to the extent that it nurtures children's physical and social environment. It could be argued that the state's focus on maternal health does not render women's health as a public concern; in fact, it could serve to negate women's visibility within policy. Bruce and Dwyer (cited in Kabeer 1994) note that although the construction of women in development policy has changed over time, dominant constructions still obscure the broad range of needs that women are likely to have. They point out that "the invisible women of the economic theorist become the all powerful mothers of the health and welfare advocates" (Bruce and Dwyer cited in Kabeer 1994: 269). It is worth considering, if in their metamorphosis as mothers, women's invisibility continue to be subtly reinforced.

The construction of women as mothers is also of interest because it directly contradicts the policy's claim to recognise that women need reproductive health care throughout their lives. Despite policy claims of being operationalised under a 'life-cycle' approach to health, there is a tendency to provide for service interventions around women's fertility and child-bearing needs. The two notions, in this context—the 'mother-child' unit and a 'life cycle' approach to health—are necessarily antagonistic to each other. The emphasis on women as mothers contradicts the state's commitment to consider women of all ages and stages of life as equally needful of public health care.

There are two perceptible outcomes arising from the state's inclination to set women's fertility as a parameter for health provision—in both, women are converted into specific 'targets' for policy intervention. First, the emphasis on the mother-child relationship encourages policy-makers to continue to think of a stratified approach to services for the population. Target groups appear to be selected on the basis of an assessment of 'risk'—the risk of AIDS, for instance. The basis for targeting contraceptive needs in the RCH, it would appear, is defined by the 'high-risk' fertility or the child-bearing propensity of women. Consequently, contraceptive programmes focus on targets such as newly-married couples, young couples, couples with one child and so on (see excerpts below). To that extent the RCH continues in the tradition of other family planning paradigms that have preceded it. Reproductive health appears to be about *health care in the reproductive ages.* Note the responses to my queries on target groups by middle-level officers at the DFW.

> What is the age group and the sex that you are focusing on in your new package—your approach?
>
> I#7: That is in the reproductive period mainly from 15–45.

I#2: ...for different programmes, different age groups are targeted. In the AIDS programme, they have [targeted] people who have high-risk behaviour. In that there is this idea to give adolescent education—you must give sex education and adolescent education. In the family welfare, married couples in the age group 15–44 are the eligible couples. Our IEC activities start from newly married couples ... the mean age at marriage [in Kerala] is above 22. So usually we approach people only after that age group for family planning.

A second outcome relates to the social reality within which women exercise their fertility—that marital status determines the state's concern with women as 'targets.' Women's reproduction, from a programme point of view, tends to be seen within the institution of marriage. At the PHC level, the 'Married Couple Registers' are the basic records for issuing contraceptive or health care. Note that the second official in the excerpt above notes that the target group of women are *married couples* (Interview I#2). The criterion for falling within the state's programme is primarily the status of marriage; sexual activity in itself is not a legitimate criterion for approaching the health system. For the policy-makers, an atypical client (a sexually active unmarried woman or man) is a 'problem' and can only be discussed under the umbrella of ill health (STD/AIDS). The following transcript reveals that the location of un-married clients, especially unmarried women, in the reproductive health discourse occupies a problematic space:

What about unmarried women? Are you saying anything about them or do you always speak in the context of husband-wife?

I#8: Sex is usually mentioned within marriage ...then within adolescent behaviour, we can talk about unmarried women.

For these unmarried women, suppose—do you give education as to where they can obtain condoms?

I#8: Yes, we are giving that.

Even if they are not married, you are giving information on what is what...

I#8: Not just unmarried women, but also men.

How do you convey it? Do you say that if they go to PHC, they will get condoms?

I#8: If we want to talk about sex, we can only [do it] in the general context of STD/AIDS. We can't tell them to go there [to the PHC] when they want sex. Because there is STD/AIDS, we tell them that sometimes people cannot control themselves ... in such situations they should go to the PHC.

The above remarks of the official offer a wealth of information regarding the construction around non-marital sex, and sexual activity in general. Although not the objective of this research, it is worth pointing to the stigma attached to non-marital sex because it is fundamental to the way that sexual/reproductive health care is formulated. Sexual health services are offered as part of a package of ill health. A disadvantage of this strategy is that it is unlikely to draw people to the programme unless they consider themselves to be a 'risk' category when engaging in sexual activity. In the end, both of these outcomes tend to exclude rather than encompass a wider range of women.

Women posited as instrumental to state's objectives

The second instrumental construction of women that the policy makes is based on women's role in supporting development efforts of the state. Three excerpts from the documents exemplify this connection:

Deficiencies in the arrangements for mother and child health care lead to higher incidence of maternal mortality and child/infant mortality and these also lead to low health status of women and children and in the long run *is a costly burden on the national system* (goi.oc.3: 2).

The RCH Programme intends to integrate fertility regulation, maternal and child health with reproductive health services... with the aim *to reduce infant and maternal mortality eventually contributing to the stabilisation of population* and improve the health status of women and children (goi.oc.1: 1).

...[w]hen she [woman] gives birth, she passes on the gift of good health to the next generation...if implemented in an integrated manner, the RCH programme will go a long way towards improving the *overall health of women and that of society as a whole* (goi.nd).

According to these extracts, maternal health is not just significant from the perspective of the privacy and intimacy of the child-mother relationship, but from a larger socio-economic perspective as well. The first piece indicates that failure to provide for maternal health is likely to have repercussions for national health, both demographically and financially. The second firmly sets the government's perspective on the rationale for the efforts to increase "safe motherhood and child survival," which, eventually, is to "stabilise" population. Document goi.oc.5: 3 explains at more length that this is likely to happen because "[I]t is now well established that *parents keep the family size small* if they are assured about the health and longevity of children, *and there is no better assurance of good health and longevity of children than health care for mothers and young children.*" The willingness of the government to spend on reproductive health was also echoed in my interviews. As I#4 emphasised:

> I#4: We believe that any woman should have an access to free family welfare services—totally free. *Because the benefit as much as it accrues to her, also accrues to society.*

A value that supports this construction of women is the unequivocal acknowledgement that women in Kerala, as a result of higher levels of literacy and education, are aware of the benefits of small families (for instance, I#12 noted: "we have 100 per cent literacy … women's literacy … so because of all that, there is a good awareness"). Women, therefore, form viable conduits for the state's population programmes. The medical officers at the PHCs were particularly emphatic about women's awareness of contraceptive and child health knowledge, and ability to take timely health measures.

> I#9: Once they [patients] have a baby, mothers come to us and ask—is there a problem if we use Cu-T? Even before we educate them, they ask us these things.
> I#11: Women, to be frank, because they have some information and ideas … they would like to do sterilisations. They know the difficulties [of continued pregnancies] more.
> I#1: Now that [intense propaganda] is not necessary. Now the mother comes to us—the family comes to us, the husband and wife comes and tell us—we want to adopt permanent methods.

In all these ground-level accounts, it is the woman in her role as a mother who is the key person enacting the state's expectation of its population programmes.[66] The instrumental construction of women has its foundation in efficiency arguments for women in development, which originated in Ester Boserup's argument that women's exclusion from development was detrimental not only to women but to the development process itself (Boserup 1970; see also Razavi and Miller 1995; Jackson 1996). Arguments favouring the efficiency rather than equality arguments were consolidated in the 1980s against the background of structural adjustment programmes (SAPs). The primary concern that has been raised about an efficiency argument is that it undermines outcomes for women on the basis of justice and equity. Women may have access to work or even credit as a result of development projects, but these may not in any way translate into transformed gender relations. For instance, Jackson (1996) cites an argument by Jeffrey (1994) regarding the widely accepted nexus between education of women and low fertility, which is seen as a statement of the empowerment of women who are now 'capable' of making decisions about contraception. Jeffrey argues that this link may speak less of empowerment of women and more of the impact of the propaganda of nuclear family ideology that is being disseminated by the state (Jackson 1996: 491). Similarly, Kabeer (1994) points out that women's reproductive roles as mothers is a deliberate move in development to capitalise on women's work for community health purposes. By assuming that women have a 'natural' willingness to undertake health responsibilities and work in the interests of the family and community, the state has the advantage of dispensing with the need to offer women any material incentives.

[66] The enthusiasm in these comments of the policy-makers counters the reluctance in the transcripts that I had reproduced in Chapter 5, where officials doubted the ability of people to make 'rational' choices. These comments may seem contradictory; however, the statements about women's awareness and practice of contraception were positive because it referred to women in Kerala. A different picture of capability (one that expressed concerns about 'responsible' behaviour) emerges when policy-makers refer to Indians in general.

A critique of the efficiency and instrumentality in development policy is located, fundamentally, not at the level of programmatic offerings, but in the positioning of women at the level of discourse. What may, at a superficial level, seem gender-sensitive is rendered antithetical to women's interests when analysing the discourses that frame these services; unless embedded within the discourses of equity, the programme can effectively limit women's agency. Some of the policy-stakeholders' comments indicate that the threat of instrumentality to the idea of agency implicit in gender-sensitivity is very real.

I asked respondents if they thought that the RCH tended to instrumentalise women, and if it did, what long-term consequences would be apparent. By and large, respondents accepted that the aims of the RCH were the result of a genuine focus on women, but at the same time, there was a recognition that the commitment to women did not go all the way. For instance, in the following exchange, the independent researcher for the government said:

> You don't see the RCH as [yet another] instrumentalist sort of policy?
>
> I#3: Well, it can work out that way, but at least the government is not—I don't think that they are thinking in that way. At least that is the impression that I get from Secretary, Family Welfare or from other people.

I raised the similar question about the instrumentality of women in my interview with this middle-level official in the DFW. I asked:

> The commitment to gender issues—is it a commitment to women or is it because of the larger problem of AIDS? [In CSSM people say it] was really a concern with the child welfare [more than the mother's welfare]. So, is the RCH something like that?
>
> I#2: No, I think in the RCH the focus is in the larger interest of the women—that's how I think. When implementation comes, how far it will be will depend on the commitment. And right now I don't think there is that commitment.

Both these responses are marked simultaneously with a faith in the state's commitment to women and a simultaneous uncertainty about the extent of that commitment. The contradiction in the response reveals a tenuous position of women in the policy that comes about because they are not central to the well-being goals that the state is interested in. The instrumental location of women can make them expendable depending on how the policy evolves. The above responses can be interpreted as the recognition of the elements in the policy that can be marshalled for women's empowerment, but which would depend largely on a deeper philosophical shift on the part of the state. I would see the official as articulating a tension in the principles and practice of the policy; in the end, the values extraneous to the policy itself, such as the aims of women's development, are likely to have significant bearing on women's reproductive health outcomes.

Ultimately, instrumental constructions in the policy influence the representation of the personhood of women within the state. In the RCH, women's instrumentality as mothers, who are seen committed to the same objectives of development as the state, underscores their invisibility as persons within the state. They continue to be 'targets' of what the state constructs as health needs. What follows is that these limited conceptualisations can limit the state's interests in women's long-term welfare.

'Equality' as a Guiding Principle in the Policy's Strategies

The third prominent theme that emerged from the data was the government's keen interest to restore reproductive 'equality' and 'parity' between the sexes. In a tone that is almost inimical to the instrumental construction of women above, the RCH also simultaneously makes emphatic gestures to define women as a distinct group whose interests have to be served, outside of any larger ends that need to be reached. 'Equality' and 'equity' of women seems to be one such goal. The policy, for example, outlines gender specific interventions to help in consciousness-raising of women in the community and among workers within the health system. In my conversations with the Mass Media department of the DFW, I was told that sex education classes being offered in the colleges in Kerala included discussions around shared decision-making and equal partnership in reproductive matters, alongside information about sexuality and reproduction. Furthermore, proposals by the Kerala Government to the UNFPA included enhancing library resource materials on gender and development, participation in seminars and workshops, increased surveillance and recording of violence and crime against women, to name a few (gok.obp.15 (g); gok.obp.12).

However, in exploring the interpretation of 'equality', my analytical interest is in the state's proposed recommendation (and interventions) in enhancing the presence of males in the reproductive health programme. The strategy to increase male presence—variously called 'male involvement,' 'male participation,' 'male responsibility' and 'men's role in decision-making' is intriguing because it has made current a novel discourse for engendering population policies. Conventional seminar/educative efforts of the state rarely address male roles and responsibilities; the discourse of equality based on male participation is new to the organisational structure of the state that normally shies away from potentially controversial issues in gender relations. In examining the discursive ethos around male involvement, I do not plan to make a study of how well such a plan has been conceived or implemented by the state. Other analyses have already critiqued the government's feeble attempts at increasing the programmatic role of men. Raju's (1999) analysis shows that the state's propaganda on male involvement has not translated into written policy or concrete plans and that there is no clear understanding of how to operationalise the joint responsibility of men and women. Instead, what I explore is how the state positions women in its discursive rhetoric of gender equality.

The role of men has been, by and large, ignored in the mother-child dyad that forms a crucial foundation for the RCH. Men do not directly form a part of the seemingly sacrosanct mother-child relationship. It is, therefore, interesting to follow the lines of argument that strive to make men an inclusive part of a reproductive health agenda of the state. Chatterjee (1996), for instance, elucidates the principles behind increased male participation in the Reproductive and Child Health Policy. She states that a basic tenet of the reproductive health approach in India is that reproduction should be based on joint decision-making between "husband" and "wife" (p. 38). As women bear the costs of pregnancy, the responsibility for planning or averting births, and for parenthood should be shared by men and women. Chatterjee identifies four ways in which male responsibility can be enhanced. First, the family welfare programme needs to give men information about family and their wives' health needs, child health care, and so on. Second, the programme must motivate men to take responsibility for obtaining preventive and curative care, including family planning. Third, it needs to propagate male methods of family planning more widely, and increase the accessibility of services to men. Finally, the system needs to focus on young males in an effort to inculcate responsible sexual behaviour and improve 'gender relations'. Pachauri (1996) argues for male involvement in programmes given the growing concern about HIV/AIDS and the unequal power that men and women wield in sexual relationships. In addition, some of my interviewees suggested that deployment of more male workers in the area of family planning might also help to engender the programme.[67]

My analysis of the interview data examined the underlying discourses in terms of the health department's shift to a strategy to involve males. Policy-makers offered explanations as to why male participation was a timely and relevant concept. A recurring theme that they alluded to was the discriminatory processes that have conventionally marked women's participation in the state's family planning programmes. Through male participation, the state strives to help women's representation be fair and equal with that of men. Some of the comments that reflected this view are given below:

---

[67] Conventionally at the PHC level the ANM is involved in family planning while the JPHN (Junior Public Health Nurse), who is the male counterpart of the ANM, engages in public health, such as ensuring appropriate sanitation practices are followed in houses, etc. The field research revealed comments among policy makers that JPHNs should also undertake family-welfare related work.

I#2: Then, more male involvement is also sought—in their sexual behaviour they (men) need to be more responsible. So also in family planning, there should be more male involvement. When the programmes first started, there were a lot of vasectomies—around 75 per cent were vasectomies. After 1975, tubectomies were done more. We get around 500-600 vasectomies in a year, of the total sterilisations. So we need more male involvement in that—rather than burden only women about these things.

I#1: In the target free and participatory planning approach, this has been emphasised. In the nine months of child bearing, women bear the brunt of all the discomfort. After that, in the lactating period, women bear the responsibility. *Without using that same woman for sterilisation again, but the benefits of population planning fall on women and men equally.* So men should accept vasectomy and other male sterilisation. As such, we are hoping to propagate this through the IEC. In the 1970s, vasectomy camps and PHC sterilisations were there. After that, there were institutional problems. Now with RCH, male sterilisation will be given more importance.

I#4: Now, even this question of making a gender bias in the case of family welfare operations was not inadvertent—it was deliberately done. Because it was found easier...to persuade the *decision-maker* in the family *to ensure that the woman gets sterilised than to make a man do it.* So the easier option was taken .... Now one of our targets is trying to persuade—increase male participation in family welfare measures.

I#3: Both men and women are (affected) and one has to look at that too. I mean involvement of men is extremely important. [After] years of working at field level and various levels, I think without men's involvement nothing can happen. So that is very important. We tend to focus just on women and forget men but we have to drag them into this too. Otherwise women are not going to go out or take decisions or they are not going to be given the kind of freedom they have. Its not only that, you know, the question of getting them vasectomised or using other contraceptive methods, its also giving support to the women and recognising their needs and giving women the freedom to make their own decisions which is not there.

The passages offer interesting insights into why the state has espoused a male involvement strategy. All the respondents above (they are all middle or senior-level officials or consultants to the government and both male and female) refer to a discriminatory attitude of the government that the state is now trying to rectify. Women have been targeted for every reproductive intervention of the state, largely because they are easier to persuade (Interview I#4). This had become more intense following "1975." The reference here is to the period of Emergency that was declared by the Indira Gandhi government from 1975–1977. Family planning excesses, especially forced vasectomies, were conducted during that period, mostly on young men. During the Emergency, compulsory sterilisation focused on men and the police force was used to round up young men for compulsory vasectomies. Ever since the government's actions became an international embarrassment, the Indian state has tried to highlight the family welfare programme as a voluntary one. The other side of this 'voluntariness' was, as the official I#4 points out, to take the easier option—i.e., "persuade" women to undergo sterilisations. Against this history, the RCH is posited as a reprieve from an ongoing legacy; through the state's efforts to increase male participation, parity and equality between the sexes will be established.

Another reason offered by the respondents why the state is embarking on a programme to ensure male participation is because without men's active involvement "nothing can happen" (Interview I#3). The state may educate and persuade women but unless men are convinced of the benefits of the programme, "women are not going to go out or take decisions" (Interview I#3). On the basis of the account of this respondent, we may infer that male involvement is another means to ensure male co-operation in the acceptance of family planning methods and family health strategies. The respondent goes on to clarify that male participation is advantageous not just directly (in that they can be vasectomised), but because male "support" is important to women, if they are to recognise their own needs or make their own reproductive decisions.

What do these ideologies of 'equality' propagated by the state imply for women? The notion of equality in feminist theory is an oft-debated issue. In the early years of the second wave of feminism, equality with men, viz., being offered the same privileges as men was the dominant interpretation of equality. The emphasis was on a formal notion of equality—same rights to vote, same status as citizens, and so on. However, recent writings have challenged this limited vision of equality because, it is argued, even though formal equality offers some protection from discrimination it fails to recognise the substantial disadvantages suffered by marginalised groups in society (MacKinnon 1989; Majury 1987; More 1993). The current debate is locked between an idea of equal treatment for men and women (a gender-neutrality of law where *sameness* between men and women are emphasised) and privileging unique rights for women (focusing on gender specific needs and *differences* from men). MacKinnon (1989) argues that a problem that has to be grappled with in this debate is that both sameness and difference of women are measured against a male-norm, and that the entire debate of equality is still trapped in a male-biased perspective. Yet, 'equality' has its relevance. As Majury (1987: 172) asserts, it is less important to define a universal framework of equality that can be applied in case of all issues; instead, she advances a practical-use perspective—that equality should be used as a strategy to rectify inequality. As she notes, "[e]quality is more effectively seen as a means that can be used to address the inequalities that women in our society experience." Feminists argue that formal equality should become the starting point for talking about rights—the plank from which law and policy can begin to offer opportunities for substantive change in the relations between men and women.

Yet, various groups tend to liberally use the concept of 'equality of women' while advocating interests that are likely to undermine the very efforts to help women gain an equal voice in society. The notion of equality is interpreted so that its progressive senses are usually substituted for narrow and more restricted meanings. Buss (1998), for instance, makes an interesting study of the use of the concept 'equality' by the Vatican during the United Nations' Fourth World Conference on Women held at Beijing (1995). She argues that the Vatican used the language of gender equality to promote conservative views on women's roles. For instance, equality was not equated with 'sameness with men'; such a connotation was rejected on grounds that it would taint the unique richness of femininity (Buss 1998: 347). It was easier to encourage an interpretation of equity for women, meaning 'similar' but not 'equal' rights. Some Islamic countries argued for granting women 'equitable' succession and inheritance rights—intended to mean 'not the same as men' (Buss 1998). Majury (1987:186) argues that the primary value of equality for women is the "forum it provides for the raising of issues and presenting of arguments on behalf of women." However, in many contexts, the notion of equality is the "packaging through which one attempts to sell a particular end result," and is used in many political and legal contexts because it is "highly marketable" (Majury 1987: 186).

A cursory reading of the RCH's offer of equality—"*but the benefits of population planning fall on women and men equally*" (Interview I#1 above) and "*both men and women are (affected) and one has to look at that too*" (Interview I#3 above)—shows that the idea of 'equality' is embedded within a framework of wanting to offer equal treatment to both sexes. What women have always experienced must be shared by men as well. The aim of the male involvement policy is driven by a desire to achieve 'sameness with women,' a reversal of the conventional feminist assertion. By making the role of men in the programme more visible, the state creates the illusion of addressing women's discriminatory position in the programme—'formal equality' has been attained. Nothing in the policy's aims seems to suggest any radical interpretation of equality; most importantly, it fails to refer to any aspect of the relationship between women and men, *or* between women and the state. For instance, the policy's reconciliation of past (and likely, present) discriminations against women is to target men, rather than address the unequal relationship that exists between women and the state. So also, equality as a notion that involves men and women is referred to in the context of sharing of the impact and benefits of population planning. The discourse of male participation positions men and women as partners in a common purpose—the pre-existing relationships between the two are not the concern here. It would appear that the state is trying to emphasise *equality of* the sexes rather than *equality between* the sexes. The former interpretation limits the conceptualisation of women's unequal status in reproductive health as a programmatic mal-design; the RCH is, then, positioned as a policy that has rectified this anomaly. The deeper layers of social processes that contribute to women's reproductive and sexual subordination are effectively left unquestioned, and are not factored into the notion of joint responsibility. Increasing the number of male vasectomies may bring a statistical parity between men and women, but in the long run, has little impact on women's position of inequality. And, as I argue in the next sub-section, this has ramifications for the way the notion of 'gender' itself is treated and depoliticised.

'Engendering' as 'Sex-Neutral' rather than as 'Sex-Specific'

A fourth dominant theme that emerged from the policy related to the construction and development of the idea of gender. The concept of 'gender' has been used in development literature over the last decade or so to draw attention to the socially constructed roles that have been assigned to men and women and their implications for social, economic and political life (Moser 1993; Kabeer 1994; Rathgeber 1990; Razavi and Miller 1995). The turn towards the concept of gender was based on the recognition that gender roles and prescribed social relations have a significant influence on the outcome of developmental efforts; in short, the 'gender' lens offered a dynamic analytical tool for women's development. The adoption of 'gender' in the development community has had mixed responses. There is, on the one hand, appreciation for the depth of understanding that accompanies an evaluation of gender relations. As Rathgeber (1990) says, "[a] gender and development perspective does not lead only to the design of intervention and affirmative action strategies to ensure that women are better integrated into ongoing developmental efforts. It leads, inevitably, to a fundamental re-examination of social structures and institutions and, ultimately, to the loss of power of entrenched elites, which will affect some women as well as men" (p. 495). On the other hand, the 'ab/use' of the notion of gender has also drawn criticism from scholars. Feminist critics have expressed reservation about the tendency in recent years for official development agencies to overwhelmingly adopt the use of the term 'gender' instead of 'woman' (Baden and Goetz

1997; Buss 1998). The main problem with this tendency to substitute one for the other is the danger that a notion that is inclusive of men could gradually edge out the interests of women. As Baden and Goetz (1997: 6) point out, "...the focus on gender, rather than women, had become counter-productive in that it had allowed the discussion to shift from a focus on women, to women and men and, finally, back to men." The engendering of development could, it seems, have either empowering or depoliticising consequences for women.

In the text of the RCH policy, 'gender,' by and large, tends to be used as a synonym for women. For instance, gender sensitivity was defined as being responsive to women's needs (goi.nd), and programmes designed to address gender issues largely consisted of issues around women's empowerment (gok.obp.12). My exploration of the gender dynamics espoused in the policy does not aim to analyse the use or context in which the term gender is used. I focus instead on the process by which the state re-writes its commitment to 'women' as a social category as it embraces the gender dimension of reproductive health. I argue that the language of equality between men and women, viz., gender equality, in the RCH has evolved into arguments for neutralising sex-specific concerns.

My interview responses showed a clear tendency among the participants to acknowledge that the RCH was an 'engendered' policy instrument. Respondents were quick to point out that the RCH, and reproductive health itself, was not the exclusive claim of women alone. For instance, a senior official highlighted that: "...[s]ee, reproductive rights [are] not for the females, but the males, too, isn't it?" (Interview I#6). Similarly, a consultant for the Government of India pointed out to me, "Why do you say only women?—RCH is for men too" (Interview I#3).[68] Both the respondents are making a valid argument here; without doubt, both men and women have the right to reproductive well-being. Consistent with the argument made in favour of equality above, the government strives to open up women's unique role in reproduction to males; recognising the gender dimension of

[68] Similar calls to attend to men's rights and women's responsibilities have come from women scholars as well. See Basu (1996).

reproductive health, to the state, means nullifying the sex-specific claims to reproduction and homogenising the experiences of men and women as reproductive beings within society. The officials are, in effect, positioning themselves within a liberal framework that advocates that all human beings have rights to freedom, regardless of sex. However, the move to equate men and women under the same umbrella is not necessarily that simple, or even desirable. The social context that has led to the consciousness for the need to have a right to reproductive health has historically been different for women and men. To assert that reproductive health (and the whole gamut of relations around it) as a right holds the same implications for women and men undermines this history of women's subordination. By according equal roles to women and men in the policy, and in the reproductive process generally, these officials are not legitimising male reproductive freedoms; they are *de-legitimising* female rights to claims for special privileges within the RCH.[69] The attempt to 'engender' the policy, in effect, de-genders reproductive rights. This was affirmed by other comments that were made by officials. For instance, I#6 (above) in a later part of the interview responded to my question:

> When you say "felt needs", are you talking about "felt needs" of women or "felt needs" of couples or…
>
> I#6: "felt needs" of the woman or … the individual. The individual.

From a claim that both women and men had a right to reproductive health, the discourse has moved to substitute the individual for woman. The concept of gender is gradually being abstracted to the general, unsexed 'individual' within society. Feminists have often pointed to discriminatory connotations for women of generalised concepts like 'citizen' and 'individual' that form the foundations for liberalism (see Fraser and Gordon 1994a, 1994b; Pateman 1988; Young 1990), arguing that the history of any society is organised around dissimilar positions for men

[69] Young (1990), for instance, argues *against* a notion of universal citizenship, and contends that the concept of equality in citizenship can, in some cases, be achieved only by according special rights to certain groups in society. Maternal benefits for women would be a case in point.

and women. The term 'individual', or 'citizen' (or even, the idealised 'client' in the neo-liberal market place) privileges a masculinist perspective and orders social organisation around a male subject. The adoption of the general subject thus only effaces the notion that there is discrimination, rather than the discrimination itself.

In the context of reproduction in India (and Kerala), there is a further ramification of introducing the generalised (male) subject within the discourse of gender. The 'individual' has always been entrenched within the community that 'he' comes from, usually a rural context. This is a tension within the policy; on the one hand, the policy discourse refers to the client as an isolated individual whose freedoms, choices, decisions, and rights are her/his own, insulated from the social context which s/he inhabits. On the other hand, the policy also repeatedly positions the individual as part of the community, so that the individual no longer has needs-claims outside of her/his community context. The state interacts essentially with the 'community', where individual interests are represented through locally elected representatives at the panchayat level. Some instances of this latter positioning of individuals are given below:

> I#11: Now, first they (the ANMs) have to go and make contact with them (the community). Contact means find out their needs. Go to each place and understand. Now there is more community participation
> I#7: ... through this participatory planning approach [with] more community involved ...

Clearly, the community and the community's voice is also a central facet of the definition of individual needs. In my analysis, I found that the shift from '*women's*' reproductive issues to '*men as well*' to '*the individual*' had one more ominous step—with the individual becoming discursively merged with the community, the distinct identity of women and their needs was being replaced by community needs. My conversation with a middle-level official in the DFW is particularly revealing in this regard. The official was telling me about the advantages of the RCH where community participation was emphasised. At that point, I asked:

> Will the Panchayat members [community leaders] ask women what their needs are?
>
> I#13: No, all the representatives will sit together and take decisions. For example, it may be that the hospital is far away. So their need may be that there should be a sub-centre where there is a high population—so that will be their need ... it is not necessarily that a hospital should be built everywhere having speciality care. It may be prevention of water-borne diseases. In Allepey, it is water contamination. So that is their need. Safe water is their need.

A key point from the passage is the shift in the way that reproductive health needs are subsumed into larger developmental needs—"safe water is their need" or a "sub-centre is their need". Reproductive health is no longer exclusively a discussion of women's reproductive or sexual needs—instead, it now encompasses community needs. It is ironic that the reproductive health movement, which began as a reaction to the neglect of women's bodies, has been subverted away from women's needs totally. Yet, such subversion is likely to find support in some contexts in developing countries where the definition of women's needs has been an issue of debate amongst feminists. Many Third World feminists resent the strong implication of individualism present in the use of the term 'reproductive rights' as used by First World feminism. Lingam (1995) points out that "... women not only want to make an informed 'choice' about contraceptives ... but also want control over their life situation, sustenance, safe work place, clean drinking water, sanitation, secure living space, harmonious gender relations, no violence, and no abuse." Although these are valid arguments especially in contexts of poverty, the state can employ the community's claims for development needs as a way of detracting from women's centrality within a reproductive policy.

The gradual process of abstraction away from women's reproductive health was evident in comments made by a senior policy-maker about the need for similar approaches (as the RCH) in general health as well. His comment was that:

I#4: As I told you, RCH is providing an opportunity for doing this *in reproductive health*. We are looking for other options so that we are able to have this quality provision *in all our health services* ...

According to this bureaucrat, the context of reproductive health can be replicated in areas of general health, because ultimately the lesson to be taken from the RCH is about quality provision of health services. The RCH and reproductive health become merely "an opportunity"—no different from cardiology, public health, or curative medicine, thereby, trivialising the social context of struggles around reproduction. The officials echo the sentiments of several writers on gender issues who with the aim to provide a holistic view of women's health associate women's reproductive concerns with a host of other social-economic conditions. Rishyasringa (2000: 440), for instance, sums up this perspective when she states that "reproductive health and rights are not issues that can be solved within the confines of population and health policies ... reproductive health and choices are fundamentally linked to opportunities for employment and income, control over productive assets and skills, and access to public goods and services." The primary danger in reducing the significance of the RCH to an improved form of health and economic service provision is that the importance of reproductive rights to women is obliterated. The process of gendering reproductive policy can become a euphemism for edging women's specific interests out of the agenda of development policy.

Gender Sensitivity, Women and Gendered Policy: A Discussion

Let me summarise the essence of the gender themes that I examined above. The analysis demonstrated the prominent ideologies that frame the RCH policy's perspective of gender, and especially, women, namely: (a) the policy strives to homogenise men and women in terms of reproductive experiences, (b) the policy promotes a conception of gender that is abstracted from embodied woman and generalised as an individual who is the member of a community, and (c) when women are referred to as a separate category, it is usually in instrumental terms, with reference to their usefulness. The analysis showed that the gender ideologies found in the RCH constitute a particular rhetoric about gender, women and their needs; the state's interpretation of gender is located within a discourse of homogeneity.[70] The discourse of gender homogeneity is dual: first, women are equated with men, and second, women are subsumed within the social and cultural context in which they live. Even when the policy recognises women's unique role as a mother, it is a process of negation of an individual identity outside of society.

The discourses around gender are important in our understanding of what the state adjudges as acting in the 'interests' of women. Feminist political theory has swayed towards a conception of women's interests that is socially contingent and reflects the multiple positions that women occupy in society, both in a material and discursive sense (Pringle and Watson 1992, 1996; Mouffe 1995). The emphasis on the different interests arising out of differential location in society is also fundamental to theorisations of women and development (Marchand and Parpart 1995). The recognition of the different social positions for need articulation supports an analysis of 'gender' in that it questions the validity of an abstracted, individualised notion of woman out of her social settings (and which resonates with the idealised notion of the Woman in western liberal feminism). Koczberski (1998), for instance, asserts that women in developmental societies cannot be compartmentalised, and must be seen as part of a larger, interactive socio-economic context. To quote her,

> [w]omen's work activities, their access to resources and their needs are not isolated fragments, rather they are intricately embedded within the communities in which they live. To ignore these linkages predisposes simplistic and unrealistic analyses and constructs images far removed from reality (p. 404).

Arguably, one can point out that what the analysis above has picked up as the varying roles of women are precisely what

---

[70] The homogeneity that is referred to here is between men and women. However, this process of discursive homogeneity can include obliterating the differences among women as well.

post-structuralists propose regarding the multiplicity of women's social locations, as citizen, mother, and members of community. And it is in each of these roles that 'women's needs' must be realised. However, what the analysis points out is (and this is where discourse converges into ideology) that in separating out women's different roles, the RCH applies a homogenising discourse so that the loss of women's specificity is accompanied by a 'scaling down' or sometimes 'scaling out' of women from the debates on needs construction. The themes from neo-liberal/neo-Malthusian development instead frame the gender agenda. In a postcolonial analysis of the Indian family welfare programme's propaganda materials, Chatterjee and Riley (2001) critique the consistency in obliterating any sense of individual agency for women in the programme. They note that although the programme exhorts Indian women to take responsibility for fertility reduction, they are not expected to become modern like other women in the world, particularly the paradigmatic "other" (in this case the 'Western' woman who represents self-seeking autonomy and untrammelled sexuality). An individual identity for women is played down, they note, in favour of "family values," which in reality reflect patriarchal interests (Chatterjee and Riley 2001: 831).

The production of a homogeneous conception of gender in the texts and practices of the RCH emphasises that women's reproductive needs are determined by their social roles and conditions. Implicitly, the state promotes the idea that women may have more in common with men (and their society, in general) than with a feminist ideal of universal sisterhood. As far as the state is concerned, there is no woman outside of certain prescribed developmental roles—as mother, as wife, and as community member—and, therefore, there is little need to provide a discursive space for women's reproductive interests in abstraction. To do so could, in fact, be antithetical to the state-defined norms of gender-sensitivity. The gender discourses in the RCH, therefore, destabilise 'women's' interests from the centre of the reproduction process. What happens is that women cannot be extricated from the needs and expectations of social institutions—women and women's needs in exclusion of their social settings are constructed as inimical to the purposes of the exercise of their reproductive rights. In effect, for the state to *engender* policy, the notion of 'woman' must be effaced.

A difficulty in critiquing the idea of 'gender' rather than 'woman' is that gender is seen to reflect a 'realistic' picture of the Third World woman. Through the 1980s and 1990s, Third World feminists resisted the valuation of cultural practices in developing contexts using the norms of the West (Mohanty 1991; Lazreg 1990). These arguments are forceful and reflect the tension in the literature on women in developing contexts between critiques of a universalistic conception of women's rights and a culturally-embedded perspective of women's needs. Increasingly, therefore, there is a move to define women's rights from within a framework of social appropriateness (e.g., Bunting 1993), that is, it should specify "gender, class, cultural, and other differences and recognise social needs" (Correa and Petchesky 1994: 107).

On the other hand, other feminist theorists have retained the value of a universalistic-based notion of rights as more effective for a politics of women's advancement (Schneider 1991; Nussbaum 1995). Schech (1998), for instance, describes instances in WID policy implementation where women were marginalised for the sake of cultural sensitivity, and points to the need for a cohesive sense of women's collective interests. Keyser (1995) makes an argument for focusing on the similarities of women's reproductive needs. She argues that:

> Despite differences in conditions, views, and power, women share an interest in sexuality and reproduction. Sexuality and reproduction are matters of life and death, of the highest fulfilment and of deep suffering, of passion and of cool calculation, of intimacy and of public policy-making.... [W] omen's decision-making in sexuality and reproduction becomes a matter of balancing personal desires and needs against socially, economically, politically defined norms and regulations which in today's world are hierarchical, patriarchal and exploitative, and not geared to people's well-being (p. v).

As Keyser notes, the ability to "balance" personal desires and needs against the norms of society (which are inherently patriarchal) is crucial to an interpretation of gender-sensitivity. The notion of autonomy must be factored into an argument for 'culturally-sensitive' interpretation of gender needs (Gaspers 1996). As Gaspers argues, " [b]asic rights include the requirements of autonomy of agency, not least the capacity and confidence to decide and act" (Gaspers 1996: 655). The requirement of an autonomous choice need not entail an atomistic self-focused individualism (Gaspers 1996: 654), but would allow women the ability to negotiate their reproductive needs within the decision-making process, including the ability to reject the choices that they are offered. A gender-sensitive perspective must allow for women to express their autonomy even within a patriarchal cultural context.

The notion of such an autonomy has been articulated within the debate of culturally-sensitive reproductive rights dominantly as the right to experience sexual pleasure. Petchesky (1998:7) reviews some feminists' concerns that there has been greater focus not on rights but on reproduction, which may reinforce ideological bias that reduces women to one aspect of their being and marginalises others, especially (non-procreative) sexuality. At a regional meeting of HealthWatch, a medical practitioner from Kerala associated with the women's movement, noted that reproductive rights should not only mean the right to have a child but should include the right to sexual pleasure (HealthWatch 1996). Sexual pleasure is but one manifestation of women's autonomous voices—the possibilities for women to express others can arise only in a discursive regime that permits the construction of women as having an interest in their reproductive well-being, outside of their roles as mothers or fertility controllers of the state.

The discourse of gender in the RCH is clearly located in the broader debate on the need to appraise gender-sensitivity from within the context of the social setting. The point to consider is if this interpretive frame is likely to advance the reproductive interests of women.

My own interviews indicated that women did seek to express an identity independent of their roles as mothers. An auxiliary nurse midwife told me that women in her 'beat' were unwilling to undergo laparoscopic tubectomoy unless they had enough information about the complications associated with the operation. The women were also anxious to recover after the operation and requested tonics and tablets to recover. These instances, I would argue, are indicative that women do have an awareness of their bodies, and a desire to do what is best for themselves. In some of my interviews with women, they expressed a keen interest in improving the interactive relationship between provider and user, especially when it came to providing information regarding contraceptives and their effects on women's bodies. One young mother told me that she was afraid of using any contraceptive other than a condom because she was afraid that it would adversely affect her health and body. She was willing to attend any class or educational programme that permitted an opportunity to obtain information about these matters. Women's consciousness of their bodies in these instances is important because (as the illustrations above show) it is an articulation of interest that is contrary to what is suggested as normalising contraceptive behaviour advocated by the state.

In sum, there are specific issues to be concerned about in advancing a 'gendered' perspective of women's needs. It is imperative to ensure that the notion of gender is not used exclusively to the state's advantage, that is, in providing for contextually relevant needs, the state is liable to focus on practical needs and ignore the issue of strategic needs (Moser 1991). Universalistic assumptions underlying women's (and human) rights can, therefore, be undermined. This analysis seeks not to marginalise debates on social rights, but rather emphasise that we should be conscious of ideologies that frame certain contexts, whether they support women's ability to negotiate their needs even when contrary to the dominant discourse. As Schech (1998: 389) so rightly points out, "a space between opposing universalist and relativist claims" can be identified. She demonstrates in the context of Australian Aid projects that the significant point to examine is who or what is being excluded when the notions of 'universality' or 'culturally appropriate' frames of reference for identifying needs are invoked.

The analysis of the RCH, thus far, seems to indicate it does not offer a broad enough berth to debate women's reproductive autonomy outside of the norms of acceptable behaviour that the state itself defines. The discourse of gender in the RCH supports the broader rhetoric of the market, and the statist discourse on development which, in fact, are crucial to the definition of 'socially contingent' gender needs. Policy makers working within the RCH policy, in particular, envisage that a market paradigm is likely to further women's interests. Comments by officials indicate that notions of gender-sensitivity are closely intertwined with the values of consumerism. Quality services, the ability to 'choose' specific contraceptive methods, and pleasing service interactions with providers are the primary criteria of gender-sensitivity. However, the market is embedded in a masculinist discourse and does not emphasise the ideology of equity and social transformation that should ground any gender-sensitive policy. The concluding line to MacKinnon's quote that began this chapter is particularly relevant here—"[t]he pursuit of the truth of women's reality is the process of consciousness; the life situation of consciousness, its determination articulated in the minutiae of everyday existence, is what feminist consciousness seeks to be conscious of" (MacKinnon 1989: 39). As long as a gender-sensitive policy does not seek to foster this consciousness, women's interests will continue to be marginalised.

Conclusion

This chapter has analysed specific ideologies around gender that have emerged from the text of the RCH. Four dominant ideological themes were abstracted; women's instrumentality as mothers and objects of development goals, erasure of women's needs as a distinct category, and the interpretation of equality for men and women in reproductive health matters. A key finding is that these ideological considerations seemed contrary to the enormous efforts of the state to ensure gender-sensitivity in the RCH. The results raise questions regarding what constitutes gender-sensitivity in development policy, and suggests that deeper layers of ideological bias can thwart the best drawn-up gender policy. The next chapter analyses the implications of these subtle constructions of gender on aspects of women's empowerment and rights.

References

Baden, S. and Goetz, A. (1997) "Who Needs [Sex] when you can have [Gender]?": Conflicting Discourses on Gender at Beijing", *Feminist Review*, No. 56, Summer, pp. 3–25.

Bang, A. and Bang, R. (1989) "WCH rather than MCH", *Lancet*, Vol. 2, No. 8672, Nov. 11, p. 1158.

Basu, A. M. (1996) "ICPD: What about men's rights and women's responsibilities?" *Health Transition Review*, No. 6, pp. 95–99.

Beall, J. (1997) "In sickness and in health: Gender issues in Health Policy and their implications for development in the 1990s" in I. Baud and I. Smyth (eds) *Searching for security: Women's responses to Economic Transformation*, Routledge: London and New York, pp. 67– 95.

Boserup, E. (1970) *Women's Role in Economic Development*, George and Allen: London.

Bunting, A. (1993) "Theorizing Women's Cultural Diversity in Feminist International Human Rights Strategies", *Journal of Law and Society*, Special Issue, Vol. 20, No. 1, pp. 6–22.

Buss, D. E. (1998) "Robes, Relics and Rights: The Vatican and the Beijing Conference on Women", *Social and Legal Studies*, Vol. 7, No. 3, September, pp. 339–364.

Chatterjee, M. (1996) "Addressing Gender and Poverty Concerns in a Reproductive Health Program", in A. R. Measham and R. A. Heaver (eds) *Supplement to India's Family Welfare Program: Moving to a Reproductive and Child Health Approach*, The World Bank: Washington, pp. 30–45.

Chatterjee, N. and Riley, N. (2001)"Planning in Indian Modernity: The Gendered Politics of Fertility Control" *Signs: Journal of Women in Culture and Society*, vol 26, no. 3, pp. 811–845

Correa, S. and Petchesky, R. (1994) "Reproductive and Sexual Rights: A feminist perspective", in G. Sen, A. Germaine and L. C. Chen (eds) *Population Policies Reconsidered: Health, Empowerment, and Rights*, Harvard Centre for Population and Development, Cambridge, MA, pp. 107–123

Dixon-Mueller, R. (1993) *Population Policy and Women's Rights: Transforming Reproductive Choice,* Praeger: Westport, Connecticut and London.

Freedman, L. and Isaacs, S. (1993) "Human Rights and Reproductive Choice" *Studies in Family Planning*, Vol. 24, No. 1, Jan/Feb., pp. 18–30.

Fraser, N. and Gordon, L. (1994a) "Civil Citizenship against Social Citizenship? On the ideology of Contract versus Charity" in

B. Steenbergen (ed.), *The Condition of Citizenship*, Sage Publications: London, pp. 90–107.

Fraser, N. and Gordon, L. (1994b) "Reclaiming Social Citizenship: Beyond the Ideology of Contract versus Charity" in P. James (ed.) *Critical Politics: From the Personal to the Global*, Arena Publications and Department of Politics, Monash University: Melbourne, pp. 59–75.

Gaspers, D. (1996) "Culture and Development Ethics: Needs, Women's Rights, and Western Theories" *Development and Change*, Vol. 27, pp. 627–661.

Hawkesworth, M. (1997) "Confounding Gender", *Signs*, Volume 22, No. 3, Spring, pp. 649–685.

HealthWatch (1996) *Proceedings of Regional Consultations: Kerala, Pondicherry and Tamil Nadu*, Chennai, October 3–5.

Jackson, C. (1996) "Rescuing gender from the poverty trap", *World Development*, Vol. 25, No. 3, pp. 489– 504.

Kabeer, N. (1994) *Reversed Realities*, Verso: London.

Keyser, L. (1995) "Sexual and Reproductive Rights instead of a Bio-Medical Fix" in *Women's Global Network for Reproductive Rights (WGNRR) newsletter*, No. 50, April–June 1995, pp. iv– viii.

Koczberski, G. (1998) "Women in development: a critical analysis", *Third World Quarterly*, Volume 19, No. 3, pp. 395–409.

Kurian, P. (2000) *Engendering the Environment? Gender in the World Bank's Environmental Policies*, Ashgate Publications: Aldershot, UK.

Lingam, L. (1995) "Reproductive Rights and More", *Radical Journal of Health*, Vol. 1, No. 2, April–June, pp. 136–144. url at http://www.hsph.harvard.edu/Organisations/healthnet/SAsia/suchana/0105/lingam.html (accessed 30.6.2005)

Lazreg, M. (1990) "Feminism and Difference: The Perils of Writing as a Woman on Women in Algeria" in M. Hirsch and E. F. Keller (eds) *Conflicts in Feminism*, Routledge: New York, pp. 326–348.

Mackinnon, C. (1989) *Towards a Feminist Theory of the State*, Harvard University Press : Cambridge, MA.

Marchand, M.H. and Parpart, J.L. (1995) *Feminist, Postmodernism, Development*, Routledge: London and New York.

Majury, D. (1987) "Strategizing in Equality", *Wisconsin Women's Law Journal*, Vol. 3, No. 147, pp. 169–188.,

Mohanty, C. T. (1991) "Under Western Eyes: Feminist Scholarship and Colonial Discourses" in C. Mohanty, A. Russo and L. Torres (eds) *Third World Women and the Politics of Feminism*, Indiana University Press : Bloomington, pp. 51 –79.

More, G. C. (1993) ""Equal Treatment" of the Sexes in European Community Law: What does "Equal" Mean?" *Feminist Legal Studies*, Vol. 1, Nos. 1–2, pp. 45–74.

Moser, C.O.N. (1991) "Gender Planning in the Third World: Meeting Practical and Strategic Needs" in R. Grant and K. Newland (eds) *Gender and International Relations*, Suffolk: Open University, Milton Keynes, pp. 83–122.

Nicholson, L. (1994) "Interpreting Gender", *Signs*, Volume 20, No. 1, Autumn, pp. 79–105.

Nussbaum, M. (1995) "Introduction" in M. Nussbaum and J. Glover (eds) *Women, Culture and Development*, Oxford University Press: Oxford.

Pateman, C. (1988) *The Sexual Contract* , Stanford University Press: Stanford, California.

Petchesky, R. (1998) "Introduction" in R. P. Petchesky and K. Judd (eds) *Negotiating Reproductive Rights: Women's Perspectives Across Countries*, Zed Books: London, pp. 1–30.

Pringle, R. and Watson, S. (1992) "'Women's Interests' and the Post-Structuralist State", in M. Barrett and A. Phillips (eds), *Destabilizing Theory: Contemporary Feminist Debates*, Polity Press: Cambridge, pp. 53–73.

Pringle, R. and Watson, S. (1996) "Feminist Theory and the State: Needs, Rights and Interests" in B. Sullivan and G. Whitehouse (eds) *Gender, Politics and Citizenship in the 1990s*, University of New South Wales Press: Australia, pp. 64–80.

Rai, S. (2003) *Mainstreaming Gender, Democratizing the State?: National Machineries for the Advancement of Women*, Manchester University Press: Manchester.

Raju, S. (1999) "Men as Supportive Partners in Reproductive Health: NGOs Pave the Way" in S. Pachauri (ed.) *Implementing a Reproductive Health Agenda in India: The Beginning*, Population Council: New Delhi, pp. 313–334.

Rathgeber, E.M. (1990) "WID, WAD, GAD: Trends in Research and Practice", *The Journal of Developing Areas*, Vol. 24, pp. 489–502.

Razavi, S. and Miller, C. (1995) *From WID to GAD: Conceptual Shifts in the Women and Development Discourse*, Occasional Paper No. 1, UNRISD: Geneva.

Rishyasringa, B. (2000) "Social Policy and Reproductive Health" in R. Ramasubban and S. J. Jejeebhoy (eds) Women's Reproductive Health in India, Rawat Publishers: New Delhi, pp. 418–445.

Schneider, E. (1991) "The Dialectic of Rights and Politics: Perspectives from the Women's Movement [1986]" in K. T. Bartlett and R. Kennedy (eds) *Feminist Legal Theory: Readings in Law and Gender*, Westview Press: Boulder, Colorado, pp. 318–322.

Schech, S. (1998) "Between tradition and post-coloniality: the location of AusAID's gender and development policy" *Australian Geographer*, Vol. 29, pp. 615–629.

Young, I.M. (1990) "Polity and Group Difference: A Critique of the Idea of Universal Citizenship" in C. R. Sunstein (ed.) *Feminism and Political Theory*, The University of Chicago Press: Chicago and London, pp. 117–139.

7

LOST IN TRANSLATION?

Ideology and Co-option in the Reproductive and Child Health Programme

> Twelve voices were shouting in anger, and they were all alike. No question, now, what had happened to the faces of the pigs. The creatures outside looked from pig to man, and from man to pig, and, from pig to man again: but already it was impossible to say which was which.
>
> George Orwell, *Animal Farm*, 1986, p. 95.

A salient point that emerges from the previous analyses is that the specific discursive influences identified in the previous chapters—of the market and of gender—inform the 'paradigm shift' towards reproductive health. The former increasingly commodifies the subject-position of the user of the state's health services, while employing the discourse of democratisation of citizenship. The ideologies of gender encourage a conceptualisation of gender that, by negating the specificity of women's diverse needs, play right into the broader priorities of state development. As a policy of the GoI, therefore, the RCH is not a direct translation of the ICPD's resolutions for population policy. The Indian reproductive health policy is the outcome of the active negotiations between competing globally and locally produced discourses and, drawing on Fraser's model elucidated in Chapter 2, is an 'interpreted' discourse.

In this chapter, I explore how these ideologies influence the way the policy is interpreted by those who practice it on an everyday basis: in their understanding, what forms the priorities and the limits of the ICPD principles? It is here that the new ideology is blended with institutional ideologies of old, where competitive discourses (of neo-liberalism and reproductive health) meet, support, merge, conflict, reflect, or produce new hybrids of ideology. These processes are reflected in individual responses as they grapple to rationalise or provide consistency to their thoughts. Although at some level their ideologies can come from personal viewpoints, it is most likely to reflect an institutional standpoint. The significant issue is if such re-interpretations eventually increase the chasm between the norms set in place for a reproductive policy at the ICPD[71] and the reality of practice in local contexts. Is the process of policy interpretation simultaneously also a process of discourse co-optation?

The analysis in this chapter has been informed by Fraser's model (see Chapter 2)—that the state's inherent ideologies will be used to interpret the rhetoric of the oppositional discourses. I have already elaborated the ideologies of the market and gender that form a dominant discursive framework for the GoI. This chapter will examine the implications of these ideologies for reproductive health as a gender discourse, and ultimately, as a political discourse. The chapter aims to demonstrate the way in which feminist and mainstream discourses are woven together creating a newer form of discourse. This is done through (a) a textual analysis of a selected piece of text from the RCH and (b) through the analysis of three keywords associated with the production of a feminist discourse of reproductive health that were widely used at the ICPD—empowerment, rights, and choices—as interpreted in the RCH documents and by policy-makers.

---

[71] This is not to suggest that the international norms for a reproductive health policy are a 'pure' discourse that address a woman's perspective absolutely. Even though the ICPD resolutions have themselves been actively negotiated (often through acrimonious debate), the emphasis of the Conference on addressing gender inequality, nonetheless, provides a firm base for promoting women's reproductive interests (see Presser 1997). For a critique of the ICPD, see Copelon and Petchesky (1995) and Petchesky (1995).

The Market as an Interpretive Framework for Reproductive Health

The discourse of the market has pervaded the construction of the user of the family welfare services as a client of the health system (see Chapter 6). Here, I look at some of the institutional outcomes—immediate and potential—of adopting market criteria. I show that in the case of the Family Welfare Services in India, the trappings of the market ideology have been central to the kinds of interventions that the state has chosen to make (or not)—some of which may positively affect users and others which may not.

A significant outcome of the integration of the discourse of market with reproductive health that emerged from my analysis is that there is a perceptible shift by the state to situate its operational efforts within a 'management' driven paradigm. The state's reproductive health policy increasingly blends the discourses of development with that of management, so that it re-writes its own and the 'client's' obligations, expectations, rights and duties within the framework of management. It is interesting to follow how the state's policy simultaneously articulates the discourses of management with efforts to improve the developmental status of the socially disadvantaged. To emphasise this point, I employed a 'structural' approach to my qualitative analysis.[72] I selected an extract from document goi.oc.3, as it is easier to work with a smaller piece of text in such analyses. The excerpt was chosen because it stated the rationale for the implementation for the RCH; in the words of the document, it provides a "description of the proposal/scheme and its objectives." I reduced the selected text by categorising sentences and parts of sentences into one of three predominant thematic discourses:

---

[72] I use the term 'structural approach' drawing on Silverman (1993). Silverman uses a structural analysis to analyse a text from within the reality of the authors of the text, rather than critiquing it using an alternative version of reality. Silverman uses simple techniques of counting, classifying and sorting to identify the ideological positions taken by authors of text. Note that this technique is not the same as the one that has been dominantly employed as part of the qualitative (theme) analysis in this book .

management discourses, development discourses, and feminist discourses. Examples of the three kinds of discourses are given in Table 7.1.

Management discourses were identified by the use of key words belonging to the discipline of management like 'integrate,' 'facilitate,' and 'optimise,' all used to describe desirable outcomes in the programme.[73] Further, sentences that referred to organisational and systemic modifications were also sorted as belonging to a management discourse. Feminist rhetoric included statements that were gender-sensitive; as shown in Table 7.1, the definition of reproductive health used in the RCH policy came

Table 7.1 Examples of Feminist, Management and Development Themes

Theme/Discourse	Examples
Feminist	• ...the basis of the RCH has been defined as "people have the ability to reproduce and regulate their fertility... • women are able to go through pregnancy and childbirth safely... • the outcome of pregnancies is successful in terms of maternal and infant survival and well-being... • couples are able to have sexual relations free of fear and pregnancy, and of contracting diseases...
Management	• integrated implementation would optimise outcomes at the field level
Development	• ...health of women in the reproductive age groups and of small children...is of crucial importance for effectively tackling the problem of growth of population...

[73] These terms may be used in all disciplines without any overt resemblance to the functional meanings of management. However, my analysis will show that, in context (in the RCH), there is a strong indication that the interpretations of the meanings (and desired programmatic effect) are from a management perspective.

from within the World Bank, but reflects the discourse of reproductive empowerment produced within the women's health movement. Development discourses reflected issues of health and social development, drawing on theorisations widely accepted within the discipline of development. In the example above, the sentence draws on the evidentiary link between perceived survival of child and fertility levels.

Once I had classified statements as belonging to one or the other discourse, I examined the data for two specific trends. The first was to see which discourse was most frequently repeated and, the second, to examine the purpose for which each discourse was being used. Using a simple count, it was clear that terms relating to the management discourse were most often repeated in the text. Some of the uses in which the management discourse emerged are as shown in Table 7.2.

The word 'integration' and its variants appear around eight times in the text, and 'efficiency/effective' around five times. However, it is in the way that the management discourse was deployed that was particularly significant. I found that each of the discourses had a distinct role to play in the text. The development discourse was presented to establish concerns and social problems, and the management discourse was used simultaneously as the cause for these social problems, as well as solutions to these developmental problems. The feminist discourse was sandwiched in between these two other discourses to assert a gender perspective. But the feminist discourse too was used primarily to support the management theme as a solution for development problems.

Some examples of how these Cause-Effect relationships were supported are given in Table 7.3.

The conjunctions 'lead to', 'is a prerequisite', and 'aimed at' link the management discourses with development problems. By merging the discourses of management and development, there was the tendency for the policy to promote management solutions for development problems—an "integrated approach", for instance, would improve the "health status of young women and children" (see Table 7.3). As in the case of other arguments made in this book , the need for the improvement of institutional

Table 7.2 *Samples of management discourses*

Sample of text	Line No.
• *separate identity* causing problems	*(ln.15)*
• (problems in) *effective management* reducing outcomes	*(ln.16)*
• programmes were i*ntegrated* under CSSM	*(ln.17)*
• process of *integration* was taken a step further (at Cairo)	*(ln.20)*
• participant countries should implement *unified* programmes for RCH	*(ln.23)*
• an integrated approach to programmes	*(ln.29)*
• integrated RCH programme	*(ln.31)*
• reducing costs of inputs	*(ln.31)*
• overlapping of expenditure would no longer be necessary	*(ln.32)*
• integrated implementation	*(ln.33)*
• optimise outcomes	*(ln.33)*
• (RCH programme conducted) within a framework of such integrated approach	*(ln.38)*
• (the proposal) integrates all the related programmes	*(ln.39)*
• an efficient arrangement	*(ln.42)*
• effectively tackling (population growth)	*(ln.43)*
• Deficiencies in arrangements	*(ln.44)*
• Effective RCH is crucially important	*(ln.48)*
• (RCH) intends to attain integration	*(ln.54)*

Table 7.3 *Linking Development and Management Discourses*

- Deficiencies in the arrangements for mother and child health care *lead to* higher incidence of maternal mortality…
- An efficient arrangement for implementing RCH programme *is a prerequisite* for tackling the problem of population growth…
- an integrated approach to the programmes *[is] aimed at improving* the health status of young women and children…

facilities *per se* is not being contested in this analysis. What I attempt to point out is that the management perspective overshadows the *causes* of developmental problems. Thus, it need not necessarily be deficiencies in the institutional arrangements alone that lead to maternal mortality, but, as Sen (1990) suggested, the ineffective entitlements that women are given in society that make it impossible to access these facilities. The broader developmental context in which poverty, unemployment and unequal social relations are crucial factors of health conditions is effectively superseded by managerial and organisational modifications.

In emphasising managerial outcomes, the state emphasises that the client's (by virtue of being a consumer in the market place) prime expectation from the health care system is that of *quality*, i.e., effective and efficient services. To quote one bureaucrat in the Ministry: "...quality service... means we have to give the quality service...technology and *modern line of management*" (Interview I#6). The "modern line of management", pointed out by the official, was associated with the idea of efficiency. As a Government of India document notes, "... without such efficiency (of the health system), the *quality of services* to citizens or *even effective access to health services cannot be assured*" (goi.oc.5: 3). Ineffective institutional structures are directly linked to the failure of the state to meet the user/client's needs. Documents, for instance, note that a major flaw in the existing infrastructure is lack of effectiveness—which is that "in almost all respects, the health care system needs upgradation and it needs to reach out to many more people" (goi.oc.5: 2). Similarly, the documents claim that, over the years, several programmes co-existed with similar objectives, independently administered, and so the "separate identity for each programme was causing problems in *effective management* and this was also reducing [somewhat] the outcomes" (goi.oc.3: 1). The "indifferent success" of the state's programmes is also attributed to the inefficiency in service delivery (goi.tm.2: 2). Further, it was pointed out that an efficient health system could be achieved by integrating various services, which "would help in reducing the cost of inputs to some extent because overlapping of expenditure would no longer be necessary and integrated implementation would *optimise* outcomes at the field level" (goi.oc.3: 2). The use of the notions of efficiency and effectiveness also permeates the state's efforts to organise institutional change. For instance, the documents note that the various health functionaries must "...acquire the knowledge and skills to *deliver the services effectively and efficiently* under the new dispensation" (goi.tm.2: 1) and that "...the achievement of these [demographic] goals necessitates improvement in the knowledge and skills of health providers both in clinical *and managerial* spheres" (goi.tm.2: 1). The discourse of management forms the methodological backdrop to resolve developmental concerns.

The implications of the managerial paradigm are clearly underwritten in the state's interpretation of its obligation to provide for the users of the family welfare services; the state, in the RCH, constructs its primary obligation as one of providing for *efficient* and *effective* services. The RCH, purportedly aiming to overcome the shortcomings of earlier programmes, claims to operate under the conditions of efficiency and effectiveness. The documents equate efficient management with the basis of the reproductive health approach—"this concept [the definition of the RCH][74] is in keeping with the evolution of an *integrated approach* to the programmes" and its centrality in the national programme—"... *effective RCH programme* is crucially important for more than one consideration in the national system" (goi.oc.3: 2).

In sum, the integration of managerial efficiency is the state's expression of neo-liberalism. The adoption of the managerial/market/neo-liberal norms, as I demonstrate below, forms the paradigmatic foundations for interpreting and designing elements of gender-sensitivity in the policy.

---

[74] Document goi.oc.3 notes that the basis of the RCH has been defined as "people have the ability to reproduce and regulate their fertility, women are able to go through pregnancy and child birth safely, the outcome of pregnancies is successful in terms of maternal and child survival and well-being and couples are able to have sexual relations free of fear of pregnancy and of contracting diseases."

Interpreting 'Empowerment'

The concept of empowerment is embedded in the text of the RCH as a goal that has to be achieved within the context of development, for citizens, in general, and women, in particular. For instance, document goi.oc.5 points out that "... while there is steady improvement due to economic development, spread of education/literacy and *empowerment of citizens*, substantial problems in regard to education/literacy particularly among the weak performing States and in regard to *empowerment of women*, remain" (goi.oc.5: 2). The emphasis on women's empowerment is a central focus of the UNFPA programme in India, which asserts that "[e]mpowerment of women and improvement of their status are important ends in themselves and are essential for the achievement of sustainable development" (unfpa.obp.2: 1). The MoHFW's references to women's empowerment are more recurrent in recent documents. The document that was presented at the ICPD 1994 (*India Country Statement for the UN Conference on Population and Development*) made only one passing reference to women's empowerment. In contrast, the RCH documents (produced by the state in the wake of the ICPD) and plan proposals to the donor agencies are more forthcoming in concrete plans to address this issue. In the Kerala government's IPD (*Integrated Population and Development*) project, for instance, the state proposes to set up a core group of resource persons in each district, who can train educators on "gender issues" (gok.obp.12). The Government of India documents note that the state plans to address empowerment of women through its IEC (Information, Education and Communication) work. Document goi.oc.5: 31 notes that the government will encourage private filmmakers "...to make films of one to one-and-a-half hours on any of the themes relating to *women's empowerment* ...[and] issues relating to the girl child...".

The government's efforts to push women's empowerment onto the mainstream agenda of population policy are laudable. For instance, a volume on the implementation of the RCH in India published by the Population Council of India (Pachauri 1999) has praised the role that NGOs play in addressing issues of empowerment and, particularly, the partnership between the state and NGOs that has marked the design of the RCH programme from the outset (Mukhopadhyay and Sivaramayya 1999). Similarly, the concept of community needs-assessment has also been highlighted as a significant aspect of empowering individuals (Mukhopadhyay and Sivaramayya 1999). Further, the authors point out that the RCH was implemented at a time when the Indian State was passing the 73rd and 74th Constitutional Amendments, which made women's representation in local *panchayats* mandatory. Thus, by the time the RCH was initiated over 800,000 women, many from socially and economically backward classes, had been chosen as people's representatives in villages across the country. The implications of women's local representation for the institutionalisation of empowering programmes under reproductive health, these authors argue, are tremendous (Mukhopadhyay and Sivaramayya 1999: 341).

Given this significance accorded to women's empowerment in texts and documents, I was keen to explore policy-makers' perspectives on empowerment—how they conceptualised the idea of empowerment in the context of the RCH, its relevance in a population policy, and how it would be strategised in implementation. From my interviews, it was clear that, by and large, policy-makers were cognisant of the relevance of the concept of empowerment for reproductive policy. One middle-level bureaucrat at the DFW assured me that "... we are giving more importance to women's empower[ment]" (Interview I#6). If, as I hypothesised, the combination of gender and market ideologies formed a framework for interpretation for policy-makers, it would be valuable to explore what aspects of empowerment were given emphasis locally and if these at all supported the discourse of Cairo. From my interviews I extrapolated the various interpretations that policy-makers used to define "empowerment." Some of the more frequently recurring descriptions of the idea of empowerment as expressed in my interviews are tabulated below (see table 7.4)[75]:

[75] It must be remembered that the interviews were not surveys or based on multi-choice questionnaires. Therefore, the responses I have tabulated should be read as patterns rather than as based on numerically significant values. The references have been ranked in terms of frequency of repetitions, i.e., those that recur more frequently are ranked higher.

Table 7.4 *Descriptions of Empowerment by Respondents*

- Increasing employment facilities
- Increasing educational facilities
- Addressing issues of violence
- Seminars for women and adolescents
- Increasing role of women's NGOs
- Legal framework within the RCH (as a Consumer Protection Act)
- Addressing intra-household gender biases
- Information about reproduction
- Reservation of seats in government bodies

The descriptions of empowerment were a mix of outcomes (such as increasing educational facilities) and objectives (to address issues of violence) and included a spectrum of issues important to women, from education to violence. The most common references, when referring to empowerment, tended to draw responses relating to opportunities for education and employment for women. Respondents also pointed to the changes in the political climate and the increased opportunities for the participation of women in the political system as empowering for women as a collective group in the nation. Some of the respondents also talked about the various forms of 'atrocities' that were being committed against women and associated measures to reduce such crimes with empowerment (Interviews I#2, I#7). Within the context of the RCH, seminars and local level training for staff of the health system, and for members of local communities were also proposed as part of a multi-pronged strategy to increase women's empowerment (Interview I#1). Still other officials felt that the provision of information about contraceptives within the RCH itself was empowering to women (Interview I#4).

While referring to education or employment as empowering devices for women, respondents were more forceful and clear about outcomes. Although there were references to empowerment as social transformation (the importance of ideas of women's *decision-making, power, bargaining ability, negotiation* at 'social' and 'household' levels were mentioned by both male and female officials of the state), respondents admitted describing empowerment in terms of power shifts often acted as barriers to change. Unlike employment or formal political participation, when these officials had to associate empowerment with transformation of gender relations, there was less clarity about how empowerment for women was to be achieved, what the end outcome was to look like, and the role of the state in this matter (i.e., to simply *address* the issues or actively *change* them?). These are deeply controversial areas, and provide instances where ideology surfaces.

The issues of discriminatory gender relations were acknowledged widely enough; several of my respondents admitted that not enough is being done to change conditions for women in Indian society. For instance, I#1 notes "... at present they (women) do not have a bargaining power. Now, as it is, to ...negotiate—that power to change things—they still don't have it. I still agree that there is male dominance." There was also recognition among policy-makers that issues of reproductive decision making, in particular, were determined by intra-household power hierarchies, and that women, quite often, did not have control over these decisions. For example, the following transcripts point out that policy-makers are aware that women have restricted control over decision-making within the family.

> I#4 ... so whatever is the power equation within the family, it [reproductive decision-making] could rest either with *the husband, or the mother-in-law or with the woman, the wife*
> I#6: No, this [decision-making for women] is ... a problem just consisting ... within the family—just limited in the family circle. *It has not come out* [been made public]
> I#8: When there is a problem in the family, decision-making may be equal. But when we consider sex behaviour, *decision-making rests with the man only* ...

The responses suggest that policy-makers did recognise that the issue of women's roles and decision-making within the conjugal and family unit was a serious one to be reckoned with. By implication, any holistic approach to reproductive well-being cannot escape addressing issues of power and substantive transformation. However, when my questions sought to ask them how the RCH had incorporated issues of power into its strategies, policy-makers were resistant to the idea that a population policy should deal with such issues. One of my respondents, the gender researcher to the Government of India, referred to another project that she was involved with in another part of the country, and where empowering women was undertaken seriously:

> I#3: ... but the way, once women have been made aware of their rights—their legal rights, their property rights, right to health. The way they have come up and the way that they are mobilising other women ... it is fantastic ... *that kind of thing is not there in the RCH project*...
>
> Do you think that it is a major lacuna?
>
> Well, it is one of the lacunae. I can't say that it is the major.

The researcher's perspective is not an isolated one; there seems to be a pattern of thought amongst the policy-makers (see the following quote) that programme interventions for women to have active control over their lives were beyond the responsibility of the state development policy because there were social boundaries that the state was obliged not to transgress. The excerpt below from a senior level bureaucrat points out that the state has a "hands-off policy" on power issues within the family:

> I#4: [Now]... why isn't it that the government doesn't want to work in this area (of addressing power relations) which, by my own admission...is an important area. The [answer] is that we will be generating *too much hostility*.
>
> How?
>
> Trying to tamper with any power equation in any society is going to engender hostility from the people who are in power
>
> ... (so) the state right now is not in a position to tamper with the empowerment issues of women?
>
> The state has not chosen to, let's put it that way
>
> ...[so] does the state have a hands-off policy?
>
> Yes, a 'hands-off' policy on that (I#4).

A similar position was taken by the researcher that I had interviewed. She felt that the processes that marked the private sphere were not the state's responsibility; rather it was the role of non-governmental organisations to take up such activities.

> I#3: I don't believe that the government can do [it]. The government can do a lot of things like providing infrastructure and training for staff, but these sensitive issues, I think NGOs and you know, other organisations will have to play a major role. Governments are not equipped to do that. They do not have the support. So the NGOs definitely have to play a role. The NGOs cannot just sit back and point their finger at the government and say "Come on, you do it". You can't. It has to be a partnership.

In both these responses, there are comparable constructions of the role of the state in empowerment of women. Both comments point to an inability of the state to cross certain social boundaries where gender relations are concerned. For a range of reasons, the state maintains a distance from the power structures within the public-private spheres. These respondents construct an image of the state that is outside of the power relationships of society. Therefore, in its limited capacity, the state is comfortable about promoting 'empowerment' measures for employment and education because these programmes do not necessarily lead to volatile transformations, that is, they do not question substantive issues around shifts in power structures. Current state discourses around empowerment consider rights to education and employment as legitimate rights which are worth supporting and which lead to empowerment in the 'public space.' After all, these efforts at empowerment are expected to alter conditions in women's economic status enough to give them leverage as social bargainers in the long run. But is this form of intervention into women's lives adequate? Scholars writing on gender and development (see Sen 1994; Kabeer 1994) have been sceptical about what they consider as passive approaches to empowerment; they argue that on their own, empowerment exercises aimed at limited engagement in the public spaces are an ineffectual strategy to address women's subordinate status in society. Wendy Brown (1992: 19) argues, "... although women have now been accorded roughly the same panoply of civil and political rights accorded to men, these rights are of more limited use to most women and have different substantive meaning in women's lives." On the contrary, interpretations of empowerment as educational or employment support can detract from addressing power issues specifically in the private sphere where women are most powerless.

Similarly, Manoranjan Mohanty (1995) writes critically of the use of the term 'empowerment' in many of the present discourses of international development. Since the 1990s, he writes, the old formulation of 'growth with social justice' is being replaced with 'development with empowerment.' The content of empowerment in the latter paradigm, when carried through, emphasises formal rather than substantive power, is usually reliant on formal institutional arrangements, and inevitably involves an external upper agency to grant power, rather than people from below seizing it in the course of a struggle. Empowerment, as a reality, does not need to address issues of power sharing or transformation. In this form, argues Mohanty, the concept of empowerment neatly fits in with the political philosophy of the new economic globalisation of western capitalism.

Through the translation of the concept of empowerment, we see one process of policy interpretation. Empowerment of women, which is to be the "cornerstone of population and development related programmes" (Preamble of the POA, ICPD 1994) confronts the limits of social disapproval in India. The response of the RCH policy is to construct a duality of private and public empowerment priorities and demarcate a position for the state to legitimately and without controversy follow through the focus of feminist rhetoric in reproductive health. In its approach to empowerment strategies for women, the Indian state (as derived from the positions of the interviewees) assumes the garb of the 'liberal' state, where its primary role is to guarantee rights for women to interact in the public sphere, where rights are a consensual currency for interchange between citizens. Therefore, the state simultaneously becomes a pro-active gender state and an advocate for status quo for the normative gender order.

Interpreting 'Reproductive Rights'[76]

Another fundamental concept that I examined in the RCH was the views of the state to provide for 'rights' as part of a gender-sensitive reproductive policy. It was noted in Chapter 2 that the POA of the ICPD locates reproductive health and rights within a broader context of women's self determination and control over their reproductive and sexual lives. It was also pointed out that the ICPD valued women's equality and empowerment as end goals of a reproductive policy. The notion of 'rights,' therefore, is central to the formulation of a reproductive health policy. Feminists argue that there are two kinds of actions that the state can undertake to provide for reproductive rights for citizens (see Cook 1995; Dixon-Mueller 1993; Correa and Petchesky 1994). First, there are positive actions or areas where the state actively intervenes and, second, there are negative actions or areas where the state refrains from acting so as to permit citizens to act in privacy. What is important is where the state draws the line regarding when to interence and when not to.

I analysed the data corpus of the RCH to assess the policy's perspective on issues of women's reproductive and sexual rights. The first striking point that emerged is that the policy documents (not the interview transcripts) do not make any direct reference to women's rights or reproductive rights. In my interviews, I tried to gauge policy-makers' perceptions of these notions of reproductive and sexual rights through direct questioning. The term 'reproductive rights' is a generic one and, despite formal definitions (as, for instance, those used by the human rights charters), is open to interpretation. In my interviews, I deliberately used the term 'reproductive rights' as a composite without expressing it as a suite of other rights (like the right to decision-making, right to choice, etc.). In two cases, respondents asked me what I intended to convey in using the term 'reproductive

[76] Note that the term 'rights' is used in many respects. The idea of the liberal notion of rights discussed in the section on empowerment is different from what is covered here. Chapter 5 refers to 'rights' of citizens and clients. My focus here is on any references to women's rights and/or reproductive and sexual rights for women. There are ultimate overlaps in all these notions.

rights.' In all other cases, the officials had formed an opinion on the basis of an interpretation that they had already formed.

As will be seen from excerpts reproduced below, the officials and providers sat uneasily with the notion of reproductive rights. The responses that I have reproduced come from the entire cross-section of respondents. They include both male and female middle-level bureaucrats, local providers and even women activists from NGOs. Some of their responses follow:

> I#7: Now, every human being has certain rights—international rights, some reproductive rights. *But at the present stage of economic level in India we will not be able to provide all those rights to people.* Everybody should be able to have a better living, better standards of living, all those things. This can be envisaged in this 'rights', reproductive rights, of the people. But these you cannot in one fine morning achieve all this things. It will take a long time, it will take some time first to achieve that. Those countries that are rich enough, it is all right for them but for us it will take some more time to reach that level ...
>
> I# 6: There are national ethics, and all have to be observed. *Along with that our cultural traditions are to be observed.* It's not just taken ... because our cultural constraints, our traditions are there and all.
>
> I # 3: It's [reproductive rights] incorporated but I can't say that's the main focus. See you also must understand one another thing—it's really easy for you and I to talk about reproductive or sexual rights ... *No ... see that is—it [rights] has nothing to do with the RCH ...*
>
> I# 9: Since I am a person who likes old-fashioned things, my opinions may be different from other people. *But when we speak of rights, I don't think that it is a good thing.*
>
> I#5: I don't think that ... *But rights—reproductive rights and sexual rights issues is ... I think it is much more of a concern in Latin American countries ... than it is here ...* but more than that, I don't know ... I keep ... whenever I read of rights, that is, when I read it in the context of Latin American countries ...

It is interesting that there is relative unanimity in the way that the notion of 'reproductive rights' was rejected across the board. The concept was seen as either alien to the Indian context, detrimental to the harmony of the family, or in some cases, as a western ideal, which could be reached at some future stage. Reproductive rights were associated, by the respondents, with culture, society, family, and even economic conditions and the nation.[77] And, all of these dimensions of life were, according to these responses, likely to be jeopardised by integrating the concept of reproductive rights into a reproductive health policy. 'Reproductive rights' was naturally assumed to be a concept that could rend the fabric of society. This could explain the cautionary note about upsetting "tradition" and "culture" and wanting to retain "old-fashioned" values that are repeatedly mentioned in the interviews.

Following on from above, a second point is that when the respondents spoke of reproductive rights, it was automatically assumed that it was something that would be endowed upon women, even without my explicitly affirming this. All of their concerns of the detrimental effects of reproductive rights were implicitly drawn because of the association of reproductive rights *with women.* It seemed as if reproductive rights could trigger a gender revolution, as an outcome of powers that women receive. Interestingly, the officials I interviewed were conscious of the discriminations that women face in the sphere of reproduction. Many of my respondents acknowledged that women, especially in marital relationships, could not make decisions about their bodies—they would have to succumb to the expectations of husbands, in-laws, and the community (see, for example, Interview I# 8 in the section above). The disparity between women and men in matters concerning sexuality and reproduction is widespread and part of the cultural landscape of Indian conservatism (see for example, Dube 1986; Krishnaraj 1995). But, despite this recognition, policy-makers were more comfortable with dealing with the issue of rights as a 'community' problem

---

[77] Underlying these concerns of 'destabilising' society, there is an implicit construction of women's sexuality as needing to be restrained or protected. Although not explored in this book, the construction of women's sexuality (particularly, as heterosexual, passive rather than expressive, and almost wholly within conditions of marriage) underpins the way women are located within the programme. The Life Cycle Approach, for instance, will not fit the sexual patterns of single women or widows who are sexually active. These statements on reproductive rights made by these officials are a manifestation of some of these ideological beliefs.

rather than as a 'woman's' problem. As the following excerpt shows, there is a reluctance to address rights specifically for women. Note the way the gender researcher simultaneously collapses women *with* and as *apart* from the community.

> I#3: ... the point is that we need to educate the community about ... their right—the right to abortion, that no doctor can charge a woman in a government sector, their right to question. Their right to whatever it is ... (but) we have not reached that stage where we are educating, will be educating women.

The respondent vacillates between "their" or "community" rights and "women's" rights. She recognises that the community needs to be educated about "their" rights—be it to abortion, or questioning the workings of the health system. A similar assertion is absent when referring to women. Notice how the gender researcher shifts positions when referring to the 'community' and 'women.' With the former, the respondent argues in favour of their rights—*we need to educate*—but when the issue is women's rights, the consultant replaces affirmative thought with inaction—*we have not reached that stage*. It is not clear if the respondent refers to the state, the health sector or the Indian society, as a whole when saying that "we" have not reached *that stage* when women will be educated. The obvious reason for the reticent attitude to educating women is that women's rights (as demonstrated in the section above) is always a cause for volatile and reactionary responses from the community, and it would not augur well for the state to be embroiled in gender politics. As in the discussion of the concept of empowerment above, the state's hesitancy to broach the public-private divide is clear. However, drawing on the ideological themes that were discussed in Chapter 6, what is interesting to note is how the community is seen as apart from women. Women are not discussed as 'the' community, but as a community within the community—a group with minority status within the community.

The third point that must be highlighted is that not one of the respondents whom I presented above felt that rights as a concept or strategy could be integrated within the ambit of a policy. The issue of reproductive rights was so embedded in a conception of upsetting the public-private divide, that it could find no place within a population policy. Their attitude indicated a tendency to distance the state and policy from 'sticky' issues of gender relations. One respondent even dismissed outright the notion that reproductive rights have anything to do with a reproductive health policy: "... that is, it has *nothing* to do with the RCH" (Interview I#3). Only one of my interviewees, the official in charge of mass media, who is not included in the excerpts above, seemed to grasp the sense in which reproductive rights could be translated into policy. When I asked the official how the concepts of reproductive and sexual rights could be integrated in the policy, I was told:

> I #8: How [do] we mention reproductive rights in the messages? We say in classes *that in a house, to have a child, it is the right of the woman.* That is how we say it. So it has to be the mother who decides when the child has to be born.

A fourth point is the reference that was made to Latin American countries by I#5. The association with the Latin American context shows that the idea of reproductive rights is associated with rights to legal abortion and contraception. Since these are already legal and available in India, 'reproductive rights' is not seen as having relevance for Indian society. The legal perspective of rights (here again the liberal view of the state is demonstrated), in reality, touches only one form of guarantees and safeguards for women to exercise control in their reproductive lives.

The multiple environments in which feminist ideas gather momentum are significant. Smyth (1998) analysed the way in which feminists and the population establishment interpreted the idea of reproductive rights. Her brief historical overview suggests that from a feminist perspective, the concept of *self-determination* continues to be a critical element of reproductive rights, where "the emphasis is on a woman's own determination against that of others, rather than of self as individual" (p. 228). This entails that women have command over material and non-material resources at the household, community and state level (in this context, gendered social relations are revealed). Smyth emphasises that from a woman-centred perspective, increasing women's life choices and reproductive rights should be the basis of any fertility programme or policy. For the population establishment, however, the notion of reproductive rights was depicted as an increase in the number and types of contraceptives primarily to ensure that all segments of the population are 'covered.' The World Bank, Smyth (1998) notes, in an attempt to address 'rights' and 'choices,' advocated reduction of the regulative constraints on contraceptives and 'unnecessary medical screening requirements.'

The interpretation of 'rights' in the RCH is, like 'empowerment,' confronted by several contradictions. Tradition vs. modernity, community vs. individual/woman, formal vs. substantive, and West vs. Third World all complicate the way policy-makers express the idea of rights in their everyday practice of reproductive health. In the present case, the easiest manner to manage the contradictory environment was for the policy-makers to deny the RCH as a rights-based instrument that supports an individualist/woman-oriented perspective of rights. Rather than setting out to alter existing social conditions, the RCH mirrors its expectations.

Interpreting 'Choices'

The concept of 'choices' is central to a feminist notion of reproductive well-being. The women's movement has seen the opportunity for women to make choices as the key to having control over their bodies. Pine and Law (1995) argue that a feminist concept of reproductive rights is constituted of three interrelated components: (a) a principle of freedom from State control, i.e., the woman, rather than the state, must have the right to make decisions that affect her reproduction; (b) a principle of governmental neutrality, which is that the State must assume an even-handedness with respect to reproductive choices; and (c) a principle of affirmative reproductive liberty, that is, the state must support a social context that enhances human freedom to make reproductive choices. The right to choice, for feminists, goes beyond an abstract conceptualisation or liberal ideal. The freedom of choice is grounded in a material and social reality, and is relevant only as long as there is the opportunity to exercise that freedom. As Petchesky (1990: 11) points out, "[t]he critical issue for feminists is not so much the content of women's choices or even the (abstract) right to choose, as it is the ... conditions under which these choices are made. The 'right to choose' means little when women are powerless." International charters and documents on human rights also endorse the centrality of a right to choose as integral to reproductive rights. The WHO, in defining reproductive rights, specifies that individuals must have the right to "have information and means" to control fertility. The ability to make informed decisions about the suitability of a contraceptive would depend greatly on how much impartial information is given to users and the range of choices offered to them. Ideally, the state ought to encourage women to make informed choices and, in order to aid them in decision-making, should provide necessary information and conditions. Coliver (1995) argues that in the past the freedom to expression has meant the right to impart and receive information without government interference. But this freedom has evolved to the point when it is both obligatory for states to provide, *and* refrain from interfering with, the communication of information that is necessary for the protection and promotion of reproductive health and choice. Population policies, in particular, have been known to promote certain contraceptives or restrict access to others by not making them available, or by giving inadequate information.

The term 'choice' has also come to be a part of everyday conversation from another quarter. The word 'choice' is a part of the growing discourse of marketisation and the consumerist culture and has, of late, trickled down from the domain of consumption of products and services to the organisation of social and political life. Phillips (1996) examining the Thatcherist discourses of the early 1990s, pointed out that choice was a key word of the Thatcherist discourse, employed by the Conservative party. Her findings showed a persistent linking of the term 'choice' with words like consumer, rights, quality, citizen and efficiency, so that the vocabulary of the market and consumerism began to define the relationships of citizenship and rights. Phillips also pointed to the novel linkages between keywords, leading to a hybrid political discourse that consisted of elements of the Thatcherist and welfare discourses.

The text of the RCH policy documents did not make explicit reference to the word 'choice' (although the interview transcripts did so). Save for a passing mention that "... couples should be able to choose from various contraceptive methods including condoms, oral pills, IUDs, male and female sterilisation" (goi.nd), the documents do not elaborate on how choices may be made, or how the cafeteria approach has been modified so as to improve choice under the new programme. However, since reproductive health as a political discourse is ineffective without the opportunity to exercise choice, whether explicitly or implicitly mentioned, the question of 'choice' formed part of my interview questions. As in the case of the concept of 'rights', the word 'choice' was used loosely in my interview questions. The statements of the respondents helped me organise the various discourses around the notion of choice, and its interpretation in policy and practice. My analysis of the interview data indicated that most interviewees were likely to interpret the concept of choice as an attribute of a consumer in a market place. However, this interpretation was mitigated by the need to be compatible with belief structures that give priority to the state's ideologies around fertility control and its developmental consequences. At the same time, the respondents were also cognisant of its meaning in an expansive sense that was associated with autonomy, freedom and liberty. Both these perspectives influenced respondents' perspectives of the idea of choice—sometimes they were complementary, but often they contradicted each other. Thus, for the most part, the interpretations of policy-makers and non-governmental personnel were marked by inconsistencies. A vital aspect of these inconsistencies was that they reproduced a discourse (and eventually, projected models of practice) that subjected individual behaviour to state ideology.

At the outset, in general, policy-makers were quick to point out that the RCH offered more opportunity for users of the family welfare services to exercise choice. The phrase 'informed decisions' accompanied the general understanding of the word 'choice.' For instance, I asked a PHC-level medical officer if the current cafeteria of contraceptive methods offered by the government was adequate to ensure people had a choice. The response was that:

> I #12: ... earlier, it was not a situation where people were told everything and *could choose*. It was more like this: "this is what is appropriate for you ... you have now two children, your younger child is this old, you are only so old, so the permanent method may be more suitable for you." We tell them that and try to promote the method. Now instead of that we [now] say ... "this is what is available to you, *you can choose* what is suitable to you. These are the pros and cons of this. This is the advantage and disadvantage of this." So they are able to say, *this is what I want*. This is what is convenient for me.

The doctor's interpretation of choice could be interpreted as falling into both a feminist understanding of choice, and a consumerist interpretation. As the former, it is reflected in the passage about removing coercive practices, and providing information so that the user can choose what is suitable to her/him. As a discourse of the market, it indicates a new set of opportunities (particularly of options) that were earlier not available to users. The doctor mentions that "earlier" it was a different situation from what it is "now." In the following passage, the gender researcher also expresses a similar understanding of choice, that it facilitates women's abilities to make decisions in a non-coercive setting.

> I#3: She is being given a chance to decide on what she should use, whether she should control her fertility. If she decides to do so, what is the method she should use. It's not that an ANM tells her, go and use an IUD. *She (the woman) makes the choice*.

An issue to point out in these accounts is that both stress the act of verbally or physically expressing a desire as the substantive content of choice. In the doctor's and consultant's view, the fact that women can, at the point of interaction with the provider, make a selection from options presented to her is indicative of choice. However, the act of choosing between alternatives is the final step in a chain of conditions that will support the individual's decisions or choice. Some of the other requisite conditions are, for instance, the range of contraceptive choices/methods available in the public sector, adequate information under the programme so as to ensure that the individual can make informed choices, and absence of any pressure to direct choices in a particular way. I specifically raised these issues in my interviews. With regard to choice as an issue of having multiple choices, respondents did not see the expansion of the range of contraceptive methods as an important aspect of a reproductive health policy. A medical officer in the PHC found the question difficult to comprehend, as if increasing the contraceptive range had never been an issue to reckon with. When I asked if,

> In our government system itself we don't have injectables. Now Depo-Provera is there, which is not available here. So as far choice is concerned, do you think that when we say reproductive health and people's needs, that this choice should be increased?
>
> I#9: Do you mean number of choices?
>
> Yes.
>
> I#9: I don't think so.

A more articulate response came from the gender researcher for the government. When I asked her:

> How much of choice does it really open up for women? Are we all of a sudden talking about a cafeteria approach that broadens the number of contraceptive methods that she (a woman) has access to?
>
> I#3: It's not that—one has not really increased the methods—let me put it that way. For various reasons, when India wanted to introduce the NORPLANT, women's groups were very much against that. Women's groups had some legitimate concerns, but I also think that they didn't give it a chance to come into the country. Of course, now the NORPLANT is also banned by the American FDA. But the injectables, which is being used in every other country—again the same problem. All these methods—it all boils down to counselling. If you do proper counselling, you know your drop-out rate will be much less. Side effects will be much less. And when you make a choice, fully realising what it can do for you. So that was one of the things. So, as far as choices of methods we still have five methods—we still have the condoms, the pills, intra-uterine device and male and female sterilisation.

There are two interesting perspectives in the researcher's response. First, the researcher responds to the question in a way that is both defensive and offensive. In admitting that the government had not really increased the number of methods, she suggests that despite the opportunity for choices, the women's groups had resisted the introduction of the NORPLANT and injectables in India. Indeed, women's groups were concerned that in the name of increasing contraceptive choices, the government was succumbing to the pressure of global pharmaceutical companies to open up the Third World markets for their products and that women's contraceptives would be provider controlled (Rao et al. 1995; Sarojini n.d.). The women's resistance obviously was well placed, because as the researcher herself points out, the NORPLANT is banned by the U.S. Food and Drug Administration (FDA). However, she continues to be critical of women's groups for the absence of the injectable drug in the Indian family welfare services, and the lack of 'choices' for women.

The consultant's condemnation of the women's groups reveals an interesting shift in the meaning of the word 'choice'. Notice how she says, "*All these methods—it all boils down to counselling ...and when you make a choice, fully realising what it can do for you.*" She shifts the discussion away from the material provision of contraceptive methods to the individual act of making decisions. The consultant's interpretation of the term 'choice' moves the discourse of *choice* from what the government must provide (methods) to what 'you' can do (individual decision-making). According to the consultant, the individual's moment of knowledge that choice has been exercised is 'realising' what the various contraceptives 'can do'—in other words, advantages and disadvantages of each contraceptive method. This information is provided by the government's counselling services. By the end of her response, she had justified that choice was not so much about what one had access to, but how well the individual (or woman) could discriminate between what was available. In the final line of the passage, when the consultant reaffirms that the contraceptive choice has not changed, "*So, as far as choice of methods...*" it is not in the same defensive tone as when she first admitted a lack of contraceptive range.

The consultant's enthusiasm about women exercising choice once information about contraceptives is provided is a bit more optimistic than is warranted. Interview questions to other participants about choice yielded a set of responses that indicated that the state interprets individual exercise of choice in a fairly restricted sense. The officials emphasised knowing the various options rather than being wholly transparent to the users about the effects of various contraceptives. In the interview exchange below, according to a senior official,

> From what I've read they (ANMs) are going to be the ones who are going to have to learn a lot of skills, have a new attitude in approach, go back to the same clients and talk about disadvantages of contraceptives where once upon a time they would talk only of advantages? ...
>
> I #4: No, we are not adopting the cafeteria approach even now. That has not been adopted in the RCH. They will not be going back and talking about disadvantages of contraceptives, they will be trying to put it to the woman and the man...
>
> You mean they are not going to talk about disadvantages? So, it's still going to be a persuasive...
>
> I#4: No, as of now we are not planned that we will be talking about the possible side effects of IUD insertion, but they (grassroots workers) are not going to scare people off by saying that .... [S]ee, what now happens is that after an IUD is inserted everybody forgets about that woman. But we are trying to build up is to ensure that the JPHN visits the woman a week later, six weeks later and then provides services in getting over the problem. But the other question of—are the different options going to be explained to her—the options will be explained to her.

The official points out that there is an element of choice presented to the woman—the options will be explained to her. But as far as talking about side effects or contra-indications, the government policy is that "they are not going to scare people off." What appears, prima facie, to be an inconsistency of thought is actually indicative of a process of interpretation of the term 'choice' by the official. The official suggests that side effects are a result of ineffective follow up services, and if those services are built-up, then side effects (and the need to dwell on them) decrease. If the consultant above had shifted the discourse of 'choice' from a *public issue* to an *individual concern*, this senior official's understanding of 'choice' moves it from the realm of *political empowerment* to *medical intervention*. Side effects should be treated as a matter of public health, but such interventions will not decrease the relevance of information (not simply options) that is offered to users.

I also perceived contradictions and inconsistencies in other participants' understanding of 'choice' when I asked several respondents specifically how choice would be interpreted in practice in interaction with a client. The following represents three responses, one from a middle-level official and the other two from PHC-level ANMs.

Excerpt 1:

In this target free method, is it that we do not tell them what contraceptive method to use?

I#2: It's not like that. This is the basis. Now if they have only one child, they will be told about temporary methods. Or else there are newly married couples. They want the first delivery only after a while. Especially we have what is called Birth Timing. Now Family Planning is expressed in three ways: Birth Timing, Birth Spacing and Birth Limiting. Limiting means permanent methods, Spacing is for after one child, Timing means even if they have married early, between the age of 20 and 30, one looks for the best time for the first delivery. So, suppose they want the first delivery only after the first year—then we advise temporary methods. Even after one child, they can use temporary methods. So they have to be targeted for temporary methods. Then to them we tell about all the temporary methods.

Excerpt 2:

I#10: What ever they are willing to do, whatever is acceptable for them, that we have to encourage. Target—there is the TC1, TC2, yes?[78] Within the targets itself there are those with one child and with two children. The mothers with one child we encourage mostly to

[78] The terms TC1, etc. refers to the informal way in which the ANMs refer to their clients. Every couple (contraceptive needs are assessed primarily for married couples) is classified in terms of the number of children they have TC1 is a target couple with one child, TC 2 is a target couple with 2 children, and so on. The classification is significant because each TC is targeted by the state for specific kinds of contraceptives. ANMs would try to promote spacing contraceptive methods like condoms and IUD among TC1, while TC2 would be urged to accept more permanent methods of contraception, such as sterilisation.

accept a Cu-T [Copper-T], a CC [Condoms] or OP [Oral Pills]. Within those three which ever they like, we leave it to their wish.

So even if is target free ...

I#10: They can do only so much.

So we are only giving them this many choices ... ?

I#10: Yes, from these three we let them make their own choices. Those who want Cu-T, can have that. Or OP, CC. After that, those who have two children, we let them have a choice of mini-lap, laparoscopy—it is their wish. What ever they like, we encourage that.

Excerpt 3:

I#15:... when we interact directly with the public, we have to provide according to their need. We won't compel them. Now those with two children we don't need to compel. Only if there is three or more—four or more we should compel them—we should direct them and bring them around.

Before I examine each of these excerpts separately, I will first highlight the inescapable similarities in the responses of the participants. In all three cases, the interviewees are describing the conditions of choice that are available to users. In each case, the description of choice is constituted by an inconsistency. The three participants speak simultaneously in terms of absolute freedom of the user and restrictive boundaries of choice. In Excerpts 1 and 2, the ANMs state the pre-determined set of options that are available to users, within which the idea of absolute freedom is constructed. For I#2, if a couple has one child, they are told only about temporary spacing methods, and their choices are limited to the frame of temporary methods. The ANM's description of choice in Excerpt 2 is more graphic—*from these three we let them make their own choice ...it is their wish.* The state provides the set of options within which 'freedom of choice' is exercised. The ANM was right in pointing out that *they (a user) can only do so much.* Excerpt 3 also depicts this remarkable scenario of contradiction. The ANM in this account begins by saying that "*we will not compel,*" only to supplement this with *if they have two children, we don't need to compel.* If a couple has more than two children, the grassroots workers can intervene into the nature of their choices. These excerpts suggest that to the provider, the idea of 'choices' was not framed in the language of rights but in terms of normalising behaviour. Consider two comments from the interviewees about choice:

> I#2: Couples are given ... freedom of choice—*freedom for "informed choice"*
> I#12: But along with that freedom—how many children to have and all—along with that thought and freedom, we should tell them the pros and cons of the problems and help them to come to *a right decision.*

Respondent I#2's statement is significant as she replaces the terms 'freedom of choice' with 'freedom for informed choice.' Choice is defined in terms of responsibility of users rather than in terms of liberty of users. A similar sentiment is expressed in the next passage where the PHC doctor emphasises that freedom of choice is contingent on the ability of users to make the "right decision." These comments reinforce the idea that *choice* is interpreted within a *discourse of normative behaviour* rather than a discourse of freedom and autonomy.

In other studies where field level interviews with clients and health providers were conducted in Rajasthan and Tamil Nadu (two other states in India), it was also affirmed that a similar approach is followed regarding the interpretation of choice. Visaria and Visaria (1999) note that a 'client segmentation' method is followed by the health provider, that is, 'choices' are offered based on the reproductive history of the client (whether s/he has one child, or two, or none). The tendency to interpret choice in this way demonstrates a continuity of thought with the state's ideology regarding the primacy of national objectives of fertility control and economic growth already explored in Chapter 5.

Old Neo-Liberal/Malthusian Wine in New Feminist Bottles?

The 'case studies' of the concepts of 'rights, empowerment, and choices' reveal a similarity of interpretations that emerge from the deconstructions of the discourses of text and talk. The understanding of these concepts by people who reside in the various spaces of the state's material and discursive locations are marked by two dominant discursive frameworks. One frame of thinking, positions state and economic development as an imperative of the RCH and women's reproductive health as aligned to those development needs. The content of reproductive health as everyday lived experience of state health providers is embedded within a neo-liberal/neo-Malthusian frame of experience. The second frame is that of cultural context; it is an indisputable set of social relations that cannot be disturbed. The infusion of feminist language, no doubt, expands the horizons of the participants' existing social, economic and cultural paradigms of thought. Unfortunately, the pre-existing value systems that ground reproductive health discourses within the familiar terrain of population containment and state imperatives, and the so-called 'new discourses' of individualisation, privatisation and consumerism limit the possibilities of reproductive health as a feminist political discourse.

It is not surprising that a senior bureaucrat summed up the comparative bottom-line of the RCH and the ICPD as follows:

> I # 4: You have seen the goals that we have defined for ourselves. They *do not—may not tally* with the Cairo declaration. *Our goal is highly restrictive* in terms of trying to ensure safe pregnancies, safe delivery, safe child who passes through the infancy and goes on to childhood. So these that we have set for ourselves do not need ... yes, to ensure safe pregnancy—if the power equations could be changed—if the woman could have access to better nutrition [and] better service ... but other than that—most of the goals that we have set for ourselves will be—can be achieved even independently of trying to work on the power equations.

This telling passage is at the heart of the Indian state's interpretation of the global change in social policy to reproductive health. The Indian state's objectives are "highly restrictive" in what the state sees as its role in enhancing individuals' reproductive well-being. It is also clear that the state's ultimate objective of a reproductive health policy is very health focused, which "can be achieved even independently of ... trying to work on power relations" in the society. The passage also points out that any changes in women's strategic positions are outside of the policy's direct intent. If women were to benefit from improved pregnancy care or better service and nutrition, that is a bonus, not a developmental goal. India's interpretation of a reproductive health policy "may not tally with the Cairo Declaration" and the core emphasis on feminist discourses around emancipation through choices, bodily integrity and rights is considerably muted, if recognisable at all. The gender dimension of reproductive policy, as noted above, is limited to "stuff related to health. So therefore, it boils down to safe motherhood and family welfare and RTIs and STIs" (Interview I#3).

Let us recapitulate here, on the basis of the last three chapters, how the RCH stands up as an integration of competing discourses. One can, with some force, assert that the RCH's implicit concern is with aspects such as awareness (knowledge of contraceptives, physiology, child health, pre-natal care, etc.), actual use of contraceptives, continuation of use, imbuing 'responsible' reproductive values, widening the definition of the reproductive target group (from the more traditional married couple to adolescents, for example), and identifying how best these programme aims can be achieved. There is less of a focus within the programme to investigate intra-household hierarchies and their implications for reproductive rights, gender relations and their influence on reproductive decision-making, and if reproductive choices engender women's empowerment. In general, therefore, the programme emphasises:

- Cost-effective interventions
- Better co-ordination of programmes
- Better interaction between client and provider
- Instrumental view of women
- Regulation and normative behaviour
- Reproductive health as a medical discourse

Conversely, the RCH does not emphasise:

- Substantive social transformation
- Choice from the standpoint of autonomy
- Reproductive rights and legal rights
- Reproductive health as gendered political discourse

The proviso here, again, is that this analysis is not intended to be a simple checklist against which the state is monitored in what it has or has not achieved. The complex environment in which the family welfare institution (or any similar institution) operates cannot be undermined, and switchovers to a new ideology, particularly one as contested as gender ideology, are not simple or easy to achieve. Moreover, in the larger scheme of nuts-and-bolts programme provision, a reality check on what can be achieved must be constantly done. As one of the interviewees rightly pointed out to me, "... you can't have just that (rights, empowerment, etc.) and no services either" (Interview I#3). As often is the case with the half full/half empty glass metaphor, one is tempted to look at the positive increments of change that the RCH has wrought in order to appreciate the fledgling but significant strides of an institution entrenched in decades of set ways of thinking.

Nonetheless, what the foregoing analysis does demonstrate is the outcome of translation of the norms of the ICPD (and the feminist conceptualisations around reproductive health) as it is institutionalised in a context that subscribes to particular ideologies. In the way the RCH is currently organised, there is a priority given to interventions that emphasise neo-Malthusian/neo-liberal agendas of the state. In the course of this translation, the state brings together certain assumptions that effectively tie in women's interests with that of its own economic priorities. The government's policy rationale builds on one key relationship, namely that addressing development issues automatically will benefit women. To support this rationale, the state capitalises on the essence of the theories of gender and development: that women's interests are grounded in their social contexts. By merging these assumptions, the policy framework reworks a woman's perspective in the RCH. The discourses of reproductive health 'needs' of women are also the discourses of state's reproductive health 'objectives.'

Can basing a reproductive health programme on neo-liberal foundations be detrimental to women's interests? Are the foundational values important as long as any programme delivers identified needs? Smyth (1998) argues,

> ... should the difference in the motive behind the support for improvements in quality of services worry the women's health

> movement? I'm inclined to say that if the population establishment can translate quality of care statements into good, comprehensive and free reproductive health services for women, which respond to their varied needs, and which are provided by adequately qualified personnel in a dignified and respectful manner, perhaps it is immaterial that this is done to achieve maximum effectiveness, rather than adhere to genuinely held feminist principles (p.231).

There is considerable merit to Smyth's contention. If indeed the programme delivers to women, do we need to trawl through the closet of the state's ideologies (or what Yeatman (1993) calls the 'core policy order') to trace where the government's motives emerge from? Perhaps not. But that is only in a best case scenario where there is a harmonious convergence between neo-liberal and gender policy. Quite often, the overt agendas of both policy structures could be quite different. In such circumstances, what should be gains for women could easily be lost as priorities of the government shift. There is, however, yet another reason to query the basis of a gender policy. Any gender policy has the goal of improving both the material conditions as well as the political positions of women. Policy that focuses only on material conditions, in the long run, may restrict women's ability to make a political difference. Yeatman (1993: 230) makes a valid argument about co-opting gender rhetoric:

> If the custodians of established policy move to foreclose politics in favour of a quick and dirty adoption of new protocols of inclusion, we can be sure that the inclusion is token only and that the core policy order remains unreformed.

A nominal shift towards gender policy eventually defeats the very purpose of its institution. The core ideologies that dominate a socio-political context (whether it is patriarchy, neo-liberalism or any other) eventually circumvent any systematic change to the gender order.

Conclusion

This chapter concludes a key task in this book—that of understanding how the Indian state would interpret the various dimensions of feminist rhetoric espoused prior to and at the

ICPD. In Deborah Stone's words, policy making is a "struggle over ideas" (1988:7); the exploration of discourses and ideology in this chapter attempted to show some of the forms in which this struggle manifests. The analysis has demonstrated that despite the various attempts to reconstitute the RCH into an accessible programme for its users, especially women, neo-liberal/neo-Malthusian doctrines underpin the core focus of the policy. The pertinent issues, in an analysis of policy struggle, then become one of understanding the appropriation of feminist rhetoric; by looking at key feminist terms related to reproductive agency, one can surmise that the process of institutionalisation of reproductive health discourse within a neo-liberal health system also signifies a process of co-option and appropriation.

The broader lesson for this book is to reflect on the relatively organic nature of policy, that development (or any public) policy is constituted by ideologies of gender and social relations and simultaneously constitutes new sets of gender and social relationships. The preceding three chapters unpicked the ideologies that constituted the Reproductive and Child Health policy, and demonstrated that when taken in its entirety, the RCH is an expression of the state's mixed political ideologies. Whether the conservative development discourses influence reproductive health policy and the political relations between women and the state is examined in the following chapter.

References

Brown, W. (1992) "Finding the man in the state", *Feminist Studies*, Vol. 18, No. 1, pp. 7–34.

Coliver, S. (ed.) (1995) *The Right to Know: Human Rights and Access to Reproductive Health Information*, edited for Article 19, University of Pennsylvania Press: London, Philadelphia.

Cook, R. (1995b) "Human Rights and Reproductive Self-Determination", *The American University Law Review*, Vol. 44, No. 975, pp. 976 – 1016.

Correa, S. and Petchesky, R. (1994) "Reproductive and Sexual Rights: A feminist perspective", in G. Sen, A. Germaine and L. C. Chen (eds) *Population Policies Reconsidered: Health, Empowerment, and Rights*, Harvard Centre for Population and Development, Cambridge, MA, pp. 107–123

Copelon, R. and Petchesky, R. (1995) "Toward an interdependent approach to reproductive and sexual rights as human rights: reflections on the ICPD and beyond" in M. A. Schuler (ed.) *Women, Law and Development*, OEF International: Washington, D.C., pp. 343–367.

Dixon-Mueller, R. (1993) *Population Policy and Women's Rights: Transforming Reproductive Choice,* Praeger: Westport, Connecticut and London.

Dube, L. (1986) "Seed and Earth: The Symbolism of Biological Reproduction and Sexual Relations of Production" in L. Dube, E. Leacock and S. Ardener (eds) *Visibility and Power: Essays on Women in Society and Development*, Oxford University Press: Delhi, pp. 22–53.

Kabeer, N. (1994) *Reversed Realities*, Verso: London.

Krishnaraj, M. (1995) "Motherhood: Power and Powerlessness", in J. Bagchi (ed.) *Indian Women: Myth and Reality*, Sangam Books : Hyderabad, pp. 34–43.

Manoranjan, M. (1995) "On the concept of 'empowerment'", *Economic and Political Weekly*, June 17.

Measham, A.R. and Heaver, R. A. (1996) *India's Family Welfare Program: Moving to a Reproductive and Child Health Approach*, World Bank, The International Bank for Reconstruction and Development: Washington, D.C.

Mukhopadhyay, S. and Sivaramayya, J. (1999) "Forging New Partnerships: Towards Empowerment" in S. Pachauri (ed.) *Implementing a Reproductive Health Agenda in India: The Beginning*, Population Council: New Delhi, pp. 335–353.

Pachauri, S. (1999)(ed.) Implementing a Reproductive Health Agenda in India: The Beginning, Population Council: New Delhi.

Petchesky, R. (1995) "From Population Control to Reproductive Rights: Feminist Fault Lines", *Reproductive Health Matters*, No. 6, November, pp. 152–161.

Pine, R.N. and Law, S. A. (1995) "Envisioning a Future for Reproductive Liberty: Strategies for Making the Rights Real", *Harvard Civil Right-Civil Liberties Law Review*, Vol. 27, pp. 408–435.

Phillips, L. (1996) 'Rhetoric and the spread of the discourse of Thatcherism', *Discourse and Society*, Vol. 7 (2): 209–241.

Petchesky, R. (1990) *Abortion and Woman's Choice: The State, Sexuality, and Reproductive Freedom*, Northeastern University Press: Boston, revised edition.

Presser, H. (1997) "Demography, feminism, and the science-policy nexus", *Population and Development Review*, Vol. 23, No. 2, pp. 295–331.

Rao, M., Nayar, K.R., Baru, R.V. and Priya, R. (1995) "Health and Structural Adjustment: Major Shifts at Policy Level", *Economic and Political Weekly*, May 20, pp. 1156–1160.

Sarojini, N.B. (n.d.) "Campaign Against Hormonal Contraceptives". Paper for distribution among women's groups in India.

Sen, G. (1994) "Population, Well-being, and Freedom" in G. Sen, A. Germaine and L. C. Chen (eds) *Population Policies Reconsidered: Health, Empowerment, and Rights*, Cambridge, MA: Harvard Centre for Population and Development, pp. 63–73.

Silverman, D. (1993) *Interpreting Qualitative Data: Methods for Analyzing Talk, Text, and Interaction,* Sage Books: London, Thousand Oaks, New Delhi.

Smyth, I. (1998) "Gender Analysis of Family Planning : Beyond the 'feminist vs. population control' debate" in C. Jackson and R. Pearson (eds) *Feminist Visions of Development : Gender Analysis and Policy*, Routledge: London and New York, pp. 217–238.

Visaria, L. and Visaria, P. (1999) "Field-Level Reflections of Policy Change", in S. Pachauri (ed.) *Implementing a Reproductive Health Agenda in India: The Beginning*, Population Council: New Delhi, pp. 77–121.

Yeatman, A. (1993) "Voice and Representation in the Politics of Difference" in S. Gunew and A. Yeatman (eds) *Feminism and The Politics of Difference*, Allen and Unwin: NSW, Australia, pp. 228–245.

8
CONCLUSION
Marketing Reproduction and the Politics of Gender Ideology

The analysis of political rhetoric reflects an emergent body of critique within development studies that questions the ideological foundations on which development theory and practice bases itself. This critical literature asserts that the collective values and beliefs held by individuals in an institutional context manifest themselves in day-to-day practice, and colours their interpretation of what constitutes the developmental needs of a community. In social contexts where there are unequal power relations, these ideologies can decide access to political bargaining and, ultimately, resources. The present study is set against the unequal relationship of power between two groups of people in the provision of public health, namely, providers of policy (or the state) and beneficiaries (or users, specifically women users). It is framed by the fundamental assumption that the ideologies that the providers subscribe to, are critical determinants of the outcome of policy decisions and practice.

Against this epistemological backdrop, this concluding chapter summarises and synthesises the various strands of analyses—both empirical and conceptual—that have been touched on in this work. It reflects on the key questions raised in the introduction, and in doing so, acknowledges the two levels at which this research is pitched: (a) deconstructing discourses and identifying traces of neo-liberalism/neo-Malthusianism in the RCH, and (b) exploring the political nature of the development state, and women as subjects. The state's historical and contemporary ideological contexts, acquire a unique focus in this enquiry as they create particular arenas for 'needs construction and talk.'

Drawing on the discourse analysis in order to undertake a conceptual exploration of state-women relationships, allows the RCH to be measured against the broader context of feminist politics that was aspired to at the Cairo Conference rather than merely against the objectives set out by the Ministry of Health and Family Welfare. Assessing the RCH against feminist politics can be a challenge; it is easy enough to point out that the RCH is not (and never overtly made the claim to be) a change instrument for social relations. One can, then, at best create an argument for a missed chance; it was an opportunity to catapult women's political interests to the fore, that was not seized. However, to solely measure a reproductive health policy against stated objectives of the RCH and conventional empirical performance overlooks an important point. Ultimately, the RCH is representative of a policy relationship between women and the state. And, despite official arguments to the contrary, the RCH is an instrument of political change, even if the 'change' is manifest as maintaining status quo. The advantages and disadvantages of the policy to women, both potential and real, must be understood in terms of strategic gains and political leverage.

The term 'conclusion' in this regard is a little misleading; this chapter does not offer the final word in the evolving framework constituted of women, state, ideology and reproductive health. If anything, it gestures toward linkages between policy and values, politics and ideology, drawing attention to processes that may otherwise be obscured or considered unimportant, even if recognised. Two main sections outline the broad arguments I wish to make in this chapter. The first provides a 'meta-analysis' of policy and of the impact of neo-liberal ideology on the gender discourse of reproductive health. The second offers some tentative thoughts on the influential nature of neo-liberalism in creating particular political contexts for women in transitional development states. A brief summary of the present research precedes these two sections.

In Summary

In 1995, the Government of India embarked on an ambitious plan to revamp the way that it had been providing family welfare services to the population. At the heart of the many changes that it proposed was the assimilation of the feminist rhetoric of sexual and reproductive health and rights that had been in vogue in international discourses around population policy since the International Conference for Population and Development (ICPD), 1994. The present study has attempted to evaluate the process of institutionalisation of the ICPD's ostensibly feminist rhetoric in the GoI's existing health and family welfare system. There are several dimensions to this process, which have offered germane topics for enquiry in this research.

First, the state and its ideologies have been a core focus of this study. The Indian state has, in its recent history, taken ambivalent stances on issues related to women. In some instances, it has proven exceedingly progressive and protective of women's rights, whereas on other issues, there has been evidence of distinct patriarchal values. A second dimension explored in this study has been the effect of the competing discourse of neo-liberalism that has, in the last decade or so, seeped into the economic and social organisation of life in India. The neo-liberal discourse (unwittingly at times) not only threatens to overturn the conventional state-citizen relationships in India, but has also proven to be a dominant ideology that influences the interpretation of reproductive health as a discourse. The emphasis of the neo-liberal discourse on efficiency, cost-effectiveness, and measurable returns to investment is an important determinant in the Indian state's decisions around designing any policy, including reproductive health policy. A third aspect evaluated in this research is the formulation of gender-sensitive policy, or policies that are likely to have maximum benefit for women. A key aim of women/gender and development scholarship is to provide the knowledge base to develop policy initiatives that are sensitive to the needs of women (as much as other marginalised groups). In this research, through the appraisal of the ideologies that have bearing on the institutionalisation of reproductive health policy in India, I hoped to bring to light the deep-rooted nature of biases in development policy that pose a challenge to developing gender-sensitivity in policy. A point that I argue repeatedly in this study is that gender sensitivity is not something that can be 'fixed' merely through technically sound methods of policy design. Gender biases in policy (as much as gender-sensitivity) occur at the level of ideology and discourse.

Fourth, a foremost factor that has an effect on how well gender sensitivity is incorporated into development policy is the political identity of women. I contend that the state produces certain constructions of women and their roles in society, which determine the way that they are positioned in policy, i.e., their political access to the state. Women's constructions as political beings, I further argue, are simultaneously framed by their roles in economic activity, and by notions of femininity and womanhood accepted within a dominant patriarchal society (Chapter 3). A fifth dimension is the global-local connection. This research provides an assessment of what ensues when a globally accepted discourse is contextualised in a local setting. What is lost in translation, what is accepted, and what new variants of discourse are produced, are empirically demonstrated through the analysis in this research. Finally, this study also offers an opportunity to debate the implications for feminist politics when empowering rhetoric is appropriated by the state and employed to benefit its own agenda, which may not directly benefit women.

Overall, this book also presents development (and particularly, reproductive health) policy as an arena of political conflict and debate. Policy goals and strategies are not determined as isolated, rational, unbiased decisions. Pre-existing biases around what women need, what the state needs, what is perceived as effective strategising, all permeate the formulation of development programmes. As these biases (and ideologies) get institutionalised, they 'locate' users (women) and providers (the state) in unequal positions of power.

Contested Ideologies and Policy

One of the central objectives of this book was to understand the policy outcomes when contradictory ideologies influenced the debate in reproductive health. There is a core incompatibility in the discourses of neo-liberalism and feminism. Bangura (1997), for instance, argues that there exists a fundamental mismatch between the basic values, premises and goals of neo-liberalism and gender discourse, making the task of integrating gender into existing policy systems a particularly contested process of struggle. Neo-liberalism makes little or no concession to the problems of disadvantaged groups, communities and countries, and is indifferent to questions of equity and participation as outcomes that should be actively sought by policy-makers. These tenets are at discord with the aims of a gender discourse, which is founded on the principles of achieving equity and social justice among women and men. Although, in reality, arguments for inducting a gender dimension into development policy have always held the efficiency rationale that such development is more efficient when gender issues are considered, social transformation and empowerment still continue to be the bedrock on which gender policy is based. A gender discourse thus is "interventionist, very multi-faceted in terms of the issues it tackles, flexible in approach, and strongly rooted in issues of social transformation and the dynamics of the moral economy" (Bangura 1997:21).

In the case of the reproductive health policy studied here, the stand-off between the two philosophical positions is especially evident. Authors referred to the schism between the two doctrines, present even at the ICPD, as "contradictions" and "fault-lines" (Amalric and Banuri 1994; Petchesky 1995). For the health providers in this research, living out this doctrinal contradiction entailed employing a range of discursive and cognitive strategies that helped reconcile the contested nature of ideas that was present in their institutional context. The reader will recall some of these mechanisms:

- *Appropriation of feminist rhetoric*: This is seen, for example, when the notions of 'equality' and 'gender' were used for promoting conservative developmental goals.

- *Maintaining the state as the benchmark*: This mechanism was evidenced, for instance, in the conflict between the idea of 'individual rights' and the stabilisation of population, the state's interests prevail.
- *Developing normative standards*: The tendency by policy staff to frame rational behaviour in terms of the small/two-family norm is an example of this mechanism.
- *Co-opting multiple paradigms*: This strategy, for example, was revealed in the way feminist, development and managerial discourses were organised to develop problems and solutions
- *Localising appropriateness*: The manner in which some policy-makers, for instance, were emphatic that 'reproductive rights', for instance, are not seen to be applicable in the Indian context expresses another way in which contradictory ideological frameworks are reconciled.
- *Collectivising the individual*: This was revealed in the case where women's needs were 'transformed' into community needs.
- *Medicalising the political*: Evidence of this strategy is seen in the emphasis of reproductive health services on childbirth and fertility.

The list of such instances can continue. If anything, these examples underscore that the RCH is a hybrid policy of contested ideological viewpoints. But is that working to women's advantage? Bangura introduces the concept of *policy dialogue*, i.e., the negotiation of diverse values among various groups, including those committed to gender issues. According to him, policy dialogue is an "organised deliberation between two or more actors on the allocation of values that is likely to result in new policies or modification of existing ones" (Bangura 1997: 2). Policy dialogue assumes willing negotiation and compromise without head-on confrontation so as to achieve the best possible gender outcome. Bangura's argument follows the tradition of the 'constructivist school' of qualitative research for whom the aim of research is to make sense of the respective worlds constructed by the key stakeholders of, say, a policy or a programme (Lincoln and Guba 1989). By understanding each participant's constructed world-view, argue constructivists, a consensus perspective can be facilitated. Despite the optimism about policy dialogue, Bangura is sceptical about how much consensus can be achieved between feminist and neo-liberal philosophies. Gender policy, according to him, is always a negotiated claim and, ultimately, a compromise. Bangura concludes that given the existing nature of policy systems, mainstreaming gender was not likely to be easy and outcomes may not be satisfactory for all participants; for instance, "progress in mainstreaming gender at the top may not easily translate into progress in enforcing gender practices at the bottom" (Bangura 1997:3).

Does the RCH represent an outcome of policy dialogue? Or, does it reflect a compromise of gender ideology? One's own perspective can decide how to weigh it up—the RCH can be an example of what Fraser (1989) neatly captured as a "depoliticised" oppositional discourse. Contrarily, the incremental shift (however marginal) towards conceptualising a population policy that is focused on individual well-being can be hailed as a significant move towards realising at least some of the goals of the ICPD. The potential improvements in the structure of the system, increased services and focus on quality of care are the likely positive outcomes in the wake of the RCH (HealthWatch 1999).

State Discourses and Women's Identity

The transformation from oppositional discourse to needs-talk and then to established policy can be paradoxical; the development into policy can simultaneously expand women's opportunities for better service provision but also limit the possibilities of emancipation. The key is to ensure that the arena for debating 'rights' is not foreclosed to women's voices, so that policy is always open to being modified. Rai (1996) asserts that, by its very nature, the 'post-structuralist' state is always opening up spaces, no matter how small, for transformation of its ideologies. What is essential for feminists to recognise is that because the state is not unified, and because its discourses are not static, there are "spaces that are available, and can be created for and through struggle for retrieving, reconstructing and regaining control over the meanings and signifiers in women's lives" (Rai 1996: 19). Yet, these spaces are not assuredly open spaces for feminist voices—context determines how much and in what form contested discourses are permitted. Yeatman (1993: 230) rightly noted that "politics is the space between established policy and an emancipatory movement's claims on equality."

To explore these possibilities for feminist emancipatory discourses, the nature of the spaces—the public spaces—that open up in the Indian neo-liberal state will be explored in this section, with a particular emphasis on the creation of women and reproduction as subjects of the neo-liberal state. What follows are some tentative thoughts aimed to generate wider debate.[79]

Earlier chapters (particularly Chapter 3) had referred to the nature of the 'state-citizen' relationship in conventional development. Using arguments raised by Jayal (1994), the point was made that the conventional developmental state differed from the western welfare state in that social intervention was not a pre-ordained right. The citizenry of India had no claims upon the state, apart from a moral basis, for access to development benefits. The relationship between state and citizen was framed in the ethos of paternal giver (the state) and receiver (people), benefactor and beneficiary. With the coming of the neo-liberal state, there was, admittedly, a shift in this paternalistic relationship. The minimalist neo-liberal Indian state of the 1990s reframed the role of the state as being responsible for administrative efficiency to provide conditions for the development of market relationships. The corollary was that the economy increasingly became the point of reference for citizenship; the mark of a good citizen was to engage in the ubiquitous and ephemeral market, and bear the transaction costs of the volatile market.

---

[79] I cover in some detail the arguments I make in this section in Simon-Kumar (2004).

The critiques of the neo-liberal development state of the 1990s, specifically with regard to women, are well-rehearsed:[80]

- That social reproduction (like childcare, care of the elderly, community work) is, without support from the state, falling on women as unpaid and unrecognised labour. Although women's unpaid labour supports the development of economy, there is no compensation by the state.
- Where women are able to enter the economy, for a large majority it is into low-paid, low-skilled and 'feminised' jobs adding to the exploitation.

In the new world of neo-liberal efficiency, therefore, there are changing notions of citizenship entitlements, the collective provision of social needs and the efficiency of the development/ welfare state. There was a disappearance of the "idea of publicness," and the sense of public obligation for individuals' well-being by the structures of the public, i.e., the state (Eisenstein cited in Petchesky 2003). Other scholars, such as Brodie (1994), argued that neo-liberalism signified a re-emergence of a privatising force that made women invisible in terms of the burdens they carried and their ability to claim rights as citizens. In sum, there is a shift in the construction of citizens' identities (including women) and notions of 'claims of rights' to the state are lost against the more dominant perspective that citizens had 'obligations' towards the state. The terms of the 'charity/contract' relationship with the state (see chapter 2) are all the more accentuated by the nature of economic contribution that citizens can make. Women, by the nature of their positioning in the sexual division of labour, are less likely to engage in a productive contractual relationship with the state.

Realistically, when we look at the RCH, there are outstanding differences to both the conventional development ideology of the state-as-benefactor and the core focus on economic value as the sole basis of citizenship in a neo-liberal state. For one thing, the RCH policy does aim to develop partnerships (in the policy

[80] For the neo-liberal western state, Brodie (1997) argues that women enter the public sphere privileging virtues of individualism, choice, competition, and independence. The shift for women in western societies is from the Keynesian 'citizen-mother' to the neo-liberal 'citizen-worker' (Roelvink and Craig 2004).

text, at least) with its users, both individual and communities. It does make an attempt to include users in its programme development and planning, and aims to focus on the relevance of its services for those it seeks to serve. Even more significant is the language reflecting gender-sensitivity and women-centeredness in the policy. In emphasising women's reproductive needs as legitimate concerns of the state, critics of the neo-liberal state (who argue that the state excludes itself from reproductive activities of women) are, understandably, silenced. In some respects, therefore, the core characteristics of a neo-liberal state do not satisfactorily explain the nature of state-women relationships and women's identity that appears to be inscribed in the RCH policy.

This book has already raised significant critique around all these aspects of the policy, and the state's genuineness in developing these partnering relationships. However, these critiques do not detract from an essential transition being made by neo-liberal states—it appears to be moving toward what writers call the "post-neoliberal state" (Roelvink and Craig 2004). The post-neoliberal state is the outcome of 'Third Way' politics (Giddens 1998) where market development is *inclusive*, i.e., market-based policies strive to fit within the social fabric and needs of the populations where it is being developed. Roelvink and Craig (2004: 7) point out "[i]nclusive" or Third Way liberalism should be understood as an attempt to re-establish the legitimacy of markets in relation to the social ...". Through strategies of involving individuals, couples, families and communities in the development of policy and programme, the moral character of the market is emphasised.[81] The post-neoliberal state is also, like its earlier variant, masculine; beneath the language of partnership

[81] The neoliberal state that heralded the structural adjustment and restructuring programmes in the 1980s is often considered to be without humanity or moral obligation to its citizens. The post-neoliberal state, in contrast, aims to position itself as a wholesome compromise between the effectiveness of market interventions and inclusive statehood. Variants of this newer version of neoliberalism are increasingly being adopted in developing countries as well. Agencies such as the World Bank are moving towards policies that balance the economic mandate and political (governance) legitimacy of the development state.

with the state, women are brought on board, as it were, to be front-runners for the state's economic development agendas. The essence of the argument to be explored here is the implication for women's identity. Through a combination of inclusive/neo-liberal policy perspectives, state-women relationships and the role of reproduction are unbundled and rewritten.

The arguments to understand women as subjects in post- and neo-liberal state have led basically to two kinds of analyses about the public space. On the one hand, authors such as Brodie (1994) argued for women's inclusion (*the inclusion perspective*) into the rapidly diminishing public space specifically through the expansion of the state. If the ideology of the market subsumed the primary mode of societal relationships, economic value as a currency for identity in the public space would be emphasised. Persons and activities falling outside of 'economic value' are more likely to be excluded as claimants to the public sphere. Feminist praxis, if anything, focused on the re-expansion of the state in various arenas of women's lives, not touched upon by the market.

The other side of the argument was informed by a widespread scepticism by feminists in the 1990s of the western welfare state. Cautious of the over-monitoring and regulation of women on welfare benefits, there was a rising concern by feminist scholars that being in the 'public eye' represented loss of a personal sense of identity. Drawing on similar themes in the context of development, writers point out that neo-liberalism does not just widen the gaps between the productive and the reproductive; it effectually erases them (Petchesky 2003). Distinctions between the 'social', the 'individual' and the 'personal' are increasingly being blurred, and there is an incursion of the social/political/economic into people's everyday lives. Consequently, the separation between the private and the public must ardently be maintained—in moving into the 'public' gaze, the risk of regulation and social governance increases (*the exclusion perspective*).[82]

[82] The idea of 'governance' is informed by the works of Michel Foucault, who saw the state as putting in place techniques and strategies which citizens comply with as part of their everyday lives. These techniques and strategies, in reality, are subtle and non-coercive forms of power structures that ensure that subjects are governed without resistance.

These contrasting perspectives offer a paradigm for me to understand the implications for reproduction (through the example of the RCH) in a neoliberal state such as India.

Women's Reproductive Identity and Neo-liberal Development Policies

Reproduction as a subject sits uneasily amidst the plethora of premises that are mushrooming about neo liberalism and women's rights. There are those who subscribe to the exclusion theory and, equally, those that argue with conviction about the dangers of inclusion. Studies in social reproduction from around the world, especially, are consistent in demonstrating that women's contributions to household and communal care are either ignored or under-supported by the public streams of funding. That is to say, they are being removed/excluded from the priorities of the public space because they are not seen as vital economic activities that are crucial to survival of market ideologies. The point about the potential dangers of inclusion are brought home by Gallin (1998) who suggests that, contrary to the widespread view that reproductive activities are unimportant and, therefore, marginalised in neo liberal states, the "control of women's reproductive powers is crucial to the maintenance of the global economy.... [T]he imperatives of this economy demand that women (and men) adjust so that they can *produce and reproduce* efficiently." Biological reproduction of labour power is crucial to capitalism and the various discourses of size and quality of the population, pro-natal/anti-natal, and controls on who can and should reproduce are all manifestations of an ideology that aims to create a labour force that meets the exigencies of contemporary capitalism. For Gallin (1998: 16) the, "mode of reproduction may be separate from the mode of production but it is regulated by the logic of accumulation." Roelvink and Craig's (2004) analysis of 'caring' post-neoliberal states that *invest* in children and families also suggest a newer and subtler form of regulation of future generations.

In India, post-independence family planning has been a 'programme' of the Government and, therefore, has been intimately connected to notions of nationalism and patriotism.

Certainly over the past four decades, there is no escaping that in order to attain levels of modernity and development, the state's subjects were required to align their reproductive behaviour with that of the priorities of the state. Family planning was a patriotic duty for the nation and a rational choice of individuals who wanted to lift themselves out of poverty. Women, particularly, were part of this grand design. Not only were the problems of under-development in India tied to their ability to reproduce, they were at the centre of a discourse that positioned them as primary agents of change. The archetypal woman subject of the Family Planning policy ideology was wife-mother, an image that stresses her familial identity, respectability, industriousness, and, most importantly, her part in the transmission of a modernised cultural tradition (Chatterjee and Riley 2001). The construction of 'mothers' and 'responsible reproducers' positions women as economic and developmental agents—actors in the population drama. Unlike in conventional nationalistic discourse, where mothers and workers were polarised identities in women's economic relationships with the state, in the reproductive health policy, to be a mother *was* to be a productive worker in nation-building. In constituting women as mothers in the reproductive health policy, the state converted women's social role/ reproductive identity (within the 'personal' domain of home and family) into an economic/productive (and public, developmental) identity. As population policy was embedded within a strong discourse of obligations that women were to discharge, for women, to be 'responsible mothers and reproducers' in development policy was also to define their political identity. The state, for its part, became the stereotypic authoritarian relentlessly persuading, and even coercing its subjects to fall in line with its policy. Through mechanisms of control, manipulation, rewards and punishments, the state assumed the role of patriarchal power, and all its subjects, the object of its command.

This duality between state and subject, in many respects, were clear-cut and, therefore, formed a firm ground on which to challenge the state's ideologies and construct a point of resistance to these roles. The alarm at excessive sterilisations, and the indifference to individual needs and people's sensitivities consumed writings critical of the state's population policy, and reflected the emerging critical mass that questioned the lines of the public space. The RCH is an interesting point of transition to these formations. The various provisions—from the idea of participatory planning to individual's choices and its efficiency discourses—seemingly makes a marked move towards expanding the public space for claiming rights. Yet because the policy's core policy order, as we have seen throughout this research, remains unchanged, the potential for political change is questionable.

If anything, the RCH forms the apposite opportunity for an image makeover for the state. In place of its representation as a totalitarian state in matters of family welfare, the use of the neo liberal discourse allows for the state to re-emerge and reconstruct its role in population ideology and its relationships with its subjects. At times the state is technocratic, at other times an arbiter of rights, and still again, a concerned interventionist 'caring' force. What I would argue is that in this transformation of the state, the conventional forms of oppressive power are converted into more complex systems of control of women's reproduction. It reifies certain constructions of women, marginalises others, regulates reproductive practice by setting norms, applauds certain behaviours—and in so doing, reiterates the traditional relationships but destabilises the conventional ideas of the public and private. An enduring bottom-line continues to be the discourses of economic growth. The state, in this avatar, follows through as keenly interested in its women subjects. However, it controls the discourses of empowerment for women so that 'emancipation' for women occurs when there is congruence between gender/reproductive subjectivities and development discourses. Women are 'freed' when they have fewer children, they are 'liberated' by their ability to make informed choices about contraceptives. As noted earlier, feminist politics is tested when women's 'acts of compliance' are reconstituted as 'acts of empowerment.'

For feminist scholars, coming to grips with this neo-liberal Indian state is the challenge of the twenty-first century. The hard lesson to be remembered is—drawing on Brown (1992)—that it is not one thread that can unravel masculinity. Rather, a complex web of relationships, ideologies and structures—across geographical space and institutional levels—must be addressed if the space of feminist reproductive politics is to be effective.

A Final Word

It is noteworthy that events following the institution of the RCH speak volumes about the embedded ideologies of the state. In late 1999, doctors in the public health sector in Kerala went on a strike for a number of issues, including their concern that "Kerala is losing ground in the area of implementing national health and family welfare programmes" (*The Hindu*, Dec. 14, 1999). The Directorate of Health Services' response was to assure the public that "the number of sterilisations, which represent a major component of nationally-implemented programmes, had registered an increase over the previous year" (*The Hindu*, Dec. 14, 1999).The role of NGOs, particularly women's groups, in relation to the programme altered significantly in the years following the RCH policy. Sen et al. (2000) note that although in the initial phases post-Cairo, the MoHFW was keen to work with women's groups in India, the early enthusiasm from the Ministry gave way to a silence. NGOs were readily 'contracted' by the state to deliver reproductive health services at the grassroots level, but not as a consulting partner in policy formulation. Rao (2004) details the changing policy context following the adoption of the two-family norm in several Indian states, inimical in every way to a gender discourse in reproductive health. Rao also quotes studies that indicate that deaths from sterilisation, abysmal conditions for operations, and corruption in the family welfare programme continue, regardless of the RCH. Buch's (2005) study provides concrete examples of the adverse implications of the two-family norm, particularly on women. She highlights the extent that individuals and families go to, in order to subvert the restrictive influence of the two-family policy and participate in the political system. Stories of women undergoing induced abortion, women being abandoned by their husbands if they have more than two children, and some families hiding away some children with relatives—in order that male and female candidates can stand for *panchayat* elections—highlight the everyday outcomes of top-down policy initiatives. From the exuberating rhetoric of gender sensitivity to reactionary population policies and practice within a decade of the ICPD, Cairo, 1994—the story of reproductive health politics in India makes tragic reading.

References

Amalric, F. and Banuri, T. (1994) "Population: malady or symptom? *Third World Quarterly*, Volume 15, No. 4, 691–706.

Bangura, Y. (1997) *Policy Dialogue and Gendered Development: Institutional and Ideological Constraints*, Discussion Paper 87, United Nations Research Institute for Social Development: Geneva.

Brodie, J. (1994) "Shifting the Boundaries: Gender and the Politics of Restructuring", in I. Bakker (ed.) *The Strategic Silence: Gender and Economic Policy*, Zed Books: London, pp. 46–59.

Brown, W. (1992) "Finding the man in the state", *Feminist Studies*, Vol. 18, No. 1, pp. 7–34.

Buch, N. (2005) "Law of Two-Child Norm in Panchayats: Implications, Consequences and Experiences", *Economic and Political Weekly*, Vol 40, No. 24, June 11.

Chatterjee, N. and Riley, N. (2001) "Planning in Indian Modernity: The Gendered Politics of Fertility Control" *Signs: Journal of Women in Culture and Society,* vol 26, no. 3, pp. 811–845

HealthWatch Trust (1999) *The Community Needs-Based Reproductive and Child Health in India: Progress and Constraints,* HealthWatch Trust: Jaipur.

Gallin, R. S. (1998) "The Gendered Nature of Globalization", Paper presented at the Annual Meeting of the American Anthropological Association, Philadelphia, Dec. 2–6.

Giddens, A. (1998) *The Third Way: The Renewal of Social Democracy*, Polity Press: Cambridge, UK.

Jayal, N. G. (1994) "The Gentle Leviathan: Welfare and the Indian State", *Social Scientist,* Vol. 22, No.9–12, pp. 18–26.

Petchesky, R. (1995) "From Population Control to Reproductive Rights: Feminist Fault Lines", *Reproductive Health Matters*, No. 6, November, pp. 152–161.

Petchesky, R. (2003) *Global Prescriptions: Gendering Health and Human Rights,* Zed Books: London.

Rai, S. (1996) "Women and the State in the Third World: Some Issues for Debate", in S. Rai and G. Lievesley (eds) *Women and the State: International Perspectives*, Taylor and Francis: London, pp. 5–23.

Rao, M. (2004) *Malthusian Arithmetic: From Population Control to Reproductive Health*, Sage Publications: New Delhi.

Roelvink, G. and Craig, D. (2004) "The Man in the Partnering State: Regendering the Social through Partnership", Research Paper Number 13, Local Partnerships and Governance website, University of Auckland, New Zealand.

Sen, G. , Gurmurthy, A., Mukherjee, V. and Ramachandran, V. (2000) "India" in Sonia Correa (compiled) *Weighing Up Cairo: Evidence from Women in the South*, DAWN: Fij.

Simon-Kumar, R. (2004) "Negotiating Emancipation: The Public Sphere and Gender Critiques of Neo-Liberal Development" *International Feminist Journal of Politics*, Vol 6, No. 3, pp. 485–506.

Yeatman, A. (1993) "Voice and Representation in the Politics of Difference" in S. Gunew and A. Yeatman (eds) *Feminism and The Politics of Difference*, Allen and Unwin: NSW, Australia, pp. 228–245.

Glossary of Acronyms/Abbreviations

AIDS	Acquired Immuno-Deficiency Syndrome
ANM	Auxiliary Nurse Midwife
CBR	Crude Birth Rate
CC	Conventional Contraceptives (Condoms)
CSSM	Child Survival and Safe Motherhood Programme
Cu- T	Copper—T (an intra-uterine device)
CHC	Community Health Centre
DANIDA	Danish Development Assistance
DAWN	Development Alternatives for Women in a New Era
DFW	Department of Family Welfare
DHS	Directorate/Director of Health Services
DMO	District Medical Office/Officer
DPP	Decentralised Participatory Planning
DPIP	District Project Implementation Plan
DRCH	District Reproductive and Child Health Programme
EC	Eligible Couple
FRU	First Referral Unit
FPP	Family Planning Programme
FWP	Family Welfare Programme
GHI	Gender Health Index
GoI	Government of India
GoK	Government of Kerala
HDI	Human Development Index
HIV	Human Immuno-Deficiency Virus
ICMR	Indian Council for Medical Research

ICPD	International Conference on Population and Development
IIPS	Indian Institute of Population Studies
IPC	Indian Penal Code
IUD	Intra-Uterine Device
ISM	Indian Systems of Medicine
IPD	Integrated Population and Development Project
IEC	Information, Education and Communication programme
IUD	Intra-Uterine Device
JPHN	Junior Public Health Nurse
MCH	Mother and Child Health
MoHFW	Ministry of Health and Family Welfare
MPW	Multi-Purpose Worker
MTP	Medical Termination of Pregnancy
NGO	Non-Governmental Organisation
NHP	National Health Policy
NPP	National Population Policy
NRR	Net Reproduction Rate
ODA	Overseas Development Assistance
OP	Oral Pills
PHC	Primary Health Centre
POA	Plan of Action of the ICPD
PPS	Post-partum Surgery
PSA	Procurement Support Agency
RCH	Reproductive and Child Health Policy
RHI	Reproductive Health Index
RTI/STI	Reproductive Tract Infection/Sexually Transmitted Infection
SIP	State Implementation Plan
SAP	Structural Adjustment Programmes
SCOVA	State Committees on Voluntary Action
TC	Target Couple
TFA	Target-Free Approach
TOA	Target-Oriented Approach
TT	Tetanus Toxoide
UIP	Universal Immunisation Programme
UNDP	United Nations Development Programme

UNICEF	United Nations Children's Fund
UNFPA	United Nations Fund for Population Assistance
USAID	United States Agency for International Development
WB	World Bank
WHO	World Health Organization

Profile of Interviewees

INTERVIEWEE	SEX	DESIGNATION
I#1	Male	Official, DFW, Kerala Middle-level bureaucrat
I#2	Female	Official, DFW, Kerala Middle-level bureaucrat
I#3	Female	Independent Consultant for MoHFW, Delhi
I#4	Male	Official, DFW, Kerala Senior-level bureaucrat
I#5	Female	Feminist activist
I#6	Male	Official, DHS, Kerala Senior-level bureaucrat
I#7	Male	Official, DHS, Kerala Middle-level bureaucrat
I#8	Female	Official, DHS, Kerala Middle-level bureaucrat
I#9	Female	Official, Medical Doctor PHC, Vellanad
I#10	Female	Official, ANM, Vellanad
I#11	Male	Official, Medical Doctor, Palathara
I#12	Male	Official Medical Doctor, Vellanad
I#13	Female	Official, ANM, Vellanad

I#14	Female	Official, ANM, Vellanad
I#15	Female(s)@	Official, ANMs, Palathara
I#16	Female	Feminist Activist
I#17	Male	Family Welfare Provider Non-Government Organisation
I#18*	Female	Official, MoHFW in Kerala Senior-level bureaucrat
I#19	Female(s)@	Official, DFW, Kerala Middle-level officers
I#20*	Male	Researcher, International Development Agency, Delhi
I#21*	Male	Official, MoHFW, Delhi Senior-level bureaucrat

*: These interviews were not recorded

@: These were group interviews involving between 2-6 participants.

Agency Documents Used in the Analysis (with respective codes)

Code Number	Name of Document
wb. 2.	World Bank (1997) Project Appraisal Document : India, Reproductive and Child Health Project, Population and Human Resources Operations Division, Country Department II, South Asia Region
wb.1	World Bank (1996) India: RCH project—Criteria for Appraisal of District/City Proposal and Guidelines to prepare State Implementation Plans under WB supported RCH Project.
unfpa.ob.2	United Nations Fund for Population and Development (undated) Integrated Population and Development—Concepts
gok.obp.9	Government of Kerala (c. July-August 1997) State and District Project Formulation Exercise : Kerala, Directorate of Health Services, Trivandrum, Kerala
gok.om.1	Government of Kerala (1997) Minutes of meeting held on 7/10/97, Department of Health and Family Welfare, Trivandrum, Kerala
goi.oc.6	Government of India (1997) Manual on Target Free Approach in F.W.P, Ministry of Health and Family Welfare, New Delhi

goi.nd Government of India (undated) Reproductive and Child Health Programme, Department of Family Welfare, Ministry of Health and Family Welfare, New Delhi

goi.tm.1 Government of India (1997) Training of Auxiliary Nurse Midwives (ANMs) for "Building Effective Community Partnerships for Implementing the Reproductive and Child Health Programme (RCH)", Ministry of Health and Family Welfare, New Delhi

goi.oc.1 Government of India (1997) Memo from Deputy Director of MoHFW officially marked as No. M. 14015/7/97 -RCH (DC), Ministry of Health and Family Welfare, New Delhi.

goi.obp. 1 Government of India (1994) India: A Country Statement, Report Presented at the ICPD, Cairo, Ministry of Health and Family Welfare, New Delhi.

goi.oc.3 Government of India (1997), Untitled Report of Financial Status under RCH marked official No, M. 15012/3/96–UIP (B& A), Ministry of Health and Family Welfare, New Delhi

goi.oc.5 Government of India (1997) Reproductive and Child Health Programme: Schemes for Implementation, Ministry of Health and Family Welfare, New Delhi.

goi.oc.6 Government of India (1997) Decentralised Participatory Planning in Family Welfare Programme under Target Free Approach, Ministry of Health and Family Welfare, New Delhi

goi.tm.2: Government of India (1996) In-Service Training under Family Welfare Programme: Guidelines for Developing in-service training plan at district level, Ministry of Health and Family Welfare, New Delhi